EQUAL CITIZENSHIP AND ITS LIMITS IN EU LAW

The research monograph *Equal Citizenship and Its Limits in EU Law: We the Burden* is a critical study of the scope of EU citizenship as an 'equal status' of all Member State nationals. The book re-conceptualises the relationship between the status of EU citizenship and EU citizens' fundamental right to equal treatment by asking what indicates the presence of agency in EU law. A thorough analysis of the case law is used to support the argument that the present view of active citizenship in EU law fails to explain how EU citizens should be treated in relation to one another and what counts as 'related' for the purposes of equal treatment in a transnational context. In addressing these questions, the book responds to the increasing need to find a more substantive theory of justice for the European Union. The book suggests that a more balanced view of agency in the case of EU citizens can be based on the inherent connection between citizens' agency and their subjectivity. This analysis provides an integrated philosophical account of transnational equality by showing that a new source of 'meaningful relationships' for the purposes of equal treatment arises from recognising and treating EU citizens as full subjects of EU law and European integration. The book makes a significant contribution to the existing scholarship on EU law, first, by demonstrating that the undefined nature of EU citizenship is fundamentally a question about transnational justice and not just about individual rights and, secondly, by introducing a framework within which the current normative indeterminacy of EU citizenship can be overcome within the existing constitutional order of the EU.

Volume 61 in the Series Modern Studies in European Law

Modern Studies in European Law
Recent titles in this series:

The EU Accession to the ECHR
Edited by Vasiliki Kosta, Nikos Skoutaris and Vassilis P Tzevelekos

The European Court of Justice and External Relations: Constitutional Challenges
Edited by Marise Cremona and Anne Thies

A Critique of Codification
Leone Niglia

Protecting Vulnerable Groups: The European Human Rights Framework
Edited by Francesca Ippolito and Sara Iglesias Sanchez

EU International Relations Law Second Edition
Panos Koutrakos

Fundamental Rights in the EU: A Matter for Two Courts
Edited by Sonia Morano-Foadi and Lucy Vickers

What Form of Government for the European Union and the Eurozone?
Federico Fabbrini, Ernst Hirsch Ballin and Han Somsen

The UK and European Human Rights: A Strained Relationship?
Edited by Katja S Ziegler, Elizabeth Wicks and Loveday Hodson

The European Union in International Organisations and Global Governance: Recent Developments
Edited by Christine Kaddous

Nudge and the Law: What Can EU Law Learn From Behavioural Sciences?
Edited by Alberto Alemanno and Anne-Lise Sibony

Fundamental Rights in EU Internal Market Legislation
Vasiliki Kosta

Uniformity of Customs Administration in the European Union
Kathrin Limbach

The Impact of Union Citizenship on the EU's Market Freedoms
Alina Tryfonidou

For the complete list of titles in this series, see
'Modern Studies in European Law' link at
www.hartpub.co.uk/books/series.asp

Equal Citizenship and Its Limits in EU Law

We The Burden?

Päivi Johanna Neuvonen

•HART•

OXFORD • LONDON • NEW YORK • NEW DELHI • SYDNEY

HART PUBLISHING
Bloomsbury Publishing Plc
Kemp House, Chawley Park, Cumnor Hill, Oxford, OX2 9PH, UK

HART PUBLISHING, the Hart/Stag logo, BLOOMSBURY and the Diana logo are trademarks of Bloomsbury Publishing Plc
First published in Great Britain 2016

First published in hardback, 2016
Paperback edition, 2018

A catalogue record for this book is available from the British Library.

Library of Congress Cataloging-in-Publication Data

Names: Neuvonen, Päivi Johanna, 1983– author.

Title: Equal citizenship and its limits in EU law : we the burden / Päivi Johanna Neuvonen.

Description: Oxford ; Portland, Oregon : Hart Publishing Ltd, 2016. | Series: Modern studies in European law ; volume 61 | Based on author's thesis (doctoral—University of Oxford, 2013) issued under title: We the burden. | Includes bibliographical references and index.

Identifiers: LCCN 2015045799 (print) | LCCN 2015046375 (ebook) | ISBN 9781782258155 (hardback : alk. paper) | ISBN 9781782258162 (Epub)

Subjects: LCSH: Citizenship—European Union countries. | Equality before the law—European Union countries. | Political rights—European Union countries.

Classification: LCC KJE5124 .N48 2016 (print) | LCC KJE5124 (ebook) | DDC 342.2408/3—dc23

LC record available at http://lccn.loc.gov/2015045799

ISBN: PB: 978-1-50992-449-3
HB: 978-1-78225-815-5

Typeset by Compuscript Ltd, Shannon

To find out more about our authors and books visit www.hartpublishing.co.uk. Here you will find extracts, author information, details of forthcoming events and the option to sign up for our newsletters.

Acknowledgements

This monograph is based on my recent doctoral thesis. I would like to express my deepest gratitude to Professor Katja Ziegler for supervising my DPhil at the University of Oxford. This research would not have been possible without her continuous support and critical insight. I am also greatly indebted to Professor Dagmar Schiek and Professor Stephen Weatherill for examining my thesis and to Dr Cathryn Costello for assessing my transfer of status and confirmation of status reports in Oxford. Their comments and criticism have shaped this work in an invaluable way. My gratitude also extends to my former supervisors. Professor Tuomas Ojanen opened my eyes to the puzzle of transnational law many years ago. Mr Colm O'Cinneide's research and seminars at UCL laid the ground for my interest in equality theory. Dr Janne Salminen encouraged me to pursue postgraduate studies and helped me forward at the beginning. The Osk Huttunen Foundation, The Emil Aaltonen Foundation, and The Finnish Lawyers' Association funded this research generously. I would also like to warmly thank my current employers, Professor Stefan Sottiaux and Dr Jogchum Vrielink, at the Institute for Constitutional Law at KU Leuven. Sinead Moloney, Mel Hamill, Tom Adams and their colleagues at Hart Publishing guided me through the publishing process with great patience. Finally, I will always remain thankful to my friends and family for their support during this project.

Contents

Table of Cases

The Court of Justice of the EU

The European Court of Human Rights

'Doublethink means the power of holding two contradictory beliefs in one's mind simultaneously, and accepting both of them.'

— G Orwell, *Nineteen Eighty-Four* (Harcourt, Brace & Co, 1949).

Introduction

THIS MONOGRAPH IS a critical study of European Union (EU) citizenship as an equal status of all Member State nationals. The difference in treatment between economically active and inactive individuals often appears as an inherent feature of European integration. But the emergence of EU citizenship has shed light on a new dilemma: the gap of entitlements between economically inactive nationals and economically inactive non-nationals, all of whom are EU citizens. The limited material scope of equal treatment has become more difficult to justify when private individuals derive their right to equal treatment from the status of citizenship instead of any direct contribution to economic integration. This ambiguity over the scope of the EU principle of equality hides a deeper philosophical question of what normative justifications, other than the participation in the internal market, can be offered for equal treatment between EU citizens at the current stage of European integration. The limits of EU citizens' right to non-discrimination and equal treatment irrespective of nationality delimit what role EU citizenship can play in the process of European integration. It is therefore important to consider why some individuals are entitled to non-discrimination and equal treatment under EU law while others are not, and how these choices in regard to equality between EU citizens shape the EU's future as a transnational polity.

The Court of Justice of the EU (the Court) frequently refers to EU citizenship as a fundamental status of all Member State nationals, but the exercise of EU citizenship rights is, in practice, limited to a select few. The fact that EU citizens' access to equal treatment seems to approach the Orwellian idea of doublethink, in accordance with which 'the aim is simultaneously recognized and not recognized' will be examined in this book through the following three inter-connected questions:

— When is differential treatment legitimate between EU citizens under EU law?
— How should EU citizens be treated in relation to one another if EU citizenship is regarded as a fundamental status of all Member State nationals?
— What counts as 'related' for the purposes of non-discrimination and equal treatment in a transnational context?

Discussing the first two questions, Part I of the book presents a critique of EU citizenship as a fundamental, let alone equal, status of all Member State nationals.

The core of this criticism is that, although EU citizenship is now 'destined to be a fundamental status of all Member State nationals', the accepted justifications for differential treatment between EU citizens reveals a narrow and individualistic approach to what constitutes agency under EU law. Shifting the focus to the third question concerning meaningful relationships between EU citizens, Part II of the book then moves from presenting yet another critique of EU citizenship to constructing a legally and philosophically coherent solution to the current indeterminacy of EU citizenship as an equal status.

The EU equality problem as discussed in this book emerges from the fact that it is far from clear what a meaningful connection between 'equality' and 'citizenship' is in a transnational context. In so far as the scope of EU citizens' right to non-discrimination and equal treatment remains limited, the status of EU citizenship also remains limited. A more inclusive personal and material scope of EU citizenship rights forms an important condition for actualising EU citizenship as a fundamental status of all Member State nationals. However, unlike much of the existing literature, this book does not focus on the limited jurisdictional scope of EU citizenship rights. Instead, it argues that the status of EU citizenship is fundamentally defined by those substantive limitations and exceptions that are used to restrict the *de facto* enjoyment of EU citizenship rights in those cases that jurisdictionally fall into the scope of equal treatment under EU law. This book is therefore primarily not a story about the scope of EU citizens' right to equal treatment under EU law, but about just and equal relationships between EU citizens.

If the goal of positivist legal research is generally to find the norm, the focus of this book lies in the 'norm behind the norm'. Both the legal and the philosophical analysis of differential treatment between EU citizens seeks to address the difficult question of why EU citizens' general/non-economic right to equal treatment exists at the current state of European integration. Or, bearing in mind the necessity of the EU to justify its existence and prove additional value, what is the *Telos* of the non-economic principle of equality in EU law? This book adopts the view that the sustainable way to face the EU equality problem is to address the even deeper question of whether, and if so how, it is possible to justify the democratic idea of just and equal relationships between citizens transnationally. The development of the European (Economic) Constitution under what is now Article 34 of the Treaty on the Functioning of the European Union (TFEU) laid the ground for the constitutionalisation of European Union law through the protection of individual rights.[1] However, this book shifts the focus of EU citizenship from individual legal rights to transnational justice. This approach does not treat 'equal treatment' and 'social justice' as synonyms, but makes a substantive claim that EU citizens' access

[1] Consolidated Versions of the Treaty on European Union (TEU) and the Treaty on the Functioning of the European Union (TFEU) [2012] OJ C326/47. See for a comprehensive analysis in Miguel Poiares Maduro, *We the Court: The European Court of Justice and the European Economic Constitution: A Critical Reading of Article 30 of the EC Treaty* (Hart Publishing, 1998).

to social equality as EU citizens is where the theory of transnational justice, or the lack of it, becomes tangible.

The Court's interpretation of equal treatment under Article 18 TFEU provides an important example of the undefined nature of EU citizenship, but these observations lead to a more fundamental question of what constitutes a meaningful relationship for the purposes of non-discrimination and equal treatment beyond ethnic and cultural and democratic belonging within the EU. Recent EU law scholarship has started to pay more attention to the lack of substance of the EU principle of equality. However, it has been argued that the formalistic interpretation of equality has its origins in the limited jurisdictional scope of EU law or, as Dimitry Kochenov has put it, in 'a situation where equality stops at the arbitrary and extremely mobile border between the legal orders'.[2] This book has its origins in the same problem, ie the lack of substance of the EU principle of equality, but it is approached from a different angle. The shift in focus from 'nationality discrimination' to 'equal citizenship' by affirming EU citizenship as a 'fundamental status' of all Member State nationals, leads to a new problem: What are the consequences of that status for the interpretation of EU citizens' right to non-discrimination and equal treatment? Our difficulties in answering this question indicate that a coherent theory of EU citizenship is still missing and this study is an attempt to contribute to that discussion in so far as equal treatment between EU citizens is concerned.

Thus, this book does not use the prohibition of nationality discrimination to argue for more equality between EU citizens. On the contrary, it explores what normative justifications can be provided for the prohibition of nationality discrimination as a means of advancing more just and equal relationships between EU citizens. Shifting the focus from individual rights to transnational justice in exploring EU citizenship means that the current highly individualistic framework of EU citizenship must be replaced with an alternative normative framework which can accommodate the political value of just and equal relations between citizens into the theory of transnational law. The EU equality problem is accordingly conceptualised as a question of which relationships are relevant for justice claims in a transnational context. A simple reference to the EU as a transnational *Demos* does not provide an adequate answer to this research question because the EU still lacks a full democratic pedigree in many respects. Moreover, the book endorses the view that a shared European identity, whether feasible or not, would not solely provide a sufficient normative tool for rethinking just and equal relations between EU citizens *as EU citizens*.

The mere reference to the status of EU citizenship as a source of more equality between private individuals within the EU remains largely pointless, unless the underlying parameters for EU citizens' agency are redefined on the basis of a

[2] Dimitry Kochenov, 'Citizenship without Respect: The EU's Troubled Equality Ideal' Jean Monnet Working Paper No 8/10, http://jeanmonnetprogram.org/paper/citizenship-without-respect-the-eus-troubled-equality-ideal/, 9.

more substantive theory of transnational political and social justice. In particular, this book suggests that the accepted parameters for EU citizens' agency must be rethought in the light of EU citizens' sense of *subjectivity* as EU citizens. The conditions for transnational political and legal subjectivity will be discussed in detail in the second part of the book. The key to this analysis is that recognising EU citizens as full and equal subjects of European integration, as opposed to being its mere objects, can ultimately strengthen their political self-determination in that capacity. The future of the EU would depend on how EU citizens practice this self-determination both nationally and transnationally, and there is no guarantee that it would necessarily result in more or deeper integration within Europe. But the becoming of EU citizens as full and equal subjects of European integration is an important step towards a more just and legitimate EU. From this starting point, the book presents a revised normative justification for the EU principle of equality as a source of EU citizens' political and legal subjectivity as EU citizens.

The limits of EU citizens' access to equal treatment have remained widely unravelled in so far as their effect on equality *between* EU citizens is concerned. Traditionally, EU law scholarship has adopted a functional perspective under which EU citizens' right to non-discrimination and equal treatment has been construed as a means of expanding the existing market freedoms beyond the strict limits of economic activity. While these approaches shed light on the historical development of the EU principle of equality, they did not adequately consider how the equality of legal relationships constitutes a transnational polity and whether the 'equality of relationships' has value as an objective of political and legal integration in itself. Both the Union legislature and the Union courts would benefit from a more nuanced understanding of what normative basis the existing legal system of the EU can provide for equal treatment between EU citizens. Union legislature may opt for a narrow interpretation of equal treatment between EU citizens, but it must take into account the constitutional safeguards for the rights of EU citizens as expressed in the general principles of EU law and EU fundamental rights. A clearer understanding about just and equal relationships between EU citizens, which should underlie the interpretation of these legal instruments, is relevant irrespective of how the competences are divided between the different levels of governance in the EU.

The concept of equality is potentially diverse,[3] or even 'empty',[4] and its content depends on more substantive non-egalitarian standards and criteria. This book adopts the view that the idea of 'significantly related people'[5] forms a logical starting point for the analysis of equality in EU law. It has been noted that

[3] There is arguably no 'pan-European consensus' on the substantive content of equality. Colm O'Cinneide, 'The Uncertain Foundations of Contemporary Anti-Discrimination Law' (2011) 11 *International Journal of Discrimination and the Law* 7, 13–14.

[4] eg Peter Westen, 'The Empty Idea of Equality' (1982) 95 *Harvard Law Review* 537 and Joseph Raz, *The Morality of Freedom* (Clarendon Press, 1986) 228–29.

[5] Kent Greenawalt, '"Prescriptive Equality": Two Steps Forward' (1997) 110 *Harvard Law Review* 1265, 1283 and 1289.

'the fundamental question of justice as equilibrium is that very old question, "who is my neighbor?"'.[6] As a comparative right, equality must be 'at bottom—relational and social'.[7] It is, therefore, important to consider what constitutes a meaningful social relationship in the context of EU law and how the basis on which 'those whom they believe to be their equals'[8] has been transformed by the creation of EU citizenship. In this book, the argument of more just and equal relationships between EU citizens as a source of their transnational subjectivity builds on a thorough legal analysis of how EU citizens' right to equal treatment is construed in European Union law in so far as the members of the unwanted and unfortunate 'underclass', that is, economically inactive and dependent Union citizens, pursue their fundamental freedom to move and reside in a Member State other than their state of origin. This analysis of EU citizenship and equality is rooted in the wider development of fundamental and human rights as part of the process of European constitutionalisation.[9]

The EU's definition of itself as a constitutional actor has become seemingly axiomatic,[10] but the legitimacy of this definition is still far from uncontroversial.[11] The constitutional perspective is nonetheless useful for understanding EU citizenship in so far as it focuses on 'conditions of membership' and 'strategies for dealing with the alien'.[12] Transnational constitutionalism in its substantive form can provide a means of redefining the relationship between the Union and private individuals and between the Member States and private individuals.[13] However, it can also be asked whether the constitutionalisation of EU law has the potential not only to redefine the vertical relationships between citizens of the Union and its Member States, but also to transform the horizontal relationships between Union citizens themselves across the borders of the Member States.[14] This is where the focus of

[6] Jan Broekman, 'Justice as Equilibrium' (1986) 5 *Law and Philosophy* 369, 390–91.

[7] Kenneth W Simons, 'Equality as a Comparative Right' (1985) 65 *Boston University Law Review* 387, 482.

[8] See eg Greenawalt (n 5) and Broekman (n 6).

[9] See eg JHH Weiler, *The Constitution of Europe* (Cambridge University Press, 1999) 19–25.

[10] For an early reference to the EEC Treaty as 'the basic constitutional charter' see eg Case 294/83 *Parti écologiste 'Les Verts' v European Parliament* [1986] ECR 1339, para 23.

[11] See eg Katja Ziegler, 'Strengthening the Rule of Law, but Fragmenting International Law: The *Kadi* Decision of the ECJ from the Perspective of Human Rights' (2009) 9 *Human Rights Law Review* 288.

[12] Nicholas Tsagourias, 'Introduction—Constitutionalism: A Theoretical Roadmap' in Nicholas Tsagourias (ed), *Transnational Constitutionalism: International and European Models* (Cambridge University Press, 2007) 4 and JHH Weiler, 'In Defence of the Status Quo: Europe's Constitutional Sonderweg' in JHH Weiler and Marlene Wind (eds), *European Constitutionalism Beyond the State* (Cambridge University Press, 2003) 19.

[13] See eg Pavlos Eleftheriadis, 'Aspects of European Constitutionalism' (1996) 21 *European Law Review* 32, 41–24 who argues that 'the endorsement of new Constitution can be evaluated and justified only by substantive criteria related to constitutionalism and the rule of law'. See also Francis Snyder, 'The Unfinished Constitution of the European Union: Principles, Processes and Culture' in Weiler and Wind (n 12) 56.

[14] eg Paul Magnette, 'How can one be European? Reflections on the Pillars of European Civic Identity' (2007) 13 *European Law Journal* 664.

critical analysis needs to shift from individual legal rights to the broader question of what access to equal treatment means for transnational polity-formation. It is therefore important to consider what kind of account of distributive justice underlies the current interpretation of EU citizens' right to non-discrimination and equal treatment irrespective of nationality and what alternatives it can have in the existing framework of EU law.

It is clear that neither the democratic nor the global theories of distributive justice provide a sufficient account of justice for the EU.[15] The ideal of EU citizenship as a source of transnational political and legal subjectivity as advanced in this book is nevertheless rooted in the democratic account of relational egalitarian social justice.[16] This account places the quality of citizens' relationships above the requirement of responsibility through individual actions in defining what is due to whom under the principles of justice. Because EU citizenship is not equal to a democratic (national) citizenship, it is important to consider how justice as a relational ideal can be justified in a transnational context in which the democratic pedigree is considerably weaker than in the context of nation states. Thus, this book does not just discuss the status of EU citizenship in light of the existing theories of distributive justice, but also makes an original contribution to developing a more substantive theory of justice for the EU by considering how the 'equality of relationships' paradigm can be justified in a transnational context. This analysis provides more philosophy to EU citizenship by critically evaluating what different 'desert-bases', such as individual responsibility, choice, or a certain status, can be utilised in justifying access to social equality transnationally.

This book argues that just and equal relationships between EU citizens can be justified as a precondition for EU citizens' political and legal subjectivity as EU citizens. From this starting point, EU citizens' general right to non-discrimination and equal treatment under Article 18 TFEU can be understood as an important platform for implementing the argument of EU citizenship as a source of transnational subjectivity. The psycho-dynamic and phenomenological analysis of subjectivity in the second part of this book draws on the view that the constitution of human subjectivity, including its social, political, legal, and cultural dimensions, happens through the self's identification with the 'Other', both within the subject and between the subjects. This analysis conceives the relationship to the 'Other' as a partly unconscious process which can be experienced as both fragmented and destructive, as suggested by the structural psycho-analytic theorists, and as positive and constructive, as discussed in phenomenological philosophy. How EU citizens are treated in relation to one another plays a central role in the becoming of EU citizens as subjects of European integration. But these relationships are challenged by the fact they may reactivate the self's complex relationship to the

[15] See more about the difference between these two forms of justice eg in Thomas Nagel, 'The Problem of Global Justice' (2005) 22 *Philosophy & Public Affairs* 113, 121 and 132.

[16] This account of egalitarian justice has been developed by such authors as Samuel Scheffler, Elizabeth Anderson, and Jonathan Wolff.

Other; namely, the relevant social relationships in and through which EU citizens' subjectivity as EU citizens is constituted mainly emerge outside any existing form of cultural, ethnic, or democratic belonging.

The relational critique of EU citizenship as presented in this book contributes to the study of EU law both substantively and methodologically. Methodologically, this analysis brings forward a strong argument for the inadequacy of a purely positivist approach in transnational legal theory. The book responds to this methodological challenge by applying critical theory to the study of EU law. This methodological perspective seeks to bring different scholarly audiences together: the book demonstrates that the methods of critical study can shed new light on the foundational questions of EU constitutional law, whilst simultaneously showing how the constructed nature of EU citizenship provides an interesting case study to critical theorists. Substantively, this study contributes to the ongoing scholarly debate on the nature of EU citizenship. Firstly, the book reconceptualises the EU equality problem as a question of meaningful relationships. Secondly, it demonstrates that EU citizenship is above all an issue of transnational justice, and not just of individual rights. Thirdly, the book provides a new substantive framework for EU citizens' agency and subjectivity. The main substantive contribution of the book is to show that reconstructing EU citizenship as a source of transnational subjectivity can provide a consistent normative justification for advancing more just and equal relationships between EU citizens.

This analysis is based on the assumption that normative and critical potential can be developed within European Union law and its constitutional order.[17] This approach can be described by referring to Kaarlo Tuori's concept of 'critical legal positivism', according to which law is a multi-layered phenomenon within which there is critical potential for ethical analysis of its limits and legitimacy.[18] But the book can also be seen as a descendant of 'new constructivism' following Alexander Somek's seminal work on EU anti-discrimination law.[19] This approach claims that the critical potential of any legal system can only be fully grasped by looking at its theoretical and philosophical foundations. These two analytical commitments together support the view that it is important to understand the internal logic and functioning of equality as part of the EU legal system, while simultaneously

[17] See for a similar methodological approach to EU constitutional law eg Dagmar Schiek, *Economic and Social Integration: The Challenge for EU Constitutional Law* (Edward Elgar Publishing, 2012).

[18] Kaarlo Tuori, *Critical Legal Positivism* (Ashgate, 2002).

[19] According to Somek, his approach is 'constructivist' because it 'avoids embracing legal positivism and natural law theory without retreating to the intellectual high ground of postmodernism' and because it 'shares the belief that legal thought is devoted to making our normative ideas clear'. However, what Somek calls the 'new constructivism' does not share the Kelsenian view that the conceptual system itself could always provide 'one right answer'. Somek nevertheless claims that 'even where legal institutions are marked by indeterminacy, this indeterminacy is bounded and the product of the work of a set of concepts and normative ideals'. For Somek, the task of scholarship is, therefore, 'to remove from the appearance of legal materials, piece by piece, the ideological distortions that originate from overconfident justifications'. Alexander Somek, *Engineering Equality: An Essay on European Anti-Discrimination Law* (Oxford University Press, 2011) 19–20.

acknowledging that the external points of view become increasingly important in assessing EU law when the analysis moves towards more critical and constructive approaches. In explaining the essence of equal citizenship in a transnational context, this book therefore combines the legal analysis of differential treatment between EU citizens with insights from political theory, phenomenological philosophy and developmental psychology.

The question of how transnational law can make sense of such concepts that usually derive their legitimacy from the democratic processes within a nation state is crucial to this book. This question cannot be avoided because many of these concepts, citizenship included, now form a central part of EU constitutional law.[20] The book's ambition is therefore to sketch one possible account of how the political ideal of just and equal relationships between citizens can be justified in a context in which its legitimacy cannot be directly derived from the existing democratic structures. The subjectivity-based approach to EU citizenship shows that the importance of just and equal relationships to the emergence of citizens' subjectivity allows us to attach a political dimension to EU citizenship even in the absence of a fully functioning transnational democracy. Moreover, strengthening EU citizens' subjectivity as EU citizens may also ultimately lead to a stronger network of democratic institutions and structures at the EU level. This is a realistic assumption if we understand European integration as a two-way process which not just accommodates the existing structures and conceptions of democracy into its own processes but also actively redefines what expressions democracy may have in a transnational world.

This book seeks to address the question of what equal treatments means as an element of EU citizenship both in practice, by examining the limits of EU citizens' general right to non-discrimination and equal treatment in the realm of social welfare benefits, and in theory, by examining the philosophical foundations of EU citizens' access to equal treatment in relation to other EU citizens, that is, on the basis of the shared status of EU citizenship. It is clear that the general scope of EU law is tied to the objectives of the EU Treaties. This means that only matters which conflict with one of the aims of the Union can be considered within the scope of the Treaties' articles. The important question to this study is therefore whether European integration aims to prevent unjust differences only if they obstruct economic integration, or whether integration in itself is about the prevention of unjust differences between the subjects of European integration. As full and equal subjects of European integration, EU citizens may contribute to a less predictable future for the EU—but that future would then be a future actively shaped by those who are affected by it, rather than a future imposed on them from above. More just and

[20] For instance, Article 9 TEU states that '[i]n all its activities, the Union shall observe the principle of the equality of its citizens', whereas Article 10(1) TEU confirms that '[t]he functioning of the Union shall be founded on representative democracy'.

equal political and legal relationships between EU citizens can provide an important step in that direction.

OUTLINE OF THE BOOK

Chapter one explains how the focus of the EU principle of equality has shifted from 'nationality discrimination' towards 'equal citizenship'. This analysis demonstrates that the meaning of 'equal citizenship' has remained unclear in the development of EU citizens' right to non-discrimination and equal treatment under EU law. The chapter conceptualises these findings by arguing that a new equality problem has emerged in EU law along with the evolution of EU citizenship: EU citizenship as the main criterion for the personal scope of the EU principle of equality necessitates a clearer articulation of what implications it may have for the substance of that right. It will be seen that this problem is actualised in defining on what basis differential treatment can be justified between those EU citizens who fall into the jurisdictional scope of EU citizens' fundamental right to non-discrimination and equal treatment irrespective of nationality under EU law. Lastly, this argument of the EU equality problem is placed into context with a description of how EU citizenship differs from a democratic national citizenship.

Chapter two provides a detailed legal analysis of EU citizens' right to non-discrimination and equal treatment in the light of the case law of the Court of Justice of the EU. This chapter focuses on the question of what is required from the different groups of economically active and inactive EU citizens to find themselves in the same situation with the nationals of the host Member State for the purposes of non-discrimination and equal treatment. From this analysis arises the argument that the accepted limitations on EU citizens' right to non-discrimination and equal treatment are problematic both structurally, in so far as the scope of EU citizens' right to equal treatment is conditional on lawful residence, and more substantively, in so far as the accepted criteria for legitimate differential treatment between EU citizens still suffer from a strong economic bias. The chapter concludes on this basis that the status of EU citizenship has not reached its full potential as a 'fundamental status' and that the mere reference to EU citizenship as a new comparison class hides the structural and substantive equality problems in EU law.

Chapter three presents a more theoretical critique of the EU principle of equality as it emerges from the case law. This chapter is based on the view that it is important to have a closer look at what philosophical conception of distributive justice underlies the EU principle of equality. The chapter engages in this task by considering what different 'desert-bases' for equal treatment between EU citizens can be induced from the case law, as discussed in Chapter two. It will be seen that, although the Court now frequently bases its decisions on the status of EU citizenship, the parameters for EU citizens' agency are still conditioned on the individual responsibility to prove value through economic and social integration. From this starting point, the chapter suggests that the EU principle of equality is vulnerable to a similar criticism that has been directed against the so-called responsibility-sensitive theories of egalitarian justice on the basis that they fail to adequately consider equality as a 'normative ideal of human relationships'.[21]

The philosophical analysis of equality in this chapter first draws the reader's attention to the several commonalities between the responsibility-sensitive theories of equal opportunities (Dworkin, Cohen, Arneson, etc) and the EU principle of equality. It then shows how an alternative, more relational, ideal of egalitarian social justice emerges from the democratic critique of egalitarian justice (Scheffler, Anderson, Wolff, etc) that emphasises the value of just and equal relationships between citizens. From this starting point, the chapter criticises the EU principle of equality for a narrow focus on responsibility through individual actions and suggests that EU citizenship could gain more substance as a 'fundamental' or 'equal' status of all Member State nationals if a more relational account of justice can be introduced to the EU, irrespective of its democratic deficit. It will conclude on this basis that the core of the EU equality problem is how the importance of just and equal relationships between citizens can be justified in a transnational context.

Chapter four moves from the critique of EU citizenship and the EU principle of equality, towards a more constructive perspective. This chapter suggests that a promising approach to justifying more just and equal relationships between EU citizens is to (re)construct EU citizenship as a source of subjectivity. This approach to EU citizenship builds on the feminist view that citizens' political and legal agency cannot be separated from their sense of subjectivity—and vice versa. This chapter uses both the psycho-dynamic and phenomenological theories of subjectivity to discuss under what conditions EU citizenship can be constructed as a source of transnational subjectivity. It will be seen that defending EU citizenship as a source of subjectivity is more complex than the voluntarist argument of choosing one's political identity would imply. The analytic categories of a 'relational subject' and the 'subject-in-process'[22] are used to explain the constitution of EU citizens' legal and political subjectivity as EU citizens. This analysis shows how the descriptive question of identity becomes less important than the relational question of how law generates and transforms social relations between EU citizens. Drawing this connection between citizens' agency and their subjectivity, the chapter argues that the normative significance of just and equal relationships between EU citizens follows from the fact that their sense of subjectivity as EU citizens only emerges in and through social relationships with other EU citizens.

Chapter five explores further the argument that a new source of 'meaningful relationships' for the purposes of non-discrimination and equal treatment can

[21] Samuel Scheffler, *Equality and Tradition Questions of Value in Moral and Political Theory* (Oxford University Press, 2007) 234.

[22] Julia Kristeva, *Desire in Language—A Semiotic Approach to Literature and Art* (Oxford, Blackwell, 1980) 135.

arise from recognising and treating EU citizens as full subjects of EU law and European integration. This chapter will conclude the book by considering what it would mean for an EU citizen to be a subject of European integration, as opposed to being its mere object, both at the level of EU law and at the level of integration theory. The chapter adopts a constitutional constructivist view that the law in general and the discrimination analysis in particular create and shape those social relationships in which the emergence of EU citizens' subjectivity as EU citizens becomes possible. From this starting point, the chapter will introduce a revised, more inter-personal, test for legitimate differential treatment between EU citizens and apply it to the recent case law. Lastly, it will briefly consider how the idea of deepening relationships of interdependence between the subjects of European integration can explain why the process of European integration took the direction of constitutionalisation instead of the more traditional forms of intergovernmentalism and how this understanding of integration would also support EU citizens' subjectivity, as discussed in this book.

Part I

EU Citizenship and the Equality Problem

1

The Evolution of Equality in EU Law: From Nationality Discrimination Towards Equal Citizenship

1.1 INTRODUCTION

THE EU PRINCIPLE of equality is a dynamic legal concept with multiple different roles in the process of European integration. This chapter follows the evolution of equal treatment irrespective of nationality in regard to private individuals from the early years of European integration through the creation of EU citizenship until the adoption of the EU Charter of Fundamental Rights[1] as a source of primary EU law and the possible future accession of the Union to the European Convention on Human Rights. A chronological perspective on these legal developments depicts how the interpretation of the EU principle of equality has shifted from non-discrimination on the grounds of nationality towards equal treatment between EU citizens. But it also reveals that a new 'equality problem' has emerged in EU law along with these developments. The core of this problem is that, although the status of EU citizenship now plays a central role in defining the personal scope of the EU principle of equality, it is not yet clear what the idea of equal citizenship means for the substance of EU citizens' right to non-discrimination and equal treatment. This normative indeterminacy over EU citizenship as an equal status forms the starting point for the doctrinal and theoretical critique of EU citizenship in the subsequent chapters.

1.2 THE MULTIPLE FACE OF EQUAL TREATMENT IRRESPECTIVE OF NATIONALITY IN REGARD TO PRIVATE INDIVIDUALS

1.2.1 An Economic Right Under Article 45 TFEU

Equal treatment irrespective of nationality between workers of the Member States has been justified as a means of first completing the common market and, then, the internal market. This requirement was included in Article 48 of the original Treaty

[1] Charter of Fundamental Rights of the European Union [2000] OJ 364/1.

of Rome (1957) and it has maintained its central role in the EU Treaties ever since.[2] Article 45(1) TFEU now secures the freedom of movement of workers within the European Union. This guarantee is completed by Article 45(2) TFEU which provides that '[s]uch freedom of movement shall entail the abolition of any discrimination based on nationality between workers of the Member State as regards employment, remuneration and other conditions of work and employment'.[3] The Court of Justice has given this provision a wide effect as one of the four fundamental economic freedoms by interpreting the concept of a 'Union worker' broadly and autonomously.[4] It is nevertheless clear that the scope of the prohibition of nationality discrimination would remain limited if it was only triggered in the context of economic activity, such as 'employment, remuneration and other conditions of work and employment'. This book wants to better understand EU citizenship as an equal status. Its main focus therefore lies in those EU citizens who do not qualify as 'Union workers' but who have recourse to the right to non-discrimination and equal treatment on the basis of their status as EU citizens. However, EU citizens' non-economic right to equal treatment is of much later origin than the right now included in Article 45(2) TFEU and, thus, can only be understood against the Union worker's more comprehensive right to non-discrimination and equal treatment irrespective of nationality.[5]

1.2.2 A Citizenship Right Under Article 18 TFEU

The original Treaty of Rome (1957) also included a prohibition of nationality discrimination with a more general scope of application.[6] Its content is now included in Article 18 TFEU which holds that 'within the scope of the Treaties, and without prejudice to any special provision contained therein, any discrimination on grounds of nationality shall be prohibited'.[7] The jurisdictional threshold for the application of the general prohibition of nationality discrimination is thus based on the scope of application of the EU Treaties themselves.[8] In practice, its potential

[2] Article 48, Treaty Establishing the European Economic Community (EEC Treaty) (Rome, 25 March 1957).

[3] Article 45, Consolidated versions of the Treaty on European Union (TEU) and the Treaty on the Functioning of the European Union (TFEU) [2012] OJ C326/47.

[4] See eg Case 66/85 *Deborah Lawrie-Blum v Land Baden-Württemberg* [1986] ECR 2121, para 20, in which the Court states that 'all that is required—is that the activity should be in the nature of work performed for remuneration, irrespective of the sphere in which it is carried out'.

[5] See more about this in Chapter 2, Section 2.2, p 41.

[6] Article 6 EEC Treaty.

[7] Article 18 TFEU.

[8] What distinguishes nationality and gender from other prohibited grounds of discrimination in EU law is their general scope of application 'within the scope of application of the Treaties'. See eg the *Phil Collins* judgment in which the Court also stated that the Treaty provision on nationality discrimination 'may be directly relied before a national court'. Cases C-92/92 and C-326/92 *Phil Collins v Imtrat Handelsgesellschaft mbH and Patricia Im- und Export Verwaltungsgesellschaft mbH and Leif Emanuel Kraul v EMI Electrola GmbH* [1993] ECR I-5145, para 35. Article 19 TFEU, which prohibits discrimination on the grounds of sex, racial or ethnic origin, religion or belief, disability, age and sexual

scope of application in regard to private individuals was considerably expanded when the Maastricht Treaty (1992) introduced the concept of EU citizenship.[9] The status of EU citizenship is now defined by Article 20 TFEU, which states that 'Citizens of the Union shall enjoy the rights and be subject to the duties provided for in the Treaties' and that these rights should *inter alia* include 'the right to move and reside freely within the territory of the Member States—in accordance with the conditions and limits defined by the Treaties and by the measures adopted thereunder'.[10] EU citizens' right to free movement and residence can now be found in Article 21 TFEU which holds that 'Every citizen of the Union shall have the right to move and reside freely within the territory of the Member States, subject to the limitations and conditions laid down in the Treaties and by the measures adopted to give them effect'.[11]

Along with the creation of a non-economic right to free movement and residence, EU citizenship made possible a new interpretation of Article 18 TFEU as a citizenship right of at least some of the economically inactive citizens of the Union. But the potential of EU citizenship to transform the prohibition of nationality discrimination into something new depends on the definition of the actual scope of Article 18 TFEU, which turned out to be an elusive task in the case of economically inactive EU citizens.[12] This can be clarified by considering the *who*, *why* and *how* questions:

— The personal scope of Article 18 TFEU defines *who* can be protected against discrimination.

orientation, has no direct effect. Directive 2000/43/EC of June 29 2000 implementing the principle of equal treatment between persons irrespective of racial or ethnic origin [2000] OJ L180/22 applies in the context of employment, vocational training, professional organisations, social protection, social advantages, education, and access to and supply of goods and services and Directive 2000/78/EC of 27 November 2000 establishing a general framework for equal treatment in employment and occupation [2000] OJ L303/16 applies in the context of employment, vocational training, and professional organisations. Although the Commission's proposal for a new Council directive on implementing the principle of equal treatment between persons irrespective of religion or belief, disability, age or sexual orientation would have extended the scope of the prohibition of discrimination to cover social protection, social advantages, education, and access to and supply of goods and services which are available to the public, it did not suggest a general scope of application for the non-discrimination principle under Article 19 TFEU. See Proposal for a Council Directive on implementing the principle of equal treatment between persons irrespective of religion or belief, disability, age or sexual orientation COM(2008) 426 final 8. For further analysis on these questions see eg Dagmar Schiek, 'A New Framework on Equal Treatment of Persons in EC Law? Directives 2000/43/EC, 2000/78/EC and 2002/???/EC changing Directive 76/207/EEC in context' (2002) 8 *European Law Journal* 290.

[9] According to Article 8(1) of the Maastricht Treaty, 'Citizenship of the Union is hereby established. Every person holding the nationality of a Member State shall be a citizen of the Union'. Article 8(2) of the Maastricht Treaty stated that 'Citizens of the Union shall enjoy the rights conferred by this Treaty and shall be subject to the duties imposed hereby'. Article 8, Treaty on European Union [1992] OJ C191/01.

[10] Article 20 TFEU.

[11] Ibid Article 21.

[12] Astrid Epiney, 'The Scope of Article 12 EC: Some Remarks on the Influence of European Citizenship' (2007) 13 *European Law Journal* 611, 612.

— The jurisdictional dimension of material scope answers the question of *why* anybody is protected under Article 18 TFEU.
— The substantive dimension of material scope defines *how* those people are protected who fall into the jurisdictional scope of Article 18 TFEU.

The status of EU citizenship has affected the answer to all three questions. At the same time, however, the way in which the scope of Article 18 TFEU is defined has significant implications for the scope of EU citizenship as an equal status.

EU citizenship as a criterion for the personal scope of Article 18 TFEU now lays the foundation for how the difference between prohibited nationality discrimination and legitimate differential treatment is defined in regard to economically inactive individuals under EU law (the *who* question). However, the limited jurisdictional scope of Article 18 TFEU means that there are instances in which differential treatment between EU citizens is implicitly classified as legitimate because there is no sufficient 'connecting factor' with EU law for the right to non-discrimination and equal treatment to apply to that specific situation (the *why* question). Moreover, a set of substantive limitations on EU citizens' right to equal treatment emerge from the objective justification test and they define more explicitly where the difference between discrimination and legitimate differential treatment lies in the case of EU citizens (the *how* question). These qualifications on EU citizens' right will be discussed in more detail in Section 1.3. However, in so far as the limited scope of Article 18 TFEU limits EU citizens' access to equal treatment, it is important to consider what other forms the non-economic prohibition of nationality discrimination can take in EU law.

Opinions differ on whether Article 18 TFEU should apply independently or whether it can only be invoked in the context of the four economic freedoms and EU citizens' right to free movement and residence under Article 21 TFEU. One argument in favour of a more independent application of Article 18 TFEU is that its mere status as a primary Treaty right can move it 'onto a different and normatively higher plane, perhaps best described as a constitutional one'.[13] This argument can be supported by the fact that the Court often refers to nationality discrimination as a specific expression of the general principle of equality in EU law.[14] The independence of Article 18 TFEU therefore also depends on how the

[13] Niamh Nic Shuibhne, 'The Outer Limits of EU Citizenship: Displacing Economic Free Movement Rights?' in Catherine Barnard and Okeoghene Odudu (eds), *The Outer Limits of European Union Law* (Hart Publishing, 2009) 175.

[14] eg Case 117/76 and 16/77 *Albert Ruckdeschel & Co, et Hansa-Lagerhaus Ströh & Co v Hauptzollamt Hamburg-St. Annen; Diamalt AG v Haupzollamt Itzenhoe* [1977] ECR 1753, para 7. See for more recent case-law eg Case C-115/08 *Land Oberösterrich v ČEZ as* [2009] ECR I-10265, para 91, according to which 'although the principle of prohibition of any discrimination on grounds of nationality within the scope of application of Community law is expressly laid down in Article 12 EC, it is a general principle'. See also Case C-101/08 *Audiolux SA and Others vs Groupe Bruxelles Lambert SA (GBL) and Others, Bertelsmann AG and Others* [2009] ECR I-9823, para 63 for the statement that '[t]he general principles of Community law have constitutional status'.

prohibition of nationality discrimination relates to fundamental rights as general principles of EU law. This is also where EU citizenship can have a central role as a normative justification for a more independent and rights-based interpretation of Article 18 TFEU.[15] Namely, the Court has recently confirmed that there are certain situations in which the scope of EU law is activated when an EU citizen is at risk of being deprived of the 'genuine enjoyment of the substance of the rights' conferred by virtue of EU citizenship under Article 20 TFEU.[16]

In the well-known *Konstantinidis* case, Advocate General Jacobs attempted in his Opinion to extend the jurisdiction of the Court and the scope of Community law by establishing a connection between European citizenship and fundamental rights.[17] The Court did not adopt this approach in *Konstantinidis*, but the status of EU fundamental rights has been considerably strengthened since then. Whether equal treatment irrespective of nationality has the potential to become an independent constitutional right is therefore closely connected to the degree to which EU citizens' right to non-discrimination and equal treatment can be characterised as a fundamental right, or even a human right, under EU law.

1.2.3 A Fundamental Right Under the EU Charter

The EU Charter of Fundamental Rights became part of EU primary law with the entry into force of the Lisbon Treaty,[18] and its Article 21(2) reiterates the wording of Article 18 TFEU by stating that '[w]ithin the scope of application of the Treaties and without prejudice to any of their specific provisions, any discrimination on grounds of nationality shall be prohibited'. Article 21 of the Charter has been criticised for failing to expand the commitment to prohibiting nationality discrimination beyond the existing Treaty provisions. The double-regulation both in the Treaty and in the Charter can nevertheless be seen as an important emphasis on the prohibition of nationality discrimination as a fundamental right. Otherwise, it would not be necessary to repeat the exact wording of Article 18 TFEU in the EU Charter of Fundamental Rights. Besides the provisions of the EU Charter of Fundamental Rights, the right to non-discrimination and equal treatment can also gain the status of a fundamental right as one of the general principles of EU law. The crucial question is just whether the general principle of equality and non-discrimination is one of those general principles of EU law which are

[15] See eg Síofra O'Leary, 'The Relationship Between Community Citizenship and the Protection of Fundamental Rights in Community Law' (1995) 32 *Common Market Law Review* 519. For a recent overview of the complex relationship between EU citizenship and fundamental rights, see also Sara Iglesias Sánchez, 'Fundamental Rights and Citizenship of the Union at a Crossroad: A Promising Alliance or A Dangerous Liaison' (2014) 20 *European Law Journal* 464.

[16] See more about this in Section 1.3, p 24.

[17] Case C-168/91 *Christos Konstantinidis v Stadt Altensteig—Standesamt and Landratsamt Calw—Ordnungsamt* [1993] ECR I-1191, Opinion of AG Jacobs.

[18] Treaty of Lisbon amending the Treaty on European Union and the Treaty establishing the European Community [2007] OJ C306/01.

simultaneously fundamental rights. In the light of Article 21 of the EU Charter, the positive answer to this question seems convincing.

The Court of Justice has traditionally held that it has competence to examine the compatibility of national rules with fundamental rights as general principles in all those cases in which national rules fall into the scope of EU law.[19] The *Fransson* judgment seemed to confirm that this is still the case, irrespective of the wording of Article 51(1) of the Charter, which states that the Charter applies to the Member States 'only when they are implementing Union law'.[20] But the Court's approach to the scope of EU fundamental rights has been cautious in other recent cases.[21] This uncertainty notwithstanding, it is important to consider what impact the recognition of EU citizens' right to non-discrimination and equal treatment as a fundamental right may have on the limits of equal treatment under Article 18 TFEU. This question relates to the more general question of whether a fundamental right can be subject to limitations and derogations to the same extent as an economic freedom.[22] It has been suggested that the legal effect of Treaty rights becoming fundamental rights should imply both a broad interpretation of the 'initial or *prima facie* right itself' (scope) and a narrow interpretation of the 'exceptions to that right' (limitations).[23] In the case of fundamental rights, limitations define the 'terms of exercise' of the right rather than the 'right itself, or to whom it belongs'.[24]

It can be argued that to articulate the prohibition of nationality discrimination as a fundamental right ought to have an impact on the way in which the scope

[19] Cases 60 and 61/84 *Cinétheèque SA and others v Fédération nationale des cinémas français* [1985] ECR 2605, para 26; Case 12/86 *Meryem Demirel v Stadt Schwäbisch Gmünd* [1987] ECR 3719, para 28; and Case C-260/89 *Ellinki Radiophonia Tileorassi AE and Panellinia Omospondia Syllogon Prossopikou v Dimotiki Etairia Pliroforissis and Sotirios Kouvelas and Nicolaos Avdellas and others* [1991] ECR I-2925, paras 41–42.

[20] C-617/10 *Åklagaren v Hans Åkerberg Fransson*, 26 February 2013, para 21. See also Case C-390/12 *Robert Pfleger and Others*, 30 April 2014, para 36.

[21] For instance, in the *Dano* judgment, the Court refused to discuss whether the Charter would support an economically inactive EU citizen's claim for non-contributory cash benefits in the host Member State and stated that the provisions of the Charter are addressed 'to the Member States only when they are implementing Union law'. Case C-333/13 *Elisabeta Dano v Jobcenter Leipzig*, 11 November 2014, para 87. For more discussion about the scope of EU law in regard to the Charter, see eg Case C-466/11 *Gennaro Currà and Others v Bundesrepublik Deutschland*, 12 July 2012, para 26; Case C-258/13 *Sociedade Agrícola e Imobiliária da Quinta de S. Paio Lda v Instituto da Segurança Social IP*, 28 November 2013, para 21; Case C-265/13 *Emiliano Torralbo Marcos v Korota SA and Fondo de Garantía Salarial*, 27 March 2014, paras 32–33 and Case C-206/13 *Cruciano Siragusa v Regione Sicilia—Soprintendenza Beni Culturali e Ambientali di Palermo*, 6 March 2014, paras 25–26. For further analysis regarding these questions, see Armin von Bogdandy, Matthias Kottmann, Carlino Antpöhler, Johanna Dickschen, Simon Hentrei, and Maja Smrkolj, 'Reverse *Solange*—Protecting the Essence of Fundamental Rights Against EU Member States' (2012) 49 *Common Market Law Review* 489.

[22] eg Steve Peers, 'Taking Rights Away? Limitations and Derogations' in Steve Peers and Angela Ward (eds), *The European Union Charter of Fundamental Rights* (Hart Publishing, 2004) 142–43.

[23] Chris Hilson, 'What's in a Right? The Relationship between Community, Fundamental and Citizenship Rights in EU Law' (2004) 29 *European Law Review* 636, 648.

[24] O'Leary (n 15) 540–41.

and the limits of equal treatment are interpreted in the case law of the Court of Justice. However, it is important to bear in mind that recognising equal treatment as a fundamental right may not provide a panacea for the interpretation of EU citizenship rights for various different reasons. Firstly, it has been noted that a 'deeper critique' of fundamental rights has traditionally been missing from EU law scholarship because almost any reference to personal rights was greeted by academic commentators as a welcome alternative to the purely economic goals of integration.[25] Secondly, it is controversial whether the assumption of 'shared values' as expressed in EU fundamental rights is simply misleading.[26] Thirdly, it is also controversial whether a rights-based model of anti-discrimination law is at all useful for redefining the EU principle of equality.[27] These concerns notwithstanding, the establishment of equal treatment as a fundamental right of all EU citizens at the level of primary law provides a logical starting point for the analysis of EU citizenship and equality. This evolution is important because it seemingly promises to transform the status of EU citizenship beyond Michelle Everson's well-known metaphor of 'Market Citizenship'.[28]

1.2.4 A Human Right Under the ECHR

In order to grasp a full picture of EU citizens' right to equal treatment irrespective of nationality, it is also important to briefly consider what role the prohibition of nationality discrimination plays in European human rights law more broadly understood. This is important not just in the light of the possible accession of the EU to the European Convention on Human Rights (ECHR), but also because the Convention has been recognised as a legitimate source of inspiration for the interpretation of EU law since the 1970s.[29] The fact that the right to non-discrimination on the grounds of nationality enjoys the status of a human right under the ECHR system could strengthen a more rights-based approach to Article 18 TFEU—despite the fact that the current level of protection against nationality discrimination under EU law is in many ways more stringent than under the ECHR, as discussed below in this section. In so far as Article 18 TFEU is primarily interpreted as a citizenship right, it can and must be critically examined through the lens of more universal human rights.

[25] eg Graínne de Búrca, 'The Language of Rights and European Integration' in Jo Shaw and Gillian More (eds), *New Legal Dynamics of European Union* (Clarendon Press, 1995) 29–30.

[26] eg JHH Weiler, 'To be a European Citizen—Eros and Civilization' (1997) 4 *Journal of European Public Policy* 495, 499–502. See also de Búrca (n 25) 45.

[27] eg Christopher McCrudden, 'Theorising European Equality Law' in Cathryn Costello and Ellis Barry (eds), *Equality In Diversity: The New Equality Directives* (Irish Centre for European Law, 2003) 20–22.

[28] Michelle Everson, 'The Legacy of the Market Citizen' in Jo Shaw and Gillian More (eds), *New Legal Dynamics of European Union* (Clarendon Press, 1995).

[29] See Opinion 2/13 of the Court (18 December 2014) for a detailed and highly critical view concerning the Union's possible accession to the ECHR.

The ECHR does not include an explicit prohibition of nationality discrimination. The European Court of Human Rights has nevertheless adopted the view that nationality can amount to 'other status' on the grounds of which discrimination is prohibited in the context of the enjoyment of Convention rights under Article 14 ECHR.[30] Moreover, Article 1 of Protocol No 12 of the Convention now includes a general prohibition of discrimination in 'the enjoyment of any right set forth by law' in all those Member States of the Council of Europe that have ratified this Protocol.[31] The Court confirmed in the *Gaygusuz* judgment that contributory social minimum benefits, such as the right to 'emergency assistance' in question, can fall into the ambit of Article 14 ECHR as 'a pecuniary right for the purposes of Article 1 of Protocol No. 1'.[32] In the later *Stec* case, the Court expanded this principle to cover all social benefits by stating that if a State 'does decide to create a benefits or pension scheme, it must do so in a manner which is compatible with Article 14 of the Convention'.[33] The prohibition of discrimination under Article 14 ECHR can, in theory, apply to some of those situations in which economically inactive and dependent EU citizens are not granted equal access to non-contributory social benefits because of their lack of integration under EU law. This argument must nonetheless be examined within the overall framework of the Convention system which currently adopts a more lenient approach to nationality discrimination than the EU framework.

It is characteristic of the Strasbourg Court that the intensity of scrutiny varies considerably between different grounds of discrimination.[34] The Court has made it clear that nationality discrimination can be justified only for 'very weighty reasons' and that the State's margin of appreciation must be applied narrowly in those cases.[35] However, the Strasbourg Court is famous for its generous interpretation of objective justifications which can be invoked both in the case of direct and indirect discrimination.[36] The EU Court of Justice holds that justifications for direct nationality discrimination can be accepted only if they take a form of statutory exceptions. Secondly, although a failure to treat different situations differently can now constitute discrimination under Article 14 ECHR,[37] it took several decades for the Strasbourg Court to recognise the harmfulness of indirect discrimination

[30] Article 14 of the European Convention of Human Rights states that 'The Enjoyment of the rights and freedoms set forth in this Convention shall be secured without discrimination on any ground such as sex, race, colour, language, religion, political or other opinion, national or social origin, association with a national minority, property, birth or other status'. European Convention for the Protection of Human Rights and Fundamental Freedoms as amended by Protocol No 11 (CETS No 155), Rome 4.XI.1950.

[31] The Protocol has already been ratified by 18 of 47 Member States of the Council of Europe.

[32] *Gaygusuz v Austria* ECHR 1996-IV, paras 39 and 41.

[33] *Stec v the UK* ECHR, 12 April 2006, para 53.

[34] Oddný Mjöll Arnardóttir, *Equality and Non-Discrimination under the European Convention on Human Rights* (Kluwer, 2003) 31 and 41.

[35] *Gaygusuz* (n 32) para 42.

[36] eg *Case 'relating to certain aspects of the laws on the use of languages in education in Belgium' v Belgium* ('Belgian Linguistic case') 23 July 1968 A6, Sec IB, para 10.

[37] eg *Thlimmenos v Greece* ECHR 2000-IV, para 44.

in the first place.[38] It has been argued that this recognition is still limited because the mere 'disparate impact' has not been regarded as sufficient proof for indirect discrimination but the applicant can be asked to prove the underlying cause of this impact.[39] This is a considerable difference with regard to EU law which prohibits nationality discrimination both in its 'overt' and 'covert' forms, as well as non-discriminatory obstacles to the freedom of movement both under Articles 21 and 45 TFEU.[40]

The Strasbourg Court has also showed deference to the limited personal scope of EU citizenship. The more beneficial treatment of Union citizens in the case of deportation came under scrutiny in the *Moustaquim v Belgium* and *C v Belgium* cases in which the Court stated that 'such preferential treatment is based on an objective and reasonable justification, given that the member States of the EU form a special legal order, which has, in addition, established its own citizenship'.[41] However, the Strasbourg Court seems less willing to defer to the limited material scope of EU citizenship. For instance, in the *Koua Poirrez* case, the Strasbourg Court found nationality discrimination in the situation in which one of the Member States had refused the allowance for disabled adults to the applicant who was resident as an adopted son of a Union citizen in the country of which the adoptive parent held the nationality.[42] This was in contrast to the fact that the Court of Justice had already decided that the case did not fall into the jurisdictional scope of the prohibition of nationality discrimination under EU law because it was a 'purely internal situation' without a sufficient connecting factor with EU law.[43] This case is an example of the different jurisdictional scopes of the prohibition of nationality discrimination under EU law and the ECHR. But it is plausible that the interpretations of what constitutes nationality discrimination under EU law and under the ECHR could also vary in so far as objective justifications for *prima facie* discriminatory treatment are concerned.

The Court of Justice has traditionally held that the protection of fundamental rights as general principles of Union law must happen within the 'structure' and

[38] *Hugh Jordan v the UK* App no 24746/94 (ECtHR, 4 May 2001) para 154. This approach was given more substance in *DH and Others v The Czech Republic* App no 57325/00 (ECtHR, 13 November 2007).

[39] Arnardóttir (n 34) 83–84 and 124.

[40] For indirect discrimination, see eg Case 152/73 *Giovanni Maria Sotgiu v Deutsche Bundespost* [1974] ECR 153, para 11 and Case C-278/94 *Commission of the European Community v Kingdom of Belgium* [1996] ECR 1-4307, para 27. For non-discriminatory obstacles to freedom of movement in the context of Article 45 TFEU, see Case C-415/93 *Union royale belge des sociétés de football association ASBL v Jean-Marc Boisman* [1995] ECR I-4921, para 96 and, in the context of Article 21 TFEU, in Case C-135/99 *Ursula Elsen v Bundesversicherungsanstalt für Angestellte* [2000] ECR I-409, para 34. The Court of Justice has held that national law can be indirectly discriminatory when 'it is intrinsically liable to' place a non-national at a particular disadvantage. Case C-237/94 *John O'Flynn v Adjudication Officer* [1996] ECR I-2617, para 20. See more about this in Chapter 2, Section 2.3.1, p 63.

[41] *Moustaquim v Belgium* 18 February 1991 A193, paras 48–49 and *C v Belgium* ECHR 1996-III, paras 37–38.

[42] *Koua Poirrez v France*, ECHR 30 September 2003, paras 16, 41 and 47–49.

[43] Case C-209/91 *Ettien Koua Poirrez v Caisse d'allocations familiales de la région parisienne* [1992] ECR I-6685, paras 10–13.

'overall objectives' of the Union.[44] A common fear is that the Court of Justice may apply the objective justification test too broadly in favour of fundamental freedoms at the expense of fundamental and human rights.[45] For instance, the *Viking* and *Laval* judgments have been criticised on the grounds that the Court of Justice justified fundamental rights on the basis of fundamental freedoms.[46] In practice, fundamental and human rights form one of the many dimensions of EU law, whereas the whole existence of the ECHR system is built upon the protection of individual rights.[47] It is therefore justified to pose the question of whether the possible accession of the Union to the ECHR would reflect any change in the 'overall objectives' of the Union. And, in particular, would it have any impact on the interpretation of Article 18 TFEU if the EU later becomes a Contracting Party to an international human rights instrument which recognises the prohibition of nationality discrimination in the field of non-contributory social benefits as a general human right and not as a mere citizenship right? These questions are important because the possible changes in the relationships between the Strasbourg and Luxembourg Courts might both reduce the Strasbourg Court's deference to the limited personal scope of the EU prohibition of nationality discrimination in regard to non-EU citizens and increase the potential for conflicts between EU law and the ECHR in so far as the scope of and the limitations on the prohibition of nationality discrimination are concerned.

1.3 BEYOND NATIONALITY DISCRIMINATION: THE EMERGENCE OF A NEW EQUALITY PROBLEM

The project of European integration arguably lacks a 'coherent political theory or philosophy' and it has been suggested that equality as a general principle of EU law could provide a way forward.[48] It has even been proposed that a general equality clause could be used to give legitimacy to the EU legal order as a whole.[49] But the

[44] Case 11/70 *Internationale Handelsgesellschaft mbH v Einfuhr- und Vorratsstelle für Getreide und Futtermittel* [1970] ECR 1125, para 4 and 4/73; *J Nold v Commission of the European Communities* [1974] ECR 491, para 14.

[45] eg John Morijn, 'Balancing Fundamental Rights and Common Market Freedoms in Union Law: Schmidberger and Omega in the Light of the European Constitution' (2006) 12 *European Law Journal* 15, 37.

[46] In the *Viking* and *Laval* judgments, the Court of Justice approached the right to collective action as a restriction to the fundamental freedom of establishment which can only be justified by an overriding public interest. See Case C-438/05 *International Transport Workers' Federation and Finnish Seamen's Union v Viking Line ABP and OÜ Viking Line Eesti* [2007] ECR I-10779, paras 75, 77 and 79; and Case C-341/05 *Laval un Partneri Ltd v Svenska Byggnadsarbetareförbundet* [2007] ECR I-11767.

[47] eg Tuomas Ojanen, *The European Way. The Structure of National Court Obligation under EC Law* (Gummerus, 1998); and Tuomas Ojanen, *EU-oikeuden perusteita* (Edita, 2006) 169.

[48] Gráinne de Búrca, 'The Role of Equality in European Community' in Alan Dashwood and Síofra O'Leary (eds), *The Principle of Equal Treatment in EC Law* (Sweet and Maxwell, 1997) 31–32 and 34.

[49] eg Erica Szyszczak, 'Building A European Constitutional Order: Prospects for a General Non-Discrimination Standard' in Dashwood and O'Leary (n 48) 35 and Catherine Barnard, 'P V. S: Kite Flying or A New Constitutional Approach?' in Dashwood and O'Leary (n 48) 67–68.

potential of equality to legitimate anything depends on whether the principle of equality provides a 'free-standing right' or merely a 'method of interpretation' in EU law.[50] The purely instrumental view of equality as a tool for completing the internal market has been challenged by the creation of EU citizenship but, at the same time, the limited competences of the EU constrain the principle of equality and non-discrimination as an 'autonomous' goal of EU law.[51] Any reference to equal treatment irrespective of nationality as a constitutional principle of EU law therefore raises a range of difficult questions: What does it mean that any citizen of the Union can rely on their right to equal treatment under Article 18 TFEU in all situations falling within the scope of the EU Treaties? Above all, what 'activates' the status of EU citizenship and, thus, EU citizens' right to non-discrimination and equal treatment? Does the judicial review under Article 18 TFEU always require a 'connecting factor' with one of the four fundamental freedoms, or shall citizens of the Union 'enjoy the rights conferred by the Treaty' as such, including the right to non-discrimination and equal treatment?

Towards the Prohibition of 'Migrant Discrimination' Between EU Citizens

The above questions show that the relationship between Article 18 TFEU and the four fundamental freedoms is a complex one. The fundamental freedoms can be understood both as prohibitions on nationality discrimination and as prohibitions on restrictions on cross-border mobility. Some commentators defend the traditional view of fundamental freedoms as prohibitions on nationality discrimination.[52] Others, however, suggest that it is better to distinguish between 'migration discrimination' and 'nationality discrimination' because the exercise of movement rights can provide an independent and self-sufficient rationale for the prohibition on discrimination.[53] On this basis, it has been argued that the general principle of non-discrimination on the grounds of nationality has become redundant because it fails to explain many of the Court's judgments in the area of 'migrant discrimination' under Article 21 TFEU.[54] At the same time, however,

[50] Barnard (n 49) 79.

[51] de Búrca (n 48) 26–27 and 30–31.

[52] eg Gareth Davies, *Nationality Discrimination in the European Internal Market* (Kluwer, 2002) and more recently eg in Gareth Davies, 'Discrimination and Beyond in European Economic and Social Law' (2011) 18 *Maastricht Journal of European and Comparative Law* 7. Davies' major concern is that '[w]here it is suggested that free movement law must go "beyond discrimination" this can only be understood as a call for positive action'. Davies argues further that 'some of the most important justifications for positive action in social law do not translate to the market context'.

[53] Anastasia Iliopoulou and Helen Toner, 'A New Approach to Discrimination against Free Movers?' (2003) 28 *European Law Review* 389, 392 and 394. For a more recent discussion see eg Niamh Nic Shuibhne, *The Coherence of EU Free Movement Law: Constitutional Responsibility and the Court of Justice* (Oxford University Press, 2013).

[54] Ferdinand Wollenschläger, 'A New Fundamental Freedom beyond Market Integration: Union Citizenship and its Dynamics for Shifting the Economic Paradigm of European Integration' (2011) 17 *European Law Journal* 1, 26. For this line of case law see eg Case C-224/02 *Heikki Antero Pusa v*

it has also been noted that the focus of the case-law has moved from 'the simple fact of movement' towards 'a more substantive or material connection'.[55] This has led some commentators to consider whether equal treatment between Union citizens and the nationals of the host Member States could be derived from their 'mere presence' in the territory of another Member State rather than the exercise of their right to free movement.[56] These different interpretations of how the non-discrimination principle relates to the fundamental freedoms illustrate the changing relationship between 'non-discrimination' and 'equal treatment' in EU law.

One way to explain the prohibition of non-discriminatory obstacles to free movement in EU law takes the form of the market access theory.[57] The Court of Justice summarised this idea in the so-called 'Gebhard test', which states that 'national measures liable to hinder or make less attractive the exercise of fundamental freedoms guaranteed by the Treaty' must *inter alia* be 'applied in a non-discriminatory manner' and 'must be justified by imperative requirements in the general interest'.[58] But several authors now agree that the traditional market access theory fails to explain the prohibition of non-discriminatory obstacles to the non-economic free movement of persons and that EU citizenship could, potentially, explain the move away from the 'internal market rationale' towards 'protecting the *individual* from disproportionate regulations imposed by Member States regardless of an effect, even only potential, on the exercise of intra-Community economic activities', as Eleanora Spaventa has put it.[59] It has also been suggested that

Osuuspankkien Keskinäinen Vakuutusyhtiö [2004] ECR I-5763, para 19; Case C-224/98 *Marie-Nathalie D'Hoop v Office national de l'emploi* [2002] ECR I-6191, para 31 and Case C-406/04 *Gérald De Cuyper v Office national de l'emploi* [2006] ECR I-6947, para 39.

[55] Niamh Nic Shuibhne, 'The European Union and Fundamental Rights: Well in Spirit but Considerably Rumpled in Body?' in Paul Beaumont, Carole Lyons and Neil Walker (eds), *Convergence and Divergence in European Public Law* (Hart Publishing, 2002) 194.

[56] Niamh Nic Shuibhne, 'Free Movement of Persons and the Wholly Internal Rule: Time to Move On?' (2002) 39 *Common Market Law Review* 731, 750.

[57] See more about the concept of 'market access' in Jukka Snell, 'The Notion of Market Access: A Concept or a Slogan?' (2010) 47 *Common Market Law Review* 437.

[58] The Court of Justice also hold that these measures 'must be suitable for securing the attainment of the objective which they pursue; and they must not go beyond what is necessary in order to attain it'. Case C-55/94 *Reinhard Gebhard v Consiglio dell'Ordine degli Avvocati e Procuratori di Milano* [1995] ECR I-4165, para 37. Other relevant cases include Case C-19/92 *Kraus* [1993] ECR I-1663; *Union royale belge* (n 40); Case C-190/98 *Volker Graf v Filzmoser Maschinebau GmbH* [2000] ECR I-493 and Case C-60/00 *Mary Carpenter v Secretary of State for the Home Department* [2002] ECR I-6279. The case law on non-discriminatory obstacles has been summarised by Stephen Weatherill as follows: 'The injection of an adequate cross-border element enables a claim not simply to an equality right, but instead to the dynamic protection of Community law on free movement, subject only to the capacity of the regulator to show justification for the restriction (when the focus shifts to the legislative role)'. Stephen Weatherill, 'After Keck: Some Thoughts on How to Clarify the Clarification' (1996) 33 *Common Market Law Review* 885, 904–05.

[59] Eleanora Spaventa, 'From Gebhard to Carpenter: Towards a (Non-)Economic European Constitution' (2004) 41 *Common Market Law Review* 743, 744 and 768. According to Spaventa, the difficulties in defining what constitutes an obstacle to market access implies that '[t]he market access test might indeed attempt to conceal the fact that the Court's interpretation of the free movement provisions might no longer be justified with regard to the internal market rationale alone'. Ibid 764.

this development can be seen as a step away from the formal concept of equality towards a more substantive concept of equality.[60] The lessening importance of the prohibition of nationality discrimination in the context of free movement of persons can thus actually imply an increasing interest in equal treatment of EU citizens.

Towards the Prohibition of 'Reverse Discrimination' Between EU Citizens

Although the right to free movement has been described as the 'core and origin'[61] of EU citizenship, EU citizenship can also be viewed as a 'non-economic *lex generalis* behind the fundamental freedoms'[62] or as 'a rearrangement of the prior distinction between *lex specialis* and *lex generalis*'.[63] In order to understand the EU principle of equality, one must, therefore, understand what consequences the shift of focus from 'nationality discrimination' towards 'equal citizenship' has on EU citizens' right to non-discrimination and equal treatment under EU law. The dynamic interpretation of EU citizenship as 'the fundamental status of nationals of the Member States' by the Court of Justice[64] has equipped the right to non-discrimination on the grounds of nationality with an entirely new tenet. At the same time, however, the meaning and purpose of 'equal treatment' has remained ambiguous in relation to EU citizens' general right to equal treatment. A common concern is that EU citizens whose situation is defined as 'purely internal' cannot invoke the right to non-discrimination and equal treatment irrespective of nationality under EU law and may thus suffer from 'reverse discrimination' in comparison with migrant EU citizens who are protected under EU law.[65]

Economically active EU citizens enjoy the right to non-discrimination and equal treatment on the basis of their status as 'Union workers' under Article 45 TFEU and Article 7 of Regulation 492/2011 or as service providers or self-employed persons under Articles 49 and 56 TFEU.[66] In the case of economically inactive EU

[60] Mattias Malmstedt, 'From Employee to EU Citizen—A Development From Equal Treatment as a Means to Equal Treatment as a Goal?' in Ann Numhauser-Henning (ed), *Legal Perspectives on Equal Treatment and Non-Discrimination* (Kluwer, 2001) 120.

[61] Hans Ulrich and Jessurun d'Oliveira, 'European Citizenship: Its Meaning, Its Potential' in Renaud Delhousse (ed), *Europe After Maastricht: An Ever Closer Union?* (Beck Law Books, 1994) 132.

[62] Wollenschläger (n 54) 30. For more discussion, see eg Pedro Caro de Sousa, 'Quest for the Holy Grail—Is a Unified Approach to the Market Freedoms and European Citizenship Justified?' (2014) 20 *European Law Journal* 499, 511–13.

[63] Sybilla Fries and Jo Shaw, 'Citizenship of the Union: First Steps in the European Court of Justice' (1998) 4 *European Public Law* 533, 559.

[64] See eg Case C-184/99 *Rudy Grzelczyk v Centre public d'aide sociale d'Ottignies-Louvain-la-Neuve* [2001] ECR I-6193, para 31; Case C-413/99 *Baumbast and R v Secretary of State for the Home Department* [2002] ECR I-7091, para 82 and Case C-148/02 *Carlos Garcia Avello v Belgian State* [2003] ECR I-11613, para 22.

[65] See eg Alina Tryfonidou, *Reverse Discrimination in EC Law* (Kluwer, 2009).

[66] See Article 45 TFEU on the freedom of movement for workers; Article 49 TFEU on the right of establishment; and Article 56 TFEU on the freedom to provide services. See also Article 7(2) of

citizens, it has been more obscure how a sufficient 'connecting factor' with EU law is established for a case to fall into the scope of the general prohibition of nationality discrimination under Article 18 TFEU. The Court's traditional understanding is that the Treaty provision on non-discrimination and equal treatment does not apply to the so-called purely internal situations 'where there is no factor connecting them to any of the situations envisaged by Community law'.[67] However, the requirement of a link to 'any of the situations envisaged by Community law' has been interpreted loosely in such familiar cases as *Surinder Singh*, *Zhu and Chen*, and *Carpenter*.[68] In practice, the requirement of a cross-border link as a 'connecting factor' now covers many situations with a 'very tenuous'[69] link with the fundamental freedoms.

EU citizenship has played an important role in transforming the requirement of a 'connecting factor' from purely activity-based standards towards a more status-based understanding of what relates an individual to the Union. At the same time, however, it has remained unclear what exactly activates the status of EU citizenship in those cases in which a Union citizen has not made use of the right to free movement but which still cannot be assimilated to purely internal situations 'for that reason alone',[70] as the Court has put it. In the more recent *Ruiz Zambrano* case, the Court of Justice seemed to finally address this question in its statement that Article 20 TFEU 'precludes national measures which have the effect of depriving citizens of the Union the genuine enjoyment of the substance of the rights conferred by virtue of their status as citizens of the Union'.[71] The Court's reasoning in this seminal case was unfortunately short-spoken, but what was noticeable was

Regulation (EU) No 492/2011 of the European Parliament and of the Council of 5 April 2011 on freedom of movement for workers within the Union [2011] OJ L141/1 and Articles 19 and 20 of Directive 2006/123/EC of the European Parliament and of the Council of 12 December 2006 on services in the internal market [2006] OJ L376/36.

[67] eg Case 175/78 *The Queen v Vera Ann Saunders* [1979] ECR 1129, para 11.

[68] In the *Zhu and Chen* case, the Court stated that '[t]he situation of a national of a Member State who was born in the host Member State and has not made use of the right to freedom of movement cannot, for that reason alone, be assimilated to a purely internal situation'. Case C-200/02 *Kunqian Catherine Zhu and Man Lavette Chen v Secretary of State for the Home Department* [2004] ECR I-9925, para 19. Similarly, the Court has accepted that the rights to free movement and establishment must not be violated by the country of origin 'when a Community national who has availed himself or herself of those rights returns to his or her country of origin'. Case C-370/90 *The Queen v Immigration Appeal Tribunal and Surinder Singh, ex parte Secretary of State for Home Department* [1992] ECR I-4265, para 23. See also *Mary Carpenter* (n 58) paras 30 and 39.

[69] Alina Tryfonidou, 'Reverse Discrimination in Purely Internal Situations: An Incongruity in a Citizens' Europe' (2008) 35 *Legal Issues of Economic Integration* 43, 44.

[70] eg *Zhu and Chen* (n 68) para 19.

[71] Case C-34/09 *Gerardo Ruiz Zambrano v Office national de l'emploi (ONEM)* [2011] ECR I-1177, paras 42 and 45. In the earlier *Rottmann* case, the Court had already decided that the decision to withdraw the naturalisation of the applicant in that case could be in breach of EU law on the basis that 'a citizen of the Union may, because he loses his nationality, lose his status of citizen of the Union and thereby be deprived of the rights attaching to that status'. Case C-135/08 *Janko Rottmann v Freistaat Bayern* [2010] ECR I-1449, para 46.

the clear emphasis on the *status* of EU citizenship, irrespective of the activities pursued by a Union citizen.[72]

However, the Court of Justice qualified the reference to the genuine enjoyment of the substance of EU citizenship rights in the later *McCarthy* and *Dereci* judgments, both of which underlined that the criterion relating to the denial of the genuine enjoyment of the substance of EU citizenship rights refers to those rather extreme situations in which 'the Union citizen has, in fact, to leave not only the territory of the Member State of which he is a national but also the territory of the Union as a whole'.[73] Moreover, in the *Ymeraga* judgment, the Court stated that, although a national of the Member State might hope, 'for economic reasons or in order to keep his family together', that his family members who are not EU citizens could reside with him in the territory of the Union, this would not suffice to support the claim that the EU citizen would need to leave the Union as a whole if such right to residence is not granted to his family members.[74] These judgments show that the new criterion of 'genuine enjoyment of the substance of EU citizenship rights' only provides an exception to the main rule that Articles 21 and 18 TFEU are not applicable to EU citizens who have not exercised their right to free movement and who have always resided in the Member State of which they are nationals.[75] It has aptly been noted that this case law seems to distinguish between the 'status of Union citizenship' and the 'exercise of certain rights which that status confers'.[76]

Despite these qualifications, the Court's reference to the 'genuine enjoyment of the substance of Union citizens' rights' provided a new tool for the assessment of the traditional distinction between the purely internal situations and a sufficient connecting factor with EU law. The broad interpretation of the *Ruiz Zambrano* case could suggest that the mere 'interaction'[77] between national law and Article 21

[72] More detailed reasoning was found in the Opinion of AG Sharpston which compensates the artlessness of the Court's judgment both in length and in breadth. The AG considered whether EU citizenship implies a 'true citizenship' beyond being merely a 'non-economic version of the same generic kind of free-movement rights as have long existed for the economically active and for persons of independent means'. Opinion of AG Sharpston in *Ruiz Zambrano* (n 71) para 3. Her suggestion was that Article 18 TFEU should be applicable if reverse discrimination is caused by the 'interaction between Article 21 TFEU and national law' and the following three 'cumulative conditions' would be met: (1) the situation of 'static' Union citizens must be 'comparable, in other material respects', to that of migrant Union citizens, (2) the case 'would entail a violation of a fundamental right protected under EU law' and (3) 'equivalent' protection would not be available under national law. Ibid, paras 144–48.

[73] Case C-256/11 *Murat Dereci, Vishaka Heiml, Alban Kokollari, Izunna Emmanuel Maduike, Dragica Stevic v Bundesministerium für Inneres*, [2011] ECR I-11315, para 66. See also Case C-434/09 *Shirley McCarthy v Secretary of State for the Home Department* [2011] ECR I-3375, paras 49–50.

[74] Case C-87/12 *Kreshnik Ymeraga, Kasim Ymeraga, Afijete Ymeraga-Tafarshiku, Kushtrim Ymeraga, Labinot Ymeraga v Ministre du Travail, de l'Emploi et de l'Immigration*, 8 May 2013, paras 38 and 45.

[75] *Murat Dereci et al* (n 73) para 74 and *Shirley McCarthy* (n 73) paras 55–56.

[76] Síofra O'Leary, 'The Past, Present and Future of the Purely Internal Rule in EU Law' in Michael Dougan, Niamh Nic Shuibhne and Eleanora Spaventa (eds), *Empowerment and Disempowerment of the European Citizen* (Hart Publishing, 2012) 58.

[77] See Opinion of AG Sharpston in *Ruiz Zambrano* (n 71) para 144.

TFEU might sometimes be enough to bring the case into the jurisdictional scope of EU citizenship rights, including the right to non-discrimination and equal treatment under Article 18 TFEU. It is therefore easy to understand why EU citizenship is seen as 'slowly but steadily evolving into a fifth Treaty freedom'.[78] Whether the non-application of EU law to 'purely internal situations' is compatible with the idea of EU citizenship has recently been discussed by several authors.[79] However, the conditions and limitations of free-movement rights can constitute an additional level of '*de facto*' discrimination, not just in the case of 'static' EU citizens who fall outside the jurisdictional scope of Article 18 TFEU, but also in the case of 'needy' migrant EU citizens.[80] The critical analysis of EU citizens' right to non-discrimination and equal treatment can therefore not be limited to the mere jurisdictional issues in regard to reverse discrimination but the question of the substantive content of the EU principle of equality, ie what rights are conferred on EU citizens and how these rights can be limited, must also be examined.

Towards Even More Substance for EU Citizenship?

Very few legal rights are absolute and the same is true for the right to non-discrimination and equal treatment under EU law. The right to equal treatment has been thoroughly analysed in recent EU law scholarship in relation to 'reverse discrimination' in what the Court of Justice calls 'purely internal situations', as discussed above. It is also clear that the limited personal scope of EU citizenship leads to the standard of mere 'near-equality' in so far as long-term resident third-country nationals are concerned.[81] This problem has been addressed by many

[78] Editorial Comments, 'Two-speed European Citizenship? Can the Lisbon Treaty Help Close the Gap?' (2008) 45 *Common Market Law Review* 1, 1.

[79] Some authors argue that the possibility of reverse discrimination is in conflict with the idea of EU citizenship, while others claim that the purely internal situation doctrine is 'a suitable instrument to meet the constitutional necessity of respecting the division of powers between the Union and its Member States'. eg Dominik Hanf, '"Reverse Discrimination" in EU Law: Constitutional Aberration, Constitutional Necessity, or Judicial Choice?' (2011) 18 *Maastricht Journal of European and Comparative Law* 29.

[80] See eg Dimitry Kochenov, '*Ius Tractum* of Many Faces: European Citizenship and the Difficult Relationship between Status and Rights' (2009) 15 *Columbia Journal of European Law* 169, 196. For further discussion see also eg Dimitry Kochenov, 'The Right to Have *What* Rights? EU Citizenship in Need of Clarification' (2013) 19 *European Law Journal* 502, 515–16.

[81] Article 20 TFEU grants the status of EU citizenship to nationals of the Member States. Those long-term resident third country nationals who fall into the scope of Directive 2003/109/EC of 25 November 2003 concerning the status of third-country nationals who are long-term residents [2004] L16/44 are now entitled to enjoy equal treatment under Article 11 of the Directive. But they fall outside the prohibition on nationality discrimination under Article 18 TFEU, as well as outside the Treaty-based free-movement provisions. The situation of those third-country nationals who do not fall into the scope of Directive 2003/109/EC is even weaker. See further eg Louise Halleskov, 'The Long-Term Residents Directive: A Fulfilment of the Tampere Objective of Near-Equality' (2005) 7 *European Journal of Migration and Law* 181. However, for a more positive approach, see eg Diego Acosta Arcarazo, 'Civic Citizenship reintroduced? The Long-Term Residence Directive as a Post-National Form of Membership' (2015) 21 *European Law Journal* 200, 207.

authors who argue for more inclusive 'postnational' or 'transnational' conceptions of EU citizenship.[82] One of the best examples is Dora Kostakopoulou's argument that the 'nationality model' of EU citizenship undermines the 'transformative' or 'constructive' potential of EU citizenship.[83] This book shares her concern that 'the normative foundations and boundaries of membership in the European polity must be rethought'.[84] Too often, however, the critical analysis has been limited to the jurisdictional scope of EU citizenship in relation to third-country nationals and in regard to purely internal situations. Despite the proliferation of academic literature on EU citizenship, EU law scholarship has failed to fully address the question of what equality means between EU citizens and how the accepted material limitations on EU citizens' right to equal treatment qualify the status of EU citizenship.

The continuous debate on the external boundaries of EU citizenship is important.[85] However, what defines EU citizenship as an equal status is how those private individuals who already hold the status of EU citizenship are treated in relation to one another. The focus of this book therefore concerns those individuals who jurisdictionally qualify for the right to non-discrimination under EU law, that is migrant EU citizens, but who are banned from equal treatment because of their lack of belonging to the society of the host Member State. Namely, only by looking at the justificatory criteria for legitimate differential treatment between different groups of Union citizens, is it possible to grasp what the *de facto* scope of EU citizenship is in the realm of non-discrimination and equality. The emerging EU equality problem can therefore be defined as the question of what the substance of EU citizenship is when it comes to equal treatment between EU citizens.

The creation of EU citizenship has inspired comments that equality has now been 'constitutionalized in favour of Union Citizens'.[86] However, the accepted conditions and limitations on EU citizens' right to non-discrimination and equal treatment qualify the nature of EU citizenship as an equal status. The limited access to EU citizenship rights in the case of non-moving EU citizens is often regarded as the main example for the lack of substance of Union citizens' rights to equal treatment. But the limitations on EU citizens' right to non-discrimination

[82] eg Dora Kostakopoulou, *The Future Governance of Citizenship* (Cambridge University Press, 2008).

[83] See eg Dora Kostakopoulou, 'European Union Citizenship: Writing the Future' (2007) 13 *European Law Journal* 623, 626–28. See further her argument of 'constructive citizenship' as a way 'to invent an alternative strategy for dealing with difference' in Dora Kostakopoulou, 'Towards a Theory of Constructive Citizenship in Europe' (1996) 4 *The Journal of Political Philosophy* 337, 341.

[84] Dora Kostakopoulou, 'Nested "Old" and "New" Citizenship in the European Union: Bringing Out the Complexity' (1998–99) 5 *Columbian Journal of European Law* 389, 413.

[85] See eg Kostakopoulou, 'European Union Citizenship' (n 83) 634 who argues that 'Processes of equalisation—co-exist with processes of exclusion, and the relativisation of the Member States' borders is accompanied by the reinforcement of the external frontiers of the Union'. A similar argument is made in Mark Bell, 'Civic Citizenship and Migrant Integration' (2007) 13 *European Public Law* 311, 314.

[86] Andrew Evans, 'Union Citizenship and the Constitutionalization of Equality in EU Law' in Massimo La Torre (ed), *European Citizenship: An Institutional Challenge* (Kluwer, 1998) 267–68.

and equal treatment can also be more substantive, stemming from the application of the objective justification test in those cases which fall into the jurisdictional scope of application of Article 18 TFEU. The dynamic interpretation of EU citizenship has influenced the so-called 'outer limits' of EU citizens' right to equal treatment, ie the requirement of a cross-border element and the non-application of EU law to 'purely internal situations'. But it is equally important to consider the question of how EU citizenship affects what has been called the 'inner limits' of EU citizens' right to equal treatment, ie those limits that 'lie inside the notion of discrimination itself'.[87] It is under these justificatory criteria for differential treatment between EU citizens that the nature of EU citizenship as an equal status is ultimately defined.

Similarly, it has been argued in the recent commentary that EU citizens' access to equal treatment, or the lack of it, can be seen as 'a barometer for the autonomous content of citizenship'.[88] In order to understand the nature of EU citizenship, more attention must therefore be directed to those situations in which 'EU citizens are treated as aliens or foreigners', as Dora Kostakopoulou has put it.[89] It has been noted that the Court's case law has recently placed more weight on the conditions and limitations on EU citizenship rights in secondary legislation and that this directly affects 'the legal shape of citizenship'.[90] As a consequence, it becomes obscure what EU citizenship as a fundamental status 'grounded in meaningful primary rights' means today.[91] For instance, Niamh Nic Shuibhne speaks of 'a more wide-scale and sustained recent shift from *predominantly* rights-opening to *predominantly* rights-curbing assessment of citizenship rights' in this context.[92] It is this question of how legitimate differential treatment between EU citizens differs from unlawful discrimination and what limitations are imposed on the right to non-discrimination and equal treatment under Article 18 TFEU which also underlies the critical analysis of EU citizenship in the next chapter.

EU citizenship has arguably created a new 'social space' within which 'our conceptions of community, membership, and democracy are reconfigured'.[93] The EU

[87] eg Anne Pieter Van der Mei distinguishes between the **'outer limits'** of Article 18 TFEU which refer to the requirement of a cross-border element and the non-application of EU law in internal situations, and the **'inner limits'** which 'lie inside the notion of discrimination itself' in the sense that differential treatment can be labelled discriminatory in so far as nationals and non-nationals are in a 'comparable position' and differential treatment 'cannot be justified'. See Anne Pieter Van der Mei, 'The Outer Limits of the Prohibition of Discrimination on the Grounds of Nationality: A Look through the Lens of Union Citizenship' (2011) 18 *Maastricht Journal of European and Comparative Law* 62.

[88] Niamh Nic Shuibhne, 'Limits Rising, Duties Ascending: The Changing Legal Shape of Union Citizenship' (2015) 52 *Common Market Law Review* 889, 915.

[89] Dora Kostakopoulou, 'When EU Citizens become Foreigners' (2014) 20 *European Law Journal* 447, 448.

[90] Nic Shuibhne (n 88) 891. See, for a similar argument, Daniel Thym, 'The Elusive Limits of Solidarity: Residence Rights of and Social Benefits for Economically Inactive Union Citizens' (2015) 52 *Common Market Law Review* 17, 25.

[91] Nic Shuibhne (n 88) 892.

[92] Nic Shuibhne (n 88) 902.

[93] Kostakopoulou (n 89) 450.

has also been described as an 'emergent polity'.[94] From this starting point, it has been noted that an important substantive question is how the 'terms of citizenship' are defined in such a polity. For instance Antje Wiener writes: 'If the definition of the polity depends not only on what constitutes a polity but also on how this polity is constituted and reconstituted through practice, then analysis of constitutional politics needs to take account of citizenship.'[95] But EU citizenship as a transformative political concept will remain largely meaningless as long as some EU citizens cannot enjoy their citizenship rights, such as the right to free movement and residence, because of their need for social assistance.[96] It is therefore important to consider what equal treatment, and not just non-discrimination, means for needy and dependent EU citizens.

When the need for a more substantive analysis of EU citizens' right to non-discrimination and equal treatment has been recognised, the focus of scholarly enquiry has typically been on EU citizens' right to reside in Member States other than their State of origin, while the Court's mantra of 'equal treatment of all those legally residing in the area of another Member State' has been taken for granted.[97] In practice, however, the right to equal treatment is far from absolute even in those cases in which an economically inactive Union citizen is legally resident in another Member State. In the case of economically inactive and dependent migrant EU citizens, the limits of the right to non-discrimination and equal treatment are defined by using the requirement of economic or social integration as a decisive criterion, as will be seen in the next chapter. But, before turning to a more detailed analysis of the EU equality problem, it is informative to briefly consider the differences between the status of EU citizenship and the status of national democratic citizenship.

1.4 THE QUEST FOR EQUAL CITIZENSHIP IN EU LAW: SOMETHING DIFFERENT?

In a modern democratic state, citizenship rights belong to everyone. This development contains its own paradox: the removal of social exclusion within a State has consolidated citizenship as a status which predominantly refers to 'membership in a *particular* community'.[98] In practice, the two meanings of citizenship as a form of membership and as a form of participation are now closely intertwined.[99]

[94] Antje Wiener, 'Constitution-making and Citizenship Practice—Bridging the Democracy Gap in the EU?' (1997) 35 *Journal of Common Market Studies* 595, 596.

[95] Ibid 598.

[96] eg Síofra O'Leary, *The Evolving Concept of Community Citizenship: From the Free Movement of Persons to Union Citizenship* (Kluwer, 1996) 99. See also Commission, 'Second Report from the Commission on Citizenship of the Union' COM(1997) 230 final.

[97] See in more detail in Chapter 2, p 40.

[98] See further eg Ulrich Preuß, 'Problems of a Concept of European Citizenship' (1995) 1 *European Law Journal* 267, 269.

[99] Massimo La Torre, 'Citizenship: A European Wager' (1995) 8 *Ratio Juris* 113, 114 and 121.

This development is vividly captured in Ulrich Preuß's statement that citizenship as including particular rights and duties and citizenship as granting a membership of a political community now present 'two sides of one and the same coin whose message is: citizenship is an exclusive status'.[100] The emphasis on exclusive national citizenship explains why the idea of transnational (let alone global) citizenship seems so controversial to many authors.[101] Although the differentiation between nationality[102] and citizenship[103] has lost much of its practical relevance in a democratic national state,[104] the conceptual and normative difference between these two statuses is still relevant for understanding what a membership of society means in practice and in theory, as well as for understanding what it could mean in the transnational context.

As national self-consciousness promises to connect those 'who had been strangers to one another' by creating a 'more abstract form of social integration', it is important to consider what type of consciousness could function as a motivating factor for new forms of integration within an emerging transnational polity, such as the European Union, and whether EU citizenship has any role to play in

[100] Ulrich Preuß, 'Citizenship and Identity: Aspects of a Political Theory of Citizenship' in Richard Bellamy, Vittorio Butacchi and Dario Castiglione (eds), *Democracy and Constitutional Culture in the Union of Europe* (Lothian Foundation Press, 1995) 107.

[101] The tension between these two approaches to citizenship is addressed by eg Michael Walzer, David Miller and Rogers Brubaker. See also Richard Bellamy, 'Evaluating Union Citizenship: Belonging, Rights and Participation within the EU' (2008) 12 *Citizenship Studies* 597, 609 for an argument that 'European citizenship must continue to be but an adjunct to national citizenship'. Along with the notions of 'origin' and 'culture', citizenship arguably forms one of the 'three major dimensions of nationalist projects'. See Nira Yuval-Davis, *Gender & Nation* (SAGE Publications, 1997) 21.

[102] *Nationality* has historically been attached to the person's origin on the basis of birth. In Roman law, the term *natio* referred to a community built upon geographical and family relations, whereas the term *civitas* referred to the political community. As time went on, it became more common to move from these concrete attributes to the use of nationality as identification for a more abstract idea of shared identity. In the aftermath of, first, the Peace of Westphalia and, then, the French Revolution, the political sovereignty of the State came to be derived directly from the ideals of nation and nationality. In other words, nationality was no longer an attribute of a pre-political community, but it was given a primary normative role in defining the political identity and democratic community. See eg Jürgen Habermas, 'Citizenship and National Identity' in Bart van Steenbergen (ed), *The Condition of Citizenship* (SAGE Publications, 1994) 22–23.

[103] *Citizenship* defines the position of an individual in relation to a political community. The dual role of citizens both as the objects and the subjects of a political community requires autonomy and loyalty. For this reason, citizenship rights were originally limited to a small elite. See Hans van Gunsteren, 'Four Concepts of Citizenship' in Bart van Steenbergen (ed), *The Condition of Citizenship* (SAGE Publications, 1994) 36. At the other end of the scale, the Enlightenment idea of citizenship started to toy with a more universalistic or cosmopolitan distribution of certain citizenship rights. It was along with the industrialisation and protectionist economic policy that the rights to free movement and residence became privileges accessible only to the members of the State community. For more detail, see Síofra O'Leary (n 96) 103–04.

[104] Preuß (n 98) 269. For the idea of nationalism as the normative source of political identity see eg David Miller, *Citizenship and National Identity* (Polity Press with Blackwell, 2000). However, it is worth noting in this context how some have convincingly developed the argument of nations as 'imagined political communities'. See Benedict Anderson, *Imagined Communities Reflections on the Origin and Spread of Nationalism* (Verso, 1983).

this task.[105] For instance, Jürgen Habermas has noted that a 'conceptual gap' between the constitutional state and the nation will always remain for the very reason that both the territorial and the social boundaries always appear as normatively 'contingent'.[106] It is this 'gap' between 'nationality' and 'constitutional citizenship' that can justify the idea of transnational citizenship. At the same time, it is clear that any attempt to expand the concept of citizenship beyond the boundaries of a nation state must address a whole range of difficult legal and political questions. The current status of EU citizenship provides an excellent example of what these difficulties and compromises are. The quest for more equal transnational citizenship lies at the cross-road of the Union's notorious democracy and justice-deficits but, for this very reason, it also has a unique potential to provide a constructive perspective on these questions, as will be shown in Chapter three.

The concept of EU citizenship can be examined both as a 'normative' and 'descriptive' concept.[107] In the absence of a clear-cut European *Demos*, the normative potential of EU citizenship has become more important than its descriptive dimensions. As a normative concept, EU citizenship can be derived from a liberal ideal of status-based citizenship rights or from a communitarian ideal of shared cultural identity.[108] This means that the rights of EU citizens can either be seen as status rights or as common rights based on the bond between EU citizens.[109] Besides these two approaches, it has also been envisioned how 'European citizenship would open the symbolic space for social activities which could finally lead to a European "*societas civilis sive politica*", ie a civil society beyond the physical boundaries of the nation-states'.[110] All of these normative approaches to EU citizenship can see the principle of equality within EU citizenship as one of the practical methods of 're-formulating' the traditional concept

[105] Jürgen Habermas, 'The European Nation State. Its Achievements and Its Limitations. On the Past and Future of Sovereignty and Citizenship' (1996) 9 *Ratio Juris* 9(2) 125, 128–29. Habermas' own focus lies in the idea of democratic citizenship which would 'generate solidarity between strangers' and under which citizens concern their citizenship as 'the frame for that dialectic between legal and actual equality from which fair and preferable living conditions for all of them can emerge'. Ibid 134–35. This vision of 'constitutional patriotism' leads Habermas to conclude that 'the nation state can no longer provide the appropriate frame for the maintenance of democratic citizenship in the foreseeable future'. Ibid 137.

[106] Ibid 131–32.

[107] For instance, Jo Shaw has pointed out that it is important to recognise the 'interaction' between 'a narrow and formal legal concept of citizenship', on the one hand, and 'a broader notion of "membership" comprising constitutional, political and socio-economic elements', on the other. Jo Shaw, 'The Interpretation of European Union Citizenship' (1998) 61 *Modern Law Review* 293, 294. See also eg Jo Shaw, 'Citizenship: Contrasting Dynamics of the Interface of Integration and Constitutionalism' in Paul Craig and Graínne de Búrca (eds), *The Evolution of EU Law* (Oxford University Press, 2011) 575–609. Similarly, Norbert Reich has formulated the question of EU citizenship by asking whether it is 'merely a legal concept which defines a formal link of European citizens via nationality' or whether it can also be 'extended to some fundamental civic, political, and social links'. Norbert Reich, 'Union Citizenship—Metaphor or Source of Rights?' (2001) 7 *European Law Journal* 4, 5.

[108] Gerard Delanty, 'Models of Citizenship: Defining European Identity and Citizenship' (1997) 1 *Citizenship Studies* 285, 285.

[109] Ulrich Preuß, 'Two Challenges to European Citizenship' (1996) *Political Studies* XLIV 534, 548–49.

[110] Preuß (n 98) 280.

of citizenship.[111] However, the reference to a new 'equality problem' above in this chapter has already pointed out that it is far from clear how far EU citizenship can go in this direction without a clearer normative justification for why EU citizenship should matter as an equal status at the current stage of European integration.

EU citizenship is inherently different from national citizenship due to its lack of independence. What applies to citizenship in a national state does not automatically apply to a 'derived'[112] citizenship or an 'intermediate status between a qualified legal subjectivity—and full citizenship'[113] in a transnational polity. Moreover, EU citizenship 'is different from "citizenship" as we know it', not just because of its complementary nature in relation to national citizenship but also because of 'its content in terms of *legal status*'.[114]

1) The rights of EU citizenship primarily advance the legal status of private individuals in countries other than their country of origin.[115] Thus, the creation of EU citizenship has challenged the link between the status of nationality and the enjoyment of citizenship rights.[116]
2) EU citizenship defines the status of Union citizens in relation to the host Member State, rather than in relation to the Union itself.[117]
3) EU citizens' primary rights to free movement, residence, and equal treatment do not just differ from universal fundamental or human rights in their 'partiality',[118] but they also differ conceptually from classic citizenship rights.[119]
4) The right of Union citizens to free movement and residence is argued to be 'highly anomalous'[120] when compared to modern citizenship rights because of a 'glaring disparity of treatment'[121] between economically active and inactive EU citizens.

[111] Carlos Closa, 'Supranational Citizenship and Democracy: Normative and Empirical Dimensions' in La Torre (n 86) 431.

[112] Carlos Closa, 'Citizenship of the Union and Nationality of the Member States' (1995) 32 *Common Market Law Review* 487, 510.

[113] La Torre (n 99) 122.

[114] Vicenzo Lippolis, 'European Citizenship: What it is and What it Could be' in La Torre (n 86) 317.

[115] Ibid 320.

[116] Andrew Evans, 'Nationality Law and European Integration' (1991) 16 *European Law Review* 190, 190.

[117] Wollenschläger (n 54) 2. The status of EU citizenship confers rights on Union citizens both directly in relation to the Union itself and by virtue of the right to equal treatment in relation to the Member States. In the latter case, the Member States are obliged to grant Union citizens the same rights and benefits as they grant to their own nationals. See further eg Anne Pieter Van der Mei, 'The Elusive and Exclusive Concept of Union Citizenship, A Review Essay' (1998) 5 *Maastricht Journal of European and Comparative Law* 391, 394.

[118] Hilson (n 23) 642. See also eg Robin CA White, 'Free Movement, Equal Treatment, and Citizenship of the Union' (2005) 54 *International and Comparative Law Quarterly* 885, 902 and Preuß (n 98) 275.

[119] Roy Davis, 'Citizenship of the Union … Rights For All?' (2002) 27 *European Law Review* 121, 121. For more recent discussion about political rights in the context of EU citizenship, see eg Hanneke van Eijken, *EU Citizenship & the Constitutionalisation of the European Union* (Europa Law Publishing, 2015) 201–4.

[120] Davis (n 119) 131.

[121] Stefano Giubboni, 'A Certain Degree of Solidarity? Free Movement of Persons and Access to Social Protection in the Case Law of the European Court of Justice' in Yuri Borgmann-Prebil and Malcolm Ross (eds), *Promoting Solidarity in the European Union* (Oxford University Press, 2010) 170.

It has been noted that the imbalance between the rights of 'citizens proper' and the rights of 'market citizens' in the realisation of the European internal market has given rise to 'a self-interested "citizen" whose allegiance to Europe may not be simply taken for granted'.[122] For some commentators, the concept of market citizenship provides both an empirically appropriate and a normatively coherent way to describe EU citizenship.[123] It is widely agreed that '"What" is grounded in constitutionalism is the substantive point'[124] but the opinions are divided when it comes to the question of what the EU constitutionalises: a market or something more? The very use of the ideologically-loaded concept of citizenship seems to confirm that at least some elements of the 'equality of relationships' between citizens in a national state were aimed to be reinforced in the context of European Union law. If this is so, it is necessary to consider what normative justifications can be provided for distributive justice in a transnational context and how our answer to this question shapes EU citizens' non-economic right to non-discrimination and equal treatment under EU law.

Equal treatment is often listed as one of the key elements of citizenship along with 'membership' and 'rights and obligations'. The quest for equal citizenship is accordingly conditioned on who is entitled to 'share in the space of civic equality'.[125] Some commentators argue that 'equality should be the goal of Union citizenship, and judicial protection its guarantee'.[126] Others suggest more moderately that '[i]f Union Citizenship is to be at all meaningful, equality of treatment must be secured for holders of this Citizenship in relation to some matters of importance'.[127] To the extent that the whole idea of transnational citizenship is still an artefact rather than a flourishing social institution, the status of EU citizenship is indeed contingent on the way in which equality and non-discrimination as rights of EU citizens are construed in EU law. This view finds support, for instance, in the *Vardyn and Wardyn* case in which the Court of Justice explained the fundamental nature of the status of EU citizenship by referring to the fact that EU citizens enjoy the right to equal treatment and a prohibition of discrimination on grounds of nationality.[128] Thus, EU citizenship as a fundamental status of all Member State nationals remains

[122] Everson (n 28) 84–85 and 89.

[123] Niamh Nic Shuibhne, 'The Resilience of EU Market Citizenship' (2010) 47 *Common Market Law Review* 1597, 1599.

[124] Ibid 1605.

[125] See eg Ruth Rubio Marin, 'Equal Citizenship and the Difference that Residence Makes' in La Torre (n 86) 201. Note also how Rubio Marin defines the term 'equal citizenship' in fn 2 as 'the membership status that results from sharing in the space of civic equality regardless of whether that status is or is not achieved directly, through the equal entitlement of rights, or indirectly, through another membership status, such as that of national citizenship'.

[126] David O'Keeffe and Antonio Bavasso, 'Fundamental Rights and the European Citizen' in La Torre (n 86) 254.

[127] Andrew Evans, 'Union Citizenship and the Constitutionalization of Equality in EU Law' in La Torre (n 86) 268.

[128] Case C-391/09 *Malgžata Runevič-Vardyn, Lukasz Pawel Wardyn* [2011] ECR I-3787, paras 60–61.

largely meaningless if it cannot develop into a genuinely equal status. At the same time, however, the transnational nature of EU citizenship means that the normative claim for equal treatment between EU citizens remains vague in comparison with a similar claim between citizens within a national democracy.

This brief analysis of national and transnational conceptions of citizenship supports the argument of the new equality problem. In sum, the EU prohibition on nationality discrimination has traditionally been selective between different groups of people and, for many commentators, its importance is gradually declining due to the increasing reliance on the broader prohibition of non-discriminatory obstacles to free movement. At the same time, however, the creation of EU citizenship has brought the equality-based argumentation back to the centre of EU law scholarship. All EU citizens who exercise their right to free movement and residence under Article 21 TFEU now fall into the personal scope of the right to non-discrimination and equal treatment under Article 18 TFEU.[129] In so far as the concept of EU citizenship defines the personal scope of the non-economic right to non-discrimination and equal treatment, it is not feasible to avoid the question of what equal citizenship means for the substantive scope of right. It has been seen in this section that this question of equal treatment between EU citizens is ultimately a question about whether justice as a political and social value can be meaningful transnationally. This means that the EU equality problem as discussed in this book is essentially a problem about the equal treatment of EU citizens *in relation to one another*.

Tying the EU equality problem with the EU's quest for more legitimacy, democracy, and justice means that it cannot be solved by providing more or broader individual rights alone. However, a closer look at the scope and the limits of EU citizens' fundamental right to non-discrimination and equal treatment

[129] However, even the personal scope of EU citizenship rights is sometimes contested. In particular, it is common amongst legal scholars to discuss the feasibility to base EU citizenship rights on residence. See eg Marie-José Garot, 'A New Basis for European Citizenship: Residence' in La Torre (n 86). Residence has been advocated as an alternative to nationality as a 'condition for access to equality'. See eg Andrew Evans, 'Union Citizenship and the Equality Principle' in Allan Rosas and Esko Antola (eds), *A Citizens' Europe: In Search of a New Order* (SAGE Publications, 1995) 110 and Davis (n 119) 135. Residence has also gained attention as a potential membership criterion for 'civic citizenship' in the case of third-country nationals. See eg Bell (n 85) 318. See also the so-called Tampere Agenda of 2000, Tampere European Council 15 and 16 October 1999, Presidency Conclusions Nr: 200/1/99. The idea of EU citizenship based on residence has been introduced as a way to expand the personal scope of EU citizenship to cover third-country nationals because it would make the right to equal treatment independent of nationality. See eg Samantha Besson and André Utzinger, 'Introduction: Future Challenges of European Citizenship—Facing a Wide-Open Pandora's Box' (2007) 13 *European Law Journal* 573, 580–82 and Gareth Davies, 'Any Place I Hang My Hat? Or: Residence is the New Nationality' 2005 11 *European Law Journal* 43. A residence-based approach would allow economically inactive Union citizens to be 'regarded as being entitled to membership rights reflecting the degree to which they are actually participating in the project that is the European Union'. Davis (n 119) 137. However, it is important to bear in mind that none of these suggestions can avoid the 'substantive equality problem'. The conditions of residence would still need to define the extent to which EU citizenship constitutes an 'equal status'. It has also been noted that '[r]esidence is indeed anchored even deeper in territorial bounds than nationality'. Besson and Utzinger (n 129) 582.

in the next chapter can help us to better understand the nature of this 'equality problem' which currently hampers the status of EU citizenship. Some argue that the focus of EU citizenship should be on the 'genuine enjoyment of the substance of the rights' conferred by virtue of that status, rather than on the 'enjoyment of rights flowing from national citizenship'.[130] However, the essence of the rights of EU citizenship depends on how we address the 'still unanswered question of what Union citizenship actually is or ought to be'.[131] The following chapters of the book will address this question from the premise that the EU principle of equality and the status of EU citizenship are so closely intertwined that one cannot be addressed without the other. Even if the reader does not share the conceptualisation of EU citizenship through the normativity of just and equal relationships between the subjects of European integration in the final chapters of the book, it is hoped that he/she will recognise why further legal and philosophical debate on these questions is still needed on the basis of the critical analysis in the preceding chapters.

1.5 CONCLUSION

This chapter first showed how the interpretation of the EU principle of equality has moved from 'nationality discrimination' towards 'equal citizenship'. It then argued that using EU citizenship as the criterion for the personal scope of Article 18 TFEU unavoidably leads to the question of what 'equal citizenship' means for the substance of EU citizens' fundamental right to non-discrimination and equal treatment. This argument was based on the view that the ideas of 'citizenship' and 'equal treatment' are so closely intertwined that one cannot be understood without the other. It followed from this starting point that the EU equality problem can be understood as a question of transnational justice, that is, as a question of how EU citizens are treated in relation to one another. A comprehensive critique of EU citizenship as a fundamental status of all Member State nationals must therefore combine the legal analysis of how differential treatment is legitimated between EU citizens with a more theoretical analysis of what kind of idea of political and social justice underlies the EU principle of equality. The next chapter will begin this task by examining in more detail how the creation of EU citizenship has modified the discrimination analysis in EU law. This analysis will shed light on the structural and substantive dimensions of the EU 'equality problem'.

[130] Van der Mei (n 87).

[131] Ibid.

2

Equal Treatment: A (Limited) Right of All EU Citizens

2.1 INTRODUCTION

CHAPTER ONE SHOWED how the development of EU citizenship has shed light on a new equality problem, ie the question of what equality means *between* EU citizens. This chapter will examine in more detail when differential treatment between EU citizens is regarded as legitimate in the case law of the CJEU and what it *de facto* takes for EU citizens to find themselves in a comparable situation for non-discrimination and equal treatment irrespective of nationality under EU law. In order to answer the question of what constitutes a violation of the EU principle of equality, it is important to understand the internal logic of discrimination analysis. In its simplest and most common form, the applicability of the non-discrimination principle is extracted from the following three steps: (1) two situations are comparable, (2) there is a difference in treatment on the basis of one of the prohibited grounds (eg nationality) and (3) there is no objective justification for differential treatment. This chapter will discuss how the concept of EU citizenship has provided the Court of Justice with a new standard of comparison and how this affects both (1) the scope of the right to equal treatment which has its basis in the comparability analysis and (2) the limitations on the right to equal treatment which depend on the accepted justifications for legitimate differential treatment.

The case law illustrates that EU citizenship as the main criterion for the personal scope of Article 18 TFEU[1] has seemingly affirmed the comparability not just between economically active nationals and non-nationals but also between economically inactive and needy migrant EU citizens and the nationals of their host Member State. In practice, however, the objective justifications for differential treatment play a central role in the discrimination analysis when economically inactive EU citizens seek to access equal treatment under EU law. The Court's rhetoric focus on EU citizenship as a fundamental status of all Member State nationals therefore hides the fact that the shift from 'nationality discrimination' towards 'equal citizenship' has changed the balance between the different levels of discrimination analysis so that the proportionality analysis has become

[1] Consolidated Version of the Treaty on the Functioning of the European Union (TFEU) [2012] OJ C326/47.

increasingly important in defining both the scope of and the limitations on the EU principle of equality. Observing these developments in the discrimination analysis gives us a clearer picture of what forms the EU equality problem takes in practice.

The analysis of the Union test for discrimination in this chapter shows that the EU equality problem emerges both at the level of the *scope* of and the *limitations* on EU citizens' right to equal treatment. Firstly, it will be seen in Section 2.2 that EU citizens' general right to equal treatment has no *de facto* independent scope, but is conditioned on the accepted limits on their right to residence and, thus, on the proportionality analysis (the structural equality problem). Secondly, it will be seen in Section 2.3 that the accepted limitations on EU citizens' right to equal treatment depend primarily on economic criteria which fail to address the question of what differential treatment means for the equality of relationships between EU citizens (the substantive equality problem). This analysis of EU citizens' right to non-discrimination and equal treatment is based on the assumption that there is more than one possible interpretation of equality in EU law and that the emergence of EU citizenship may transform what equality means in the context of EU law. Examining the shift of balance between different levels of discrimination analysis in the interpretation of EU citizens' right to equal treatment will lay the foundations for theorising the EU equality problem in Chapter three.

2.2 THE SCOPE OF THE RIGHT: COMPARABILITY BETWEEN EU CITIZENS

2.2.1 A Personal Right to Equal Treatment—Comparability Based on What?

The notion of discrimination usually refers to decision-making on arbitrary or irrelevant grounds, whereas the notion of equality can vary from a purely formal definition of 'like should be treated alike' to different ideas of substantive equality.[2]

[2] On the one hand, the principle of non-discrimination may go further than the mere requirement of formal equality, because non-discrimination can derive its content from substantive values such as autonomy and dignity, whereas equality is often based on the formal idea of treating like cases alike. See eg Elisa Holmes, 'Anti-Discrimination Rights without Equality' (2005) 68 *Modern Law Review* 175 and Tarunabh Khaitan, 'An Autonomy-Based Foundation for Legal Protection against Discrimination' (D Phil thesis, University of Oxford, 2010). On the other hand, different notions of substantive equality can go far beyond the mere requirement of non-discrimination or equal treatment because they can also legitimate positive action under discrimination law. Unlike its formal counterpart, the principle of substantive equality recognises that there is no axiomatic or uncontroversial comparability between different groups and that social circumstances play an important role when actual comparability or similarity is defined. See eg Sandra Fredman, *Discrimination Law*, 2nd edn (Oxford University Press, 2011) 7–15. However, the relationships between 'equality' and 'non-discrimination' can also be defined more technically. Under this approach, equality represents a principle or value which is materialised within the prohibition of discrimination. For instance, Catharine Barnard has described the non-discrimination principle as 'the framework for enforcing legal rights to equality', whereas the principle of equality is argued to serve 'a political or symbolic purpose rather than a legal function'. Catherine Barnard, 'The Principle of Equality in the Community Context: *P*, *Grant*, *Kalanke*, and *Marschall*: Four Uneasy Bedfellows?' (1998) 57 *Cambridge Law Journal* 352, 353. Similarly, L Betten notes that the prohibition of discrimination on arbitrary grounds is the 'consequence' of the requirement of equal treatment. Lammy Betten, 'New Equality Provisions in European Law: Some Thoughts on the

Comparability of situations as the first stage of discrimination analysis refers to the question of 'which features of persons it takes to be relevantly alike or unlike'.[3] The operation of formal equality therefore depends on finding a 'suitable comparator'.[4] Equal treatment is required in those cases which are relevantly alike and differential treatment is required in those cases which are relevantly unlike each other. The Court of Justice has given the EU principle of equality a primarily formal meaning by stating that similar situations must be treated similarly and different situations differently, unless there are objective justifications for differential treatment of similar situations or similar treatment of different situations.[5] The prohibition of nationality discrimination has been referred to as a 'specific enunciation' of the general principle of equality since the early years of European integration.[6] From this starting point, the Court of Justice has defined nationality discrimination by stating that 'discrimination can arise only through the application of different rules to comparable situations or the application of the same rule to different situations'.[7] The idea of comparability therefore plays a central role in defining the scope of EU citizens' fundamental right to non-discrimination and equal treatment.

This section discusses how EU citizenship has changed the comparability analysis in EU law and whether this change has actually led to more equality between EU citizens. In a series of cases beginning with the seminal *Martínez Sala* and *Grzelczyk* judgments, the Court of Justice underlined the importance of EU citizenship as 'the fundamental status of nationals of the Member States, enabling those who find themselves in the same situation to enjoy the same treatment in law irrespective of their nationality, subject to such exceptions as are expressly provided for'.[8] EU citizenship as a 'fundamental status' has added a new strand into the definition

Fundamental Value of Equality as a Legal Principle' in Kim Economides, Lammy Betten, John Bridge, Andrew Tettenborn and Vivien Shrubsall (eds), *Fundamental Values* (Hart Publishing, 2000) 71, fn 12.

[3] See eg Carl Knight, 'Describing Equality' (2009) 28 *Law and Philosophy* 327, 331.

[4] See eg Gavin Barret, 'The Concept of Equality in European Community Law' in Cathryn Costello and Eilis Barry (eds), *Diversity in Equality: The New Equality Directives* (Irish Centre for European Law, 2003) 105.

[5] eg Case 13/63 *Italy v Commission* [1963] ECR 165, para 4 which stated: 'The different treatment of non-comparable situations does not lead automatically to the conclusion that there is discrimination. An appearance of discrimination in the form may therefore correspond in fact to an absence of discrimination in substance. Discrimination in substance would consist in treating either similar situations differently or different situations identically'.

[6] See eg Case 117/76 and 16/77 *Albert Ruckdeschel & Co, et Hansa-Lagerhaus Ströh & Co v Hauptzollamt Hamburg-St Annen; Diamalt AG v Haupzollamt Itzenhoe* [1977] ECR 1753, para 7. For more recent case law, see eg Case C-115/08 *Land Oberösterrich v ČEZ as* [2009] ECR I-10265, para 91, according to which 'although the principle of prohibition of any discrimination on grounds of nationality within the scope of application of Community law is expressly laid down in Article 12 EC, it is a general principle'. See also Case C-101/08 *Audiolux SA and Others vs Groupe Bruxelles Lambert SA (GBL) and Others, Bertelsmann AG and Others* [2009] ECR I-9823, para 63 for the statement that '[t]he general principles of Community law have constitutional status'.

[7] Case C-279/93 *Finanzamt Koln-Altstadt v Roland Schumacker* [1995] ECR I-225, para 30.

[8] Case C-184/99 *Rudy Grzelczyk v Centre public d'aide sociale d'Ottignies-Louvain-la-Neuve* [2001] ECR I-6193, paras 30–31. See also Case C-85/96 *María Martínez Sala v Freistaat Bayern* [1998] ECR I-2691, paras 61–63.

of comparability between private individuals within the EU. However, it has been noted that '[i]t is by no means obvious'[9] what the provisions of EU citizenship add to the principle of non-discrimination or what the relationship between EU citizens' general right to equal treatment under Article 18 TFEU and their non-economic right to residence and free movement under Article 21 TFEU is.

Defining the relevant parameters for comparability between EU citizens is crucial for understanding discrimination analysis as currently applied in the Court's case law, although the analysis of EU citizens' right to equal treatment through the concept of 'meaningful relationships' in the later chapters of this book will challenge the traditional, assimilationist, idea of comparability as a prerequisite for equal treatment under EU law. The prohibition of migration discrimination, that is, the prohibition of non-discriminatory obstacles to EU citizens' free movement, is not dependent on comparability in the same way. However, it has been seen in Chapter one that there is a clear need to examine what the idea of 'equal citizenship' can add to the traditional market access theory. Understanding the limits of EU citizenship as an equal status depends on understanding on what basis EU citizens can claim that they 'find themselves in the same situation to enjoy the same treatment' under EU law. It is therefore important to examine in more detail what is required from the holders of EU citizenship to find themselves in the same situation as the nationals of the host Member State. This is where the comparability analysis merges with the objective justification test and reasonableness analysis in the EU test for discrimination, as will be seen below in this section.

It has been noted that the difficulties in defining a 'coherent proxy' for comparing nationals and non-nationals follow from the undefined nature of Union citizenship.[10] To the extent that a 'Union Citizen' is a descendant of a 'Market Citizen',[11] it is logical to begin the analysis of the EU equality problem by examining how the discrimination analysis varies between economically active and inactive EU citizens. In Sections 2.2.2 and 2.2.3, it will be shown how the relationship between scope of and limitations on the right to non-discrimination and equal treatment depends on whether the right to equal treatment is derived from the status of a 'Union worker' or from the mere status of a 'Union citizen'. Here the important distinction is drawn between Union workers' status-based right to equal treatment and EU citizens' residence-based right to equal treatment. The way in which the residence-based right to equal treatment lacks an independent scope of application reveals the structural side of the EU equality problem in Section 2.2.4.

[9] FC Jacobs, 'Citizenship of the European Union—A Legal Analysis' (2007) 13 *European Law Journal* 591, 594.

[10] Floris de Witte, 'The End of EU Citizenship and the Means of Non-Discrimination' (2011) 18 *Maastricht Journal of European and Comparative Law* 86.

[11] Michelle Everson, 'The Legacy of the Market Citizen' in Jo Shaw and Gillian More (eds), *New Legal Dynamics of European Union* (Clarendon Press, 1995) 79. Everson points out that 'the rights of the market citizen, particularly that of free movement, have not merely been transferred to the Union citizen but continue to form the very core of that citizenship'. See also Niamh Nic Shuibhne, 'The Resilience of EU Market Citizenship' (2010) *Common Market Law Review* 1597.

2.2.2 Union Workers and the Status-Based Right to Equal Treatment: A Story of Strong Comparability

It has been crucial to the EU principle of equality that the Community institutions, above all the European Commission, refused to see the free movement of workers in 'macroeconomic terms' but instead underlined the right to free movement as a 'personal freedom' to choose the country in which citizens of the Member States want to work.[12] The objective of the original Treaty right to free movement was clarified with the adoption of Regulation 1612/68 on the freedom of movement for workers within the Community (now Regulation 492/2011) and Directive 68/360 on the abolition of restrictions on movement and residence within the Community for workers of Member States and their families.[13] The preamble to Regulation 1612/68 made it clear that the exercise of the right to freedom of movement 'in freedom and dignity' requires equal treatment. In practice, this has meant that the discrimination analysis under Regulation 1612/68 and now Regulation 492/2011 builds on the status of a 'Union worker' and any limitations on Union workers' status-based right to equal treatment have been interpreted strictly.

The Status of a Union Worker

The economic rights to establish residence and to enjoy equal treatment are conditioned on the status of a Union worker which requires the pursuit of 'effective and genuine economic activities' as opposed to 'marginal and ancillary activities'. In the *Levin* case, the Court emphasised that the pursuit of an 'effective and genuine' economic activity leads to the status of a Union worker even in a situation which 'yields an income lower than that which, in the latter State, is considered as the minimum required for subsistence'.[14] Moreover, the Court has adopted a generous interpretation of the temporal dimension of the 'worker' status. In the *Leclere* case, it was established that the status of a Union worker 'may produce certain effects' even after the actual employment relationship has ended. The Court also noted that the person must be classified as a worker if he/she is 'genuinely' seeking work after the previous employment relationship has ended.[15] The Court has examined

[12] Anne Pieter Van der Mei, *Free Movement of Persons within the European Community—Cross-Border Access to Public Benefits* (Hart Publishing, 2003) 26–27.

[13] Regulation (EEC) No 1612/68 of the Council of 15 October 1968 on freedom of movement for workers within the Community [1968] OJ L257/2; Regulation (EU) No 492/2011 of the European Parliament and of the Council of 5 April 2011 on freedom of movement for workers within the Union Text with EEA relevance [2011] OJ L141/1; Council Directive 68/360/EEC of 15 October 1968 on the abolition of restrictions on movement and residence within the Community for workers of Member States and their families [1968] OJ L257/13. Directive 68/360 was repealed by Directive 2004/38 of the European Parliament and of the Council of 29 April 2004 on the right of citizens of the Union and their family members to move and reside freely within the territory of the Member States [2004] OJ L158.

[14] Case 53/81 *DM Levin v Staatssecretaris van Justitie* [1982] ECR 1035, para 18. See also Case 53/81 *Deborah Lawrie-Blum v Land Baden-Württemberg* [1982] ECR 2121, para 22.

[15] Case C-43/99 *Ghislain Leclere and Alina Deaconescu v Caisse nationale des prestations familiales* [2001] ECR I-4265, para 55. The Court clarified this statement further by noting that a former worker

the retention of the 'worker' status in the case of voluntary and involuntary unemployment. In the *Raulin* case, the status of a Union worker was retained during the studies which were pursued after voluntary unemployment on the basis that there was a 'link between the previous occupational activity and the studies in question'. Moreover, the Court emphasised that the requirement of a 'link' could not be imposed on a migrant worker who seeks vocational training in another field of activity in the case of involuntary unemployment.[16]

In the light of these cases, it is clear that the Court has made a great effort to interpret the status of a Union worker in a wide and inclusive manner. However, this does not mean that the status would be all-inclusive. It is clear that this status is only available to those nationals of the Member States who engage in economic activity effectively and genuinely across the borders of the Member States. In the *Brown* case, a national of another Member State, who had entered into an employment relationship in the host State for eight months and who would not have been employed by his employer if he had not already been accepted for admission to university, was regarded to be a 'worker' according to Article 7(2) of Regulation No 1612/68. However, the Court concluded that the Member State could refuse to grant him a grant for studies under Article 7(2) of Regulation 1612/68 on the basis that the employment relationship was 'merely ancillary to the studies to be financed by the grant'.[17] In other words, even the pursuit of those activities which were categorised as 'marginal and ancillary' would entitle the applicant to equal treatment in employment-related issues. But these activities would not entitle the applicant to equal access to social advantages under Article 7(2) of Regulation 1612/68.[18] In these situations, they would need to rely on the general right to equal treatment as EU citizens.[19]

In order to understand the differences in discrimination analysis in the case of Union workers and in the case of EU citizens as EU citizens, it is important to have a closer look at the Court's interpretation of the scope of Union workers' right to equal treatment. The right to take up employment in another Member State under EU law includes the right to establish residence for that purpose. In the case of those EU citizens who hold the status of a 'Union worker', the need for social assistance does not terminate the right to establish residence in another Member

must be protected against 'any discrimination affecting rights acquired during the former employment relationship but, since he is not currently engaged in an employment relationship, cannot thereby claim to acquire new rights having no links with his former occupation'. Ibid para 59.

[16] Case C-357/89 *VJM Raulin v Minister van Onderwijs en Wetenschappen* [1992] ECR I-1027, para 21. Similarly, In the *Lair* case, the Court stated that no link between the previous employment and university studies could be required from a claimant who had become involuntarily unemployed, but that 'a worker who is a national of another Member State and has exercised his right as such to freedom of movement is entitled in the same way as national workers to all the advantages available to such workers for improving their professional qualifications and promoting their social advancement'. Case 39/86 *Sylvie Lair v Universität Hannover* [1988] ECR 3161, para 22.

[17] Case 197/86 *Steven Malcolm Brown v The Secretary of State for Scotland* [1988] ECR 3205, paras 23 and 27.

[18] See further eg Van der Mei (n 12) 35–37 and 42.

[19] See Section 2.2.3, p 50.

State.[20] And the established employment in another Member State under Article 45 TFEU grants Union workers the right to equal treatment in many cases which are not directly related to the employment issues.[21] Under Article 7(2) of Regulation 492/2011 (ex Article 7(2) of Regulation 1612/68), migrant Union workers are granted the right to equal treatment in relation to social advantages. Moreover, unlike the coordination system for social security which only applies to benefits covering one of the risks explicitly specified in Regulation 883/2004,[22] Regulation 492/2011 also applies to general social benefits, such as benefits guaranteeing a minimum means of subsistence.[23]

The case law shows that the Court has adopted a notably wide interpretation of what is meant by 'social advantages' under Article 7(2) of Regulation 1612/68 and now Article 7(2) of Regulation 492/2011, as well as a narrow interpretation of the accepted conditions and limitations on the status-based right to equal treatment in the case of Union workers. In the *Ugliola* case, the Court underlined that the principle of equal treatment in Article 7(2) of Regulation 1612/68 is based on the Treaty Article and 'prescribes the abolition of any discrimination based on nationality between workers of the Member States as regards employment, remuneration and other conditions of work and employment'.[24] This interpretation was taken further in the *Cristini* case where the Court stated that Article 7(2) cannot be interpreted 'restrictively' and that 'in the view of the equality of treatment which the provision seeks to achieve, the substantive area of application must be delineated so as to include all social and tax advantages, whether or not attached to the contract of employment'.[25] In the *Even* case, the Court formulated a more specific test, according to which the material scope of Article 7(2) would cover all those benefits

> which, whether or not linked to a contract of employment, are generally granted to national workers primarily because of their objective status as workers or by virtue of

[20] *Levin* (n 14) paras 11–16 and Case 139/85 *RH Kempf v Staatssecretaris van Justitie* [1986] ECR 1741, paras 14–15.

[21] See more about this eg Van der Mei (n 12) 31.

[22] Regulation (EC) No 883/2004 of the European Parliament and of the Council of 29 April 2004 on the coordination of social security systems [2004] OJ L166/1.

[23] In practice, this means that the provisions of Regulation 1612/68 and now Regulation 492/2011 on freedom of movement for workers within the Union have provided a tool for the Court of Justice to soften the material limits of the coordination system by giving a wide interpretation to the concept of 'social advantages' in the context of the principle of equal treatment under what used to be Article 7(2) of Regulation 1612/68 and is now Article 7(2) of Regulation 492/2011. The Court has confirmed that Article 7(2) of Regulation 1612/68 can be applied to those 'social advantages' which simultaneously fall within the scope of Regulation 1408/71 (now Regulation 883/2004). For instance, Josephine Steiner has described the situation between the two regulations as follows: 'Basing its arguments on the aims of the Treaties and the preambles and general scheme of Regulations 1408/71 and 1612/68 the Court remedies the deficiencies of each Regulation by arguing by analogy from one to the other—and building imperceptibly on its own case law'. Josephine Steiner, 'The Right to Welfare: Equality and Equity under Community Law' (1985) 10 *European Law Review* 21, 39.

[24] Case 15/69 *Württembergische Milchverwertung-Südmilch AG v Salvatore Ugliola* [1969] ECR 363, para 3.

[25] Case 32/75 *Anita Cristini v Société nationale des chemins de fer français* [1975] ECR 1085, paras 12–13.

> the mere fact of their residence on the national territory and the extension of which to workers who are nationals of other Member States therefore seems suitable to facilitate their mobility within the Community.[26]

Despite the wide interpretation of the concept of a 'social advantage', there must still be a benefit 'flowing from the migrant worker, albeit indirectly' for Article 7(2) to apply.[27] For instance, in the *Lebon* case, the Court rejected the right of family members to equal treatment in the context of minimum subsistence in those cases in which they were no longer dependent on the Union worker.[28] However, in the same case, the Court underlined that the principle of equal treatment 'contributes to the integration of migrant workers in the working environment in the host country in accordance with the objectives of the free movement of workers'.[29] It has been suggested on this basis that the Court's case law on social advantages under Article 7(2) of Regulation 1612/68 includes a 'shift from the criterion of assistance of mobility to facilitation of the integration of the migrant worker into the host State'.[30] The Court has clearly not been disturbed by the fact that many of the social benefits falling into the scope of its broad definition of 'social advantages' under Article 7(2) of Regulation 1612/68 (now 492/2011) do not explicitly fall into the scope of the EU Treaties.[31] Instead, the scope of equal treatment is defined by using a criterion under which the right to equal treatment covers all rights and benefits which seem to facilitate the integration of the worker into the society of the host Member State.[32]

Accepted Limitations: A Narrow Approach

The Court of Justice has expanded the Union workers' right to equal treatment not just by interpreting the personal scope of the Treaty provisions and the material scope of the equal treatment provision of Regulation 1612/68 broadly, but also by

[26] Case 207/78 *Criminal proceedings against Gilbert Even and Office national des pensions pour travailleurs salariés (ONPTS)* [1979] ECR 2012, para 22. See also Case C-249/83 *Vera Hoeckx v Openbaar Centrum voor Maatschappelijk Welzijn, Kalmthout* [1985] ECR 973, para 20.

[27] Evelyn Ellis, 'Social Advantages: A New Lease of Life?' (2003) 40 *Common Market Law Review* 639, 643.

[28] Case 316/85 *Centre public d'aide sociale de Courcelles v Marie-Christine Lebon* [1987] ECR 2811, para 13.

[29] Ibid para 11.

[30] Ellis (n 27) 652.

[31] It has even been claimed that the Court of Justice has constitutionalised Article 7(2) of Regulation 1612/68 by interpreting it as an expression of the principle of equal treatment in the EU Treaties. Stefano Giubboni, 'A Certain Degree of Solidarity? Free Movement of Persons and Access to Social Protection in the Case Law of the European Court of Justice' in Yuri Borgmann-Prebil and Malcolm Ross (eds), *Promoting Solidarity in the European Union* (Oxford University Press, 2010) 189. As an example, see Case C-287/05 *DPW Hendrix v Raad van Bestuur van het Uitvoeringsinstituut Werknemersverzekeringen* [2007] ECR I-6909, para 53.

[32] Van der Mei (n 12) 34.

developing more nuanced jurisprudence on indirect discrimination.[33] The Court has confirmed that the rules of equal treatment under Article 7(2) of Regulation 1612/68 'forbid not only overt discrimination by reason of nationality but also all covert forms of discrimination which, by the application of other criteria of differentiation, lead in fact to the same result'.[34] In practice, the prohibition of indirect discrimination has directed attention towards residence conditions.[35] The Court has assessed the compatibility of residence requirements with Union workers' right to non-discrimination and equal treatment in several cases, all of which adopt a narrow interpretation of the accepted limitations. This is notable because, as will be seen in Section 2.3, the discrimination analysis for EU citizens' general right to equal treatment has adopted a lenient approach to objective justifications for differential treatment, including different types of integration requirements.

In the *Meeusen* case, the Court concluded that the requirement of residence as a condition for financing the studies of the children of non-national workers was (directly) discriminatory on the basis that national legislation did not impose such conditions on the children of national workers.[36] In the *Meints* case, the Court highlighted that a residence condition cannot be accepted unless it is objectively justified and proportionate to its aim because it could be more easily met by national workers than by those from other Member States.[37] In this case, the Court rejected the residence condition on the basis that it was 'neither necessary nor appropriate, in order to achieve the aim of excluding persons laid off as a result of their own action from entitlement to the benefit'.[38] In the *Commission v France* case, the Court similarly held that 'criteria such as the place of origin or residence of a worker may, according to the circumstances, be tantamount, as regards their practical effect, to unlawful discrimination on the grounds of nationality'.[39] Moreover, the Court underlined the priority of equal treatment by stating that the 'financial consequences' may never alone suffice to justify such limitations.[40] The strict view on integration requirements in regard with Union workers' right to non-discrimination and equal treatment has nevertheless been qualified in the case of so-called frontier workers.

[33] Kay Hailbronner, 'Union Citizenship and Access to Social Benefits' (2005) 42 *Common Market Law Review* 1245, 1246.

[34] Case C-111/91 *Commission of the European Communities v Grand Duchy of Luxembourg* [1993] ECR I-817, para 9 and Case C-237/94 *John O'Flynn v Adjudication Officer* [1996] ECR I-2617, para 17.

[35] See eg Maurizio Ferrera, 'European Integration and National Social Citizenship: Changing Boundaries, New Structuring?' (2003) 36 *Comparative Political Studies* 611, 636 notes that 'the line of defense on the side of national systems thus shifted to control over rules of residence'.

[36] Case C-337/97 *CPM Meeusen v Hoofddirectie van de Informatie Beheer Groep* [1999] ECR I-3289, para 23.

[37] Case C-57/96 *H Meints v Minister van Landbouw, Natuurbeheer en Visserij* [1997] ECR I-6689, paras 45–46.

[38] Ibid para 48.

[39] Case C-35/97 *Commission of the European Communities v French Republic* [1998] ECR I-5325, para 51.

[40] Ibid para 52.

In the *Hartmann* case, the Court held that the Member State could not refuse to pay a child-raising allowance to a spouse of a migrant worker on the basis that 'he did not have his permanent or ordinary residence in the former State'.[41] However, the Court did not reject the use of integration requirements in this context, provided that 'residence was not regarded as the only connecting link with the Member State concerned, and a substantial contribution to the national labour market also constituted a valid factor of integration into the society of that Member State'.[42] In the *Geven* case, the Court outlined that a Member State can exclude a national of another Member State 'who is in minor employment' from receiving a child-raising allowance 'on the ground that he does not have his permanent or ordinary residence in the former State'.[43] The *Hendrix* case concerned a situation in which a national of one Member State maintained paid employment in that State and transferred his residence to another Member State, after which he found other employment in his Member State of origin.[44] According to the Court, the Member State could refuse to pay him a benefit for disabled young people only if the residence requirement as a condition for that benefit does not lead to 'an unacceptable degree of unfairness' and takes into account the fact that the applicant had 'exercised his freedom of movement as a worker' and had 'maintained all of his economic and social links to the Member State of origin'.[45] This line of case law has provoked the question of whether the Court is developing a more lenient approach to integration requirements in the case of Union workers. However, all of these cases concern frontier workers, whose situation is, in many ways, different from those migrant Union workers who both work and reside in the same Member State.[46]

The Court of Justice later confirmed that those rights and benefits which fall into the material scope of Article 7(2) of Regulations 1612/68 and 492/2011 can also fall into the material scope of the general prohibition of discrimination under Article 18 TFEU.[47] Despite the shared material scope, the discrimination analysis under Article 7(2) differs from the discrimination analysis under Directive 2004/38, which regulates the free movement and equal treatment of economically inactive Union citizens.[48] The most important difference between these legal instruments concerns the definition of objective justifications, above all residence conditions, in the context of indirect discrimination. EU citizens who hold the status of a 'Union worker' enjoy a broad right to equal treatment and the Court

[41] Case C-212/05 *Gertraud Hartmann v Freistaat Bayern* [2007] ECR I-6303, para 38.

[42] Ibid para 36.

[43] Case C-231/05 *Wendy Geven v Land Nordrhein-Westfalen* [2007] ECR I-6347, para 30.

[44] *Hendrix* (n 31), para 46.

[45] Ibid, paras 57–58.

[46] eg Hanneke van Eijken, *EU Citizenship and the Constitutionalisation of the European Union* (Europa Law Publishing, 2015) 90.

[47] See more about this in Section 2.2.3, p 50.

[48] Directive 2004/38/EC of the European Parliament and of the Council of 29 April 2004 on the right of citizens of the Union and their family members to move and reside freely within the territory of the Member States [2004] OJ L158/77.

of Justice has adopted a narrow approach to objective justifications for differential treatment between national workers and non-national workers when it comes to their access to social assistance.[49] The focus of discrimination analysis in the case of Union workers lies in the establishment of the 'worker' status which, then, grants a broad status-based right to equal treatment. The Union workers' right to equal treatment provides an example of *strong comparability* which escapes the structural equality problem, as will be discussed in Section 2.2.4. The next section shows that this is not the case with the EU citizens' general right to equal treatment.

2.2.3 Union Citizens and the Residence-Based Right to Equal Treatment: A Story of Weak Comparability

The discrimination analysis in relation to EU citizens' general right to equal treatment differs from the discrimination analysis in the case of Union workers. The status-based right to equal treatment in the case of Union workers has been considerably modified in the case of economically inactive EU citizens. The key to understanding EU citizens' general right to equal treatment is that lawful residence in another Member State brings economically inactive EU citizens into the personal scope of the right to equal treatment when they apply for social welfare benefits covered by the material scope of the EU Treaties. In the *Martínez Sala* judgment, the Court confirmed that a 'national of a Member State lawfully residing in the territory of another Member State' comes within the personal scope of the rights attached to EU citizenship under Articles 18 and 21 TFEU.[50] In this case, the Court extended the scope of the non-discrimination principle by deriving the legality of residence from the sources which fell outside EU law and by stating that, within this extended personal scope of Article 18 TFEU, EU citizens can rely on the general prohibition of nationality discrimination in all situations which fall within the *ratione materiae* scope of EU law.[51] However, in the light of more recent case law, it is unclear whether 'lawful residence' can still be derived from national law, or, whether it needs to be based on the provisions of EU law, as discussed below in this section.

The Court could have limited EU citizens' general right to equal treatment to those rights which fall into the material scope of the Treaty provisions on EU citizenship in Articles 22–25 TFEU.[52] But the case-law has adopted a wide

[49] This also applies to the coordination system on social security as a point of comparison.

[50] *Martínez Sala* (n 8), paras 61–62.

[51] Ibid.

[52] For this observation, see eg Síofra O'Leary, 'Putting Flesh on the Bones of European Union Citizenship' (1999) 21 *European Law Review* 68, 77–78 and Síofra O'Leary, 'Developing an Ever Closer Union between the Peoples of Europe? A Reappraisal of the Case Law of the Court of Justice on the Free Movement of Persons and EU Citizenship' (2008) 27 *Yearbook of European Law* 167, 179–80.

interpretation of the material scope of the Treaty articles in the context of free-movement, residence and non-discrimination. It was confirmed in the *Martínez Sala* and *Grzelczyk* cases that the question of whether a social benefit falls into the material scope of the right to equal treatment under Article 18 TFEU must be defined by using the same criteria as in the context of Union workers and their right to equal treatment. In practice, EU citizens who are lawfully resident in the territory of another Member State can now rely on their fundamental right to equal treatment and non-discrimination in all those cases which fall into the material scope of the EU Treaties and not just in those cases which fall into the material scope of the citizenship provisions of the Treaty.[53] Most disputes concerning social benefits will therefore come within the jurisdictional scope of Union law both *ratione personae* and *ratione materiae*, but it is less clear when EU citizens will actually have access to those benefits.[54]

EU citizens' general right to non-discrimination and equal treatment is not protected as 'securely' as in the case of Union workers.[55] In the context of Union citizens, unlike in the case of Union workers, the right to equal treatment is 'premised on residence'.[56] It has been noted that EU citizenship can paradoxically provide a justification for the general right to non-discrimination under what is now Article 18 TFEU, while the exercise of their right to free movement and residence under Article 21 TFEU is 'still ever subordinate to the economic imperatives'.[57] However, as EU citizens' access to equal treatment depends on lawful reference, these 'economic imperatives' also qualify EU citizens' fundamental right to non-discrimination and equal treatment. Opinions are divided on the question of whether the requirement of lawful residence should be considered as a 'prerequisite' for the application

[53] In the literature, it has been asked how social benefits, such as minimum subsistence benefits 'lex generalis' come within the material scope of the Treaties so that the applicant can rely on his/her general right to non-discrimination. For instance, James Mather has noted that it is possible to find two explanations for the material scope of Article 18 TFEU in the case law of the Court of Justice. In the first case (in *Martínez Sala* (n 8)), the social benefit would fall into the material scope of the Treaty on the basis that it constitutes a social advantage under Article 7(2) of Regulation 1612/68, irrespective of the fact that the applicant is not economically active. In the second case (in *Grzelczyk* (n 8)), the exercise of fundamental freedoms provided for in the Treaty would suffice to bring the case into the material scope of the Treaty on the basis that 'the benefit in question necessarily had some connection to the exercise of the right'. See James Mather, 'The Court of Justice and the Union Citizen', (2005) 11 *European Law Journal* 722, 736–38. It has been widely accepted in academic commentary that it is the second, broader definition, of the material scope of the EU Treaties which has been accepted in the Court's more recent case law. See eg Mel Cousins, 'Citizenship, Residence and Social Security' (2007) 32 *European Law Review* 386, 389–90. In practice, this means that '[t]he essential requirement for a measure to fall within the scope of Article 12 is that it affects negatively the access to, or the exercise of the fundamental freedoms'. Catherine Jacqueson, 'Union Citizenship and the Court of Justice: Something New under the Sun? Towards Social Citizenship' (2002) 27 *European Law Review* 260, 273 and Christian Tomuschat, 'Comment on Case C-85/96, María Martínez Sala v Freistaat Bayern, Judgment of 12 May 1998, Full Court. [1998] ECR I-2691' (2000) 37 *Common Market Law Review* 449, 451.

[54] Matthew Elsmore and Peter Starup, 'Union Citizenship—Background, Jurisprudence, and Perspective: The Past, Present, and Future of Law and Policy' (2007) 26 *Yearbook of European Law* 57, 105.

[55] Van der Mei (n 12) 50.

[56] Elsmore and Starup (n 54) 101.

[57] Mather (n 53) 742.

of EU citizens' right to non-discrimination and equal treatment under Article 18 TFEU, or whether it should rather be considered as a 'condition' which can limit access to social benefits under the right to equal treatment.[58] But, in so far as the host Member States can legitimately terminate the right to residence in the case of 'needy' migrant EU citizens who do not have sufficient resources not to become an 'unreasonable burden' on their social assistance system, they can also restrict the *de facto* scope of his/her right to equal treatment, as will be seen below in this section.[59]

The Requirement of Lawful Residence

The 1957 Treaty of Rome only granted free movement and equal treatment rights to workers, self-employed persons and providers of services. In 1979, the European Commission made a proposal for a directive on the general right of residence for nationals of the Member States in the territories of other Member States.[60] This proposal was never adopted and the Commission replaced it with three separate proposals concerning the rights of residence of students, pensioners, and all other Community citizens in 1989.[61] Economically inactive individuals gained the right to free movement and residence with the adoption of the three Residence Directives in 1990, but their rights under these directives were dependent on the possession of sickness insurance and sufficient financial resources.[62]

[58] For instance, Kay Hailbronner has argued that these provisions do not just restrict the exercise of the right to reside ('conditions') but have a limiting impact on the very establishment of the right to reside ('limitations'). This argument derives its normative force from the claim that EU citizenship and the principle of proportionality must not be 'used to rewrite the rules laid down in secondary Community law'. Hailbronner (n 33) 1253–54. See also Mather (n 53) 727 who speaks of a derived right of residence upon Article 18 EC 'through' the application of secondary legislation. It has, nonetheless, been observed that the residual right of the Member State to terminate residence on the basis of the 'unreasonable burden' test constitutes a 'more promising point of departure' for the debate on the autonomous nature of Article 21 TFEU than the arguments about the conceptual difference between 'conditions' and 'limitations'. Yuri Borgmann-Prebil, 'The Rule of Reason in European Citizenship' (2008) 14 *European Law Journal* 328, 336–37.

[59] This is so even if it is only the exercise and not the existence of the right to residence which is conditional. See more about this latter argument eg Van der Mei (n 12) 148.

[60] See 'Proposal for a Council Directive on a right of residence for nationals of Member States in the territory of another Member State' [1979] OJ C207/14 and COM(79) 215 final, 26 July 1979. See also 'European Union. Report by Mr Leo Tindemas, Prime Minister of Belgium, to the European Communities', Bulletin of the European Communities, Supplement 1/76 (Bull.EC 8 -1975), ie 'the Tindemas Report'.

[61] 'Proposal for a Council Directive on the right of residence for students' [1989] OJ C 191/2; 'Proposal for a Council Directive on the right of residence for employees and self-employed persons who have ceased their occupational activity' [1989] OJ C191/3; and 'Proposal for a Council Directive on the right of residence' [1989] OJ C191/5. See further on the historical background of these directives in, Van der Mei (n 12) 44–46.

[62] Directive 90/364 on the right of residence [1990] OJ 180/26: Directive 90/365 on the right of residence for employees and self-employed persons who have ceased their occupational activities [1990] OJ L180/28 and Directive 90/366 on the right of residence of students [1990] OJ L180/30, readopted as Directive 93/96 [1993] OJ L317/54. These three directives were repealed by Directive 2004/38 on the right of citizens of the Union and their family members to move and reside freely within the territory of the Member States [2004] OJ L158/77.

Meanwhile, the general Treaty-based right to free movement and residence was included in the EC Treaty when the concept of EU citizenship was created by the Maastricht Treaty in 1992.[63] The three separate Residence Directives were later replaced by Directive 2004/38 on the right of citizens of the Union and their family members to move and reside freely within the territories of the Member States.[64]

The limitations and conditions of Union citizens' right to reside in the territory of another Member State under Article 21 TFEU now find their expression both in the wording of Directive 2004/38 and in the proportionality assessment by the Court of Justice. In practice, the right to residence is limited by the concept of a 'burden' which first emerged from the case-law and is now included in Article 7(1)(b) of Directive 2004/38. According to this provision, all EU citizens have the right of residence in the territory of another Member State for a period longer than three months if they are workers, self-employed persons or 'have sufficient resources for themselves and their family members not to become a burden on the social assistance system of the host Member State during their period of residence and have comprehensive sickness insurance cover in the host Member State'.[65] Article 8(4) of the same Directive clarifies that Member States 'may not lay down a fixed amount which they regard as "sufficient resources" but they must take into account the personal situation of the person concerned'. It is also noteworthy that Recital 10 of the preamble to Directive 2004/38 talks about an 'unreasonable burden' and not just about a 'burden' in this context.[66]

Directive 2004/38 also regulates the retention of the right to residence in more detail. Article 14(1) of Directive 2004/38 holds that Union citizens have the right to reside up to three months under Article 6 'as long as they do not become an unreasonable burden on the social assistance system of the host Member State'. According to Article 14(2), after three months they have the right to reside under Article 7 'as long as they meet the conditions set out therein'. Article 14(3) of the same Directive clarifies that an expulsion measure 'shall not be the automatic consequence of a Union citizen's or his or her family member's recourse to the social assistance system of the host Member State'. In the famous *Grzelczyk* case, which pre-dated Directive 2004/38, the Court of Justice had stated that the decision to withdraw a residence permit or not to renew it must not become 'the automatic consequence of a student who is a national of another Member State having recourse to the host Member State's social assistance system'.[67] Instead, the host

[63] Treaty on European Union [1992] OJ C191/01.

[64] Directive 2004/38/EC.

[65] These conditions do not apply to those EU citizens who gain the right of permanent residence after a continuous period of five years under Article 16 of Directive 2004/38/EC. In practice, however, the conditions laid down in Article 7 of the Directive have a considerable impact on whether the continuous residency of five years can be reached in practice and, thus, on whether a migrant Union citizen will ever reach the stage of full assimilation with the nationals of the host Member State in so far as access to social minimum benefits is concerned.

[66] See also Opinion of AG Wahl in *Pensionsversicherungsanstalt v Peter Brey* (C-140/12) 29 May 2013, para 76.

[67] *Grzelczyk* (n 8) para 42–43.

Member State must show that the applicant has become an 'unreasonable burden' before it can terminate his/her residence on the basis of the recourse to social assistance.[68] Whether or not this is the case is subject to the proportionality analysis. However, the Court's more recent references to 'automatic' acquisition and loss of free movement rights may indicate that the lack of sufficient resources can have direct implications for 'residence status', instead of just providing an accepted justification for terminating the right to residence.[69]

Migrant EU citizens' non-economic right to equal treatment and its limitations are also included in Directive 2004/38. According to Article 24(1) of the Directive, 'all Union citizens residing on the basis of this Directive in the territory of the host Member State shall enjoy equal treatment with the nationals of that Member State within the scope of the Treaty'. Article 24(2) of the same Directive qualifies this right by stating that 'the host Member State shall not be obliged to confer entitlement to social assistance during the first three months of residence or, where appropriate, the longer period provided for in Article 14(4)(b)' which regulates the work-seeker's right to residence in the area of another Member State.[70] Article 24(2) also includes a provision stating that the Member States are not obliged to 'grant maintenance aid for studies, including vocational training, consisting in student grants or student loans to persons other than workers, self-employed persons, persons who retain such status and members of their family'.

Some argue that the principle of equal treatment must not apply under any circumstances to those EU citizens who belong to the groups mentioned in Article 24(2) of Directive 2004/38, namely short-term residents, work-seekers, and students.[71] However, the Court of Justice has adopted a more flexible approach by which the derogation clause must not be applied in a disproportionate manner.[72] But even those EU citizens who enjoy the 'full' right to equal treatment under Article 24(1) of Directive 2004/38/EC may find that their right is limited either (1) on the basis that their residence is terminated because they have become a 'burden' or an 'unreasonable burden'[73] to the welfare system of the host Member State or (2) on the basis that the host Member State uses their lack of integration as an objective justification for differential treatment. Objective justifications for legitimate differential treatment between EU citizens are discussed in more detail in Section 2.3. The rest of this section will focus on the question of how conditions of EU citizens'

[68] Ibid para 44.

[69] For this observation, see Daniel Thym, 'The Elusive Limits of Solidarity: Residence Rights of and Social Benefits for Economically Inactive Union Citizens' (2015) 52 *Common Market Law Review* 17, 40.

[70] The concern is that the definition of 'social advantages' under the limitation clause of Article 24(2) of Directive 2004/38 'is much broader than the rather marginal and residual concept traditionally used by the Court of Justice in interpreting Regulation 1408/71'. See eg Stefano Giubboni, 'Free Movement of Persons and European Solidarity' (2007) 13 *European Law Journal* 360, 372.

[71] Hailbronner (n 33) 1262.

[72] See more about the case-law in Section 2.3, p 63.

[73] It is not clear whether the references to a 'burden' in Article 7(1)(b) and an 'unreasonable burden' in Article 14(1) are interchangeable, but both of them depend on the proportionality analysis.

right to residence qualify EU citizens' general right to equal treatment in the light of the Court's case law.

Unequal Treatment Between EU Citizens as an 'Inevitable Consequence' of EU Law?

The recent *Dano* case illustrates how EU citizens' general right to equal treatment is dependent on the right to residence in EU law. In this case, the central question was whether a general exclusion from access to social assistance in the case of those economically inactive EU citizens who, according to the national authorities, have entered the host Member State 'to obtain social assistance' or 'whose right of residence arises solely out of the search for employment' is acceptable in the light of Directive 2004/38 and the principle of proportionality. In his Opinion, Advocate General Wathelet outlined that the general criterion can be legitimate if it demonstrates 'the absence of a genuine link with the territory of the host Member State and of integration in it' and grants that 'the system is economically viable and that its financial balance is not undermined'.[74] Moreover, the Advocate General found the general criterion in question proportionate because, in his view, there was no risk for 'automatic expulsion' based on the mere recourse to social assistance in so far as the competent authorities are 'to a certain extent' required to examine the applicant's personal circumstances.[75]

This analysis was based on the presumption that EU citizens can claim equal treatment with nationals of the host Member State under Article 24(1) of Directive 2004/38 only if his/her residence in this Member State complies with the conditions laid down in Article 7(1)(b) of that Directive.[76] According to the Advocate General, the 'particular aim' of that provision is 'to prevent economically inactive Union citizens from using the welfare system of the host Member State to finance their livelihood'.[77] For the Advocate General, the potential to unequal treatment between other EU citizens and nationals of the host Member State is therefore 'an inevitable consequence of Directive 2004/38'.[78] The Court's Grand Chamber agreed on Advocate General Wathelet's conclusion that the potential to unequal treatment between EU citizens necessarily follows from the link between the requirement of sufficient resources and the concern not to create a burden in Article 7(1)(b) of Directive 2004/38 and that German legislation in question therefore served a legitimate aim and was proportionate in regard to that aim.[79]

The judgment also pointed out that persons who are working have the right to residence 'without having to fulfil any further condition', whereas persons who are

[74] Opinion of AG Wathelet in *Elisabeta Dano and Florin Dano v Jobcenter Leipzig* (C-333/13) 20 May 2014, para 135.

[75] Ibid paras 137–38.

[76] Case C-333/13 *Elisabeta Dano and Florin Dano v Jobcenter Leipzig*, 11 November 2014, para 69.

[77] Opinion of AG Wathelet in *Dano* (n 74) para 94.

[78] Ibid para 93.

[79] *Dano* (n 76) paras 77–78.

economically inactive, and whose residence has been longer than three months but shorter than five years, have to meet the condition of sufficient resources.[80] According to the Court, this condition 'seeks to prevent economically inactive Union citizens from using the host Member State's welfare system to fund their means of subsistence'.[81] In his Opinion, the Advocate General underlined that the existing case law demonstrates that the right of economically inactive EU citizens to access social benefits 'is, in general, dependent on a certain degree of integration in the host Member State'.[82] In his view, it would thus be acceptable 'to prevent persons exercising their right to freedom of movement without intending to integrate themselves from becoming a burden on the social assistance system'.[83] The interesting question is how 'a certain degree of integration' between the EU citizen and the host Member State was defined in this context and what considerations could contribute to establishing relevant integration.

In practice, the Court accepted the reason for entering the territory of the host Member State, together with the lack of economic resources, as a means of demonstrating the absence of a genuine link with the host Member State. In so far as the possibility of more individual assessment was discussed by the Advocate General, the focus of that discussion was on the 'economic capability' of the EU citizen. The Advocate General noted that the Court's earlier case law[84] requires the Member States to carry out an 'overall assessment' of the proportionality of such exclusions in the light of the applicant's 'personal circumstances' and the 'specific burden which granting that benefit would place on the social assistance system as a whole'.[85] However, he argued that the 'individual assessment of a Union citizen's economic capability' beyond the requirement of sufficient resources and comprehensive sickness insurance under Article 7(1)(b) of Directive 2004/38 would 'lead to an impasse',[86] in which the condition of sufficient resources could be 'artificially fulfilled' when Union citizens move to another Member State 'merely in order to obtain social assistance' from that State in question.[87] Neither the Advocate General nor the Court of Justice addressed the question of whether, and if so how, access to equal treatment could facilitate integration in the case of EU citizens *qua* EU citizens—as clearly is the case in regard to Union workers.

[80] Ibid para 75.

[81] Ibid, para 76.

[82] Opinion of AG Wathelet in *Dano* (n 74) para 127–29. See also Case C-209/03 *The Queen, on the application of Dany Bidar v London Borough of Ealing and Secretary of State for Education and Skills* [2005] ECR I-2119, paras 56–57; Case C-138/02 *Brian Francis Collins v Secretary of State for Work and Pensions* [2004] ECR I-2703, para 67; Cases C-22/08 and C-23/08 *Athanasios Vatsouras, Josit Koupatanze v Arbeitsgemeinschaft (ARGE) Nürnberg 900* [2009] ECR I-4585, para 38; and Case C-158/07 *Jacqueline Förster v Hoofddirectie van de Informatie Beheer Groep* [2008] ECR I-8507, paras 48–49.

[83] Opinion of AG Wathelet in *Dano* (n 74), para 131.

[84] See in particular Case C-140/12 *Pensionsversicherungsanstalt v Peter Brey*, 19 September 2014, para 76, in which the Court states that, in the light of Recital 16 of Directive 2004/38, the criteria for determining whether an EU citizen is a disproportionate unreasonable burden on the social assistance system in the host Member State include 'whether the difficulties are temporary; the duration of residence; personal circumstances; and the amount of aid granted'.

[85] Opinion of AG Wathelet in *Dano* (n 74) paras 99–100.

[86] Ibid, para 113.

[87] Ibid.

It has been suggested in academic commentary that different degrees of equal treatment in regard to different groups of EU citizens are softened because residence conditions are not self-contained but a 'conventional discrimination analysis' is used to define their acceptability.[88] However, this safeguard remains unfortunately vague in so far as EU citizens' general right to non-discrimination and equal treatment is not even fully materialised in these cases and the Court will therefore not engage with the discrimination analysis proper. The *Dano* judgment depicts EU citizens' non-economic right to non-discrimination and equal treatment as a derived right which is conditional on lawful residence under EU secondary legislation. Conversely, this means that the *de facto* scope of the fundamental right to non-discrimination and equal treatment is made contingent on the proportionality analysis which defines the limits of the right to residence. This indicates that the comparability on the basis of the status of EU citizenship is much weaker than comparability between Union workers.

2.2.4 EU Citizens' Derived Right to Equal Treatment: The Structural Equality Problem

In Sections 2.2.2 and 2.2.3 above, it has been made clear that the scope of the EU principle of equality is different for economically active and inactive EU citizens. The difference between EU citizens' status-based and residence-based rights to equal treatment has considerable implications on equality between different groups of EU citizens. The main division happens between those EU citizens who hold the status of a Union worker and those who do not. In academic commentary, this disparity in the legal status between Union workers and Union citizens as Union citizens has been described by referring to 'the distinction between guaranteed, specific rights and general, highly conditional ones'.[89] However, as will be shown in the next section, the interpretation of EU citizens' right to equal treatment also distinguishes between citizens *sensu stricto* as different criteria for legitimate differential treatment are imposed on different groups of economically inactive EU citizens under Directive 2004/38. The differences in the scope of EU citizens' economic and non-economic right to equal treatment imply different degrees of comparability between different groups of EU citizens. This section will further consider what these differences mean for EU citizenship as an equal and/or fundamental status.

In the case of Union workers, the Court of Justice has widely rejected the use of durational residence as a condition for equal treatment and the interests of the Member States are accommodated in the interpretation of the status of a Union

[88] Catherine Barnard, 'EU Citizenship and the Principle of Solidarity' in Michael Dougan and Eleanora Spaventa (eds), *Social Welfare and EU Law* (Hart Publishing, 2005) 174.

[89] Charlotte O'Brien, 'Social Blind Spots and Monocular Policy Making: The ECJ's Migrant Worker Model' (2009) 46 *Common Market Law Review* 1107, 1109.

worker.[90] The question of the personal scope of equal treatment is therefore crucial and the Court has established a *strong comparability* between nationals of the host Member State and those individuals who fall within the personal scope of Article 7(2) of Regulation 1612/68 and now Regulation 492/2011, ie who qualify for the status of a Union worker. Strong comparability means that the status of a Union worker has been given priority over objective justifications, such as residence requirements. The Court has made it clear that, with the exception of frontier workers, an additional residence requirement imposed on non-national Union workers 'constitutes a clear case of discrimination on the basis of the nationality of workers'.[91] The wide interpretation of equal treatment under Article 7(2) of Regulation 1612/68 underlines the fact that the receipt of the social benefits under this Article is seen as a way to 'promote' integration in the future and no requirement of a 'real link' is therefore imposed on migrant workers under this provision.[92]

Strong comparability can be contrasted with *weak comparability* under which the right to non-discrimination and equal treatment is extensively conditioned on the proportionality analysis at the expense of initial comparability between EU citizens. The current interpretation of EU citizens' general right to equal treatment in the light of Directive 2004/38 will only allow us to speak of weak comparability between economically inactive nationals and non-nationals. Their right to non-discrimination and equal treatment is made dependent on legal residence which is defined by the Member States on the basis of the requirement of proportionality. Moreover, as will be discussed in Section 2.3, their access to social minimum benefits can be limited further by the requirement of already achieved social integration into the society of the host State.[93] Unlike in the case of Union workers, the integrative force of equal treatment is clearly considered to be less relevant in the case of EU citizens as EU citizens.[94]

It needs to be asked *on what basis* EU citizens find themselves in the same situation with the nationals of the host Member State and how this may qualify EU citizenship as the fundamental status of all Member State nationals. The Court began its substantive analysis in the *Dano* judgment by referring to the right of all those EU citizens 'who find themselves in the same situation' to enjoy equal treatment within the material scope of the EU Treaties.[95] In practice, however, the *de facto* scope of EU citizens' general right to equal treatment under EU law depends on the reasonableness analysis which defines the limits of the right to residence and, thus, the boundaries within which EU citizens can rely on their

[90] Van der Mei (n 12) 130–31.

[91] *Vera Hoeckx* (n 26), para 24.

[92] O'Leary, 'Developing an Ever Closer Union' (n 52) 171.

[93] See more about this in Sections 2.3 and 3.3.

[94] See also O'Leary, 'Developing an Ever Closer Union' (n 52) 183–91 about the risk that the case law on Union citizenship may have a restrictive impact on the principles of free movement of economically active persons which, so far, has been interpreted as not allowing any additional requirement of integration or residence.

[95] *Dano* (n 76) para 58.

right to equal treatment. This slip away from the strong and status-based comparability in the case of EU citizens as EU citizens to a much weaker form of comparability directs our attention to what can be called the structural dimension of the EU equality problem.

The core of the structural EU equality problem is that the residence-based scope of EU citizens' general right to equal treatment can easily lead to circularity in the application of the EU principle of equality. This risk of circularity is particularly clear in the older *Trojani* case. Mr Trojani was a French national who resided in Belgium and who, in the context of a personal reintegration programme, did various jobs for about 30 hours a week in a Salvation Army hostel where he was given accommodation in Brussels. The Court confirmed that Mr Trojani's right to reside in the territory of the host Member State under Article 18 EC (now Article 21 TFEU) was limited due to his lack of sufficient resources under Directive 90/364.[96] But the Court also pointed out that, since Mr Trojani was nevertheless issued a residence permit by the municipal authorities, he was able to rely on Article 12 EC (now Article 18 TFEU) in order to be granted the minimum social assistance benefits.[97] Instead of considering how this right to equal treatment could be limited under the objective justification test, the Court stated that 'it remains open to the host Member State to take the view that a national of another Member State who has recourse to social assistance no longer fulfils the conditions of his right to residence'.[98]

The *Trojani* case is exceptional because the applicant had been granted the right to residence on the basis of national law and not on the basis of EU law. However, the judgment shows not just that the right to equal treatment depends on the right to residence but also that the use of the right to equal treatment can lead to the termination of that residence on the basis of the 'unreasonable burden' test. The legal effect of Treaty rights becoming fundamental rights should arguably imply both a broad interpretation of the 'initial or *prima facie* right itself' and a narrow interpretation of the 'exceptions to that right'.[99] An important difference is that, in the case of fundamental rights, limitations define the 'terms of exercise' of the right rather than the 'right itself, or to whom it belongs'.[100] But the case law seems to confirm that EU citizens' fundamental right to equal treatment is not just limited in regard to the exercise of that right, but the very enjoyment of the right is now restricted under Directive 2004/38.[101] The connection between EU citizens' right to equal treatment and their right to residence means that EU citizens'

[96] Case C-456/02 *Michel Trojani v Centre public d'aide sociale de Bruxelles (CPAS)* [2004] ECR I-7573, para 36.

[97] Ibid, para 40.

[98] Ibid, para 45.

[99] Chris Hilson, 'What's in a Right? The Relationship between Community, Fundamental and Citizenship Rights in EU Law' (2004) 29 *European Law Review* 636, 648.

[100] See eg Síofra O'Leary, 'The Relationship between Community Citizenship and the Protection of Fundamental Rights in Community Law' (1995) 32 *Common Market Law Review* 519, 540–41.

[101] For a similar argument, see eg Niamh Nic Shuibhne, 'Limits Rising, Duties Ascending: The Changing Legal Shape of Union Citizenship' (2015) 52 *Common Market Law Review* 889, 915.

fundamental right to non-discrimination and equal treatment appears as a *derived right*, which is contingent on the proportionality analysis in defining the limits of the right to residence.

The structural equality problem is also illustrated in the Opinion of Advocate General Wahl in the recent *Brey* case. In his Opinion, the Advocate General held that the principle of equal treatment was not 'directly relevant' to granting the benefit in question, because the main discussion concerned the conditions for obtaining the right to reside in the host Member State.[102] The structural equality problem becomes obvious in his statement that

> so long as Union citizens reside lawfully under EU law in another Member State, they may rely on EU law, including the principle of equal treatment, in order to receive social benefits, *notwithstanding that this may subsequently compromise their right of residence* [italics added].[103]

In the words of the Advocate General, 'the loss of sufficient resources is always an underlying risk'.[104] This indicates that the exercise of the right to equal treatment may indeed 'subsequently compromise' the very same right of residence from which the right to equal treatment derives its scope of application under Directive 2004/38.

Thus, what is noteworthy is that the exercise of proportionality analysis in the context of the right to residence has direct implications on the actual scope of EU citizens' general right to equal treatment in so far as that right depends on residence. In his Opinion on the *Morgan and Bucher* case, Advocate General Ruiz-Jarabo Colomer referred to EU citizenship as a fundamental status 'which has gained in significance from the prohibition of discrimination laid down by Article 12 EC [now 18 TFEU]'.[105] He based this view of EU citizenship on the above-mentioned *Trojani* case by noting that '[t]he combined reference to the exclusion of discrimination and the freedom of movement is no obstacle to the independence of those principles, each of which may be evaluated on its own'.[106] In practice, however, the slip away from the status-based comparability between EU citizens as EU citizens can easily lead to the circularity of the EU principle of equality because the use of the right to equal treatment can lead to the termination of the same right of residence from which the right to equal treatment derives its *de facto* scope of application.

The relationship between proportionality and equality is closely connected to the broader question of whether, and if so how, the interpretation and application of concrete provisions of secondary legislation, above all Directive 2004/38, should fall within the more abstract general principles of Union law. The general principles of EU law include both administrative principles and fundamental

[102] Opinion of AG Wahl in *Brey* (n 66) para 95.
[103] Ibid, para 94.
[104] Ibid.
[105] Opinion of AG Ruiz-Jarabo Colomer in *Rhiannon Morgan v Bezirksregierung Köln* and *Iris Bucher v Landrat des Kreises Düren* (C-11/06 and C-12/06) 20 March 2007, para 65.
[106] Ibid, para 67.

rights. The crucial question is how the general principles of EU law as 'optimization requirements'[107] are weighted against each other in the context of EU citizens' equal treatment. It has been argued that using the principle of proportionality to interpret EU citizenship rights must not be used to 'rewrite' the provisions of EU secondary legislation.[108] In practice, the Court must therefore carefully demarcate between 'constitutional' and 'legislative' matters.[109] Where this line is drawn will have significant consequences for the rights of EU citizens. Above all, if the right to reside is terminated on the basis of reasonableness analysis under Article 7(1)(b) of Directive 2004/38, do migrant EU citizens lose their right to equal treatment altogether under Article 18 TFEU? The *Dano* judgment does not provide a direct answer to this question, although the Court's reasoning approaches Directive 2004/38 as a specific expression of Article 18 TFEU.[110]

There is nothing surprising in the fact that the Court of Justice interprets secondary legislation in the light of the general principles of EU law, including the principle of proportionality, if the general principles are regarded as having a direct effect under EU law.[111] The Court's reliance on the proportionality analysis in this context has even been seen as a sign of 'the application of the rule of reason to Article 18(1) EC [now 21 TFEU] and its limitations analogous to the established four freedoms'.[112] However, the critics have pointed out that, instead of applying the 'less restrictive alternative test', proportionality review is often reduced to the less intense 'manifestly inappropriate test' when individual rights are balanced against the Union's or Member State's interests.[113] It is therefore important to critically assess what it means for equal treatment as a fundamental right of all EU citizens that it has *de facto* no independent scope, but the scope of the non-discrimination and equality principles in the case of 'needy' EU citizens is made dependent on the proportionality analysis under the 'unreasonable burden' test.[114]

[107] Robert Alexy, *A Theory of Constitutional Rights* (Oxford University Press, 2002).

[108] Hailbronner (n 33) 1253–54.

[109] Koen Lenaerts and José A Gutierrez-Fons, 'The Constitutional Allocation of Powers and General Principles of EU Law' (2010) 47 *Common Market Law Review* 1589, 1667.

[110] For more discussion about this, see Herwig Verschueren, 'Preventing "Benefit Tourism" in the EU: A Narrow or Broad Interpretation of the Possibilities Offered by the ECJ in *Dano*?' (2015) 52 *Common Market Law Review* 363.

[111] For a more critical opinion, see eg Michael Dougan, 'The Spatial Restructuring of National Welfare States within the European Union: The Contribution of Union Citizenship and the Relevance of the Treaty of Lisbon' in Ulla Neergaard, Ruth Nielsen and Lynn Roseberry (eds), *Integrating Welfare Functions into EU Law From Rome to Lisbon* (DJØF Publishing, 2009).

[112] Borgmann-Prebil (n 58) 330.

[113] Takis Tridimas, 'Proportionality in Community Law: Searching for the Appropriate Standard of Scrutiny' in Evelyn Ellis (ed), *The Principle of Proportionality in the Laws of Europe* (Hart Publishing, 1999) 66.

[114] Proportionality as one of the general (administrative) principles of EU law can be defined by referring to the German concept of proportionality as a three-fold test: the measure must be (1) 'appropriate for attaining the objective', (2) 'necessary, in the sense that no other measure is available' and (3) 'must not be disproportionate to its aim'. Jürgen Schwarze, *European Adiminstrative Law* (Sweet & Maxwell, 1992) 678. See also eg FG Jacobs, 'Recent Developments in the Principle of Proportionality in European Community Law' in Ellis (n 113). The difference between these 'levels' of proportionality

The relationship between the non-discrimination principle and proportionality was originally raised in the aftermath of the so-called 'skimmed-milk powder cases' in the 1970s when prohibited discrimination was assimilated with disproportionality.[115] Both the criteria of non-discrimination and the criteria of proportionality may lose their specific character if they are entangled with each other.[116] Firstly, it has been argued that the 'test of discrimination' ought to be more about the 'effect' on relationships between persons and undertakings than about the relationship between the impact on the 'material sphere of the affected persons' and the 'aim underlying the measure'.[117] Secondly, the criticism of proportionality can also be derived from the failure to 'capture the agent-relative (subjective) aspects of human rights claims'.[118] It has also been noted that the proportionality principle remains meaningless unless the 'supervision of the objectives' under the 'strong' version of proportionality is adopted in addition to the 'weak' proportionality analysis of the mere 'means chosen to pursue those objectives'.[119]

Robert Alexy, the well-known advocate of proportionality analysis, claims that there is no morality without balancing.[120] The logical conclusion is that, equally, there is no balancing without morality. More substantive values and principles than the mere principle of proportionality are needed to guide the Court of Justice through its difficult task of defining the scope of EU citizens' right to non-discrimination and equal treatment. We can share Kay Hailbronner's concern that

> [e]ven if one were to accept the Court's use of proportionality principle, the question remains what criteria can be derived from the principle when it comes to determining the rights of students and other non-economically active Union citizens to social benefits.[121]

However, here the concern is not so much that proportionality 'may again serve as an almost unlimited instrument to amend secondary Community law'[122] but that,

review has been explained by stating that under the first two levels the limitation of rights is required to be 'as small as possible', whereas the third level, ie the balancing test, asks whether the limitation 'adequately compensates for the loss to rights'. Julian Rivers, 'Proportionality and Variable Intensity of Review' (2006) 65 *Cambridge Law Journal* 174, 201.

[115] See eg Case 114/76 *Bela-Mühle Josef Bergmann KG v Grows-Farm GmbH & CO KG* [1977] ECR 1211, para 7. There are nevertheless other cases in which these two areas have been kept more strictly apart. See eg Case 15/83 *Denkavit Nederland BV v Hoofproduktschap voor Akkerbouwprodukten* [1984] ECR 2171, paras 22–23 and 24–25.

[116] Nicholas Emiliou, *The Principle of Proportionality in European Law: A Comparative Study* (Kluwer Law, 1996) 155.

[117] Matthias Herdegen, 'The Relation between the Principles of Equality and Proportionality' (1985) 22 *Common Market Law Review* 683, 685.

[118] Basak Çali, 'Balancing Human Rights? Methodological Problems with Weights, Scales and Proportions' (2007) 29 *Human Rights Quarterly* 251, 263.

[119] Sheldon Leader, 'Proportionality and the Justification of Discrimination' in Janet Dine and Bob Watt (eds), *Discrimination Law: Concepts, Limitations and Justifications* (Longman, 1996) 115.

[120] Alexy (n 107) 193–96 and 363.

[121] Hailbronner (n 33) 1256–57.

[122] Ibid, 1264.

under the proportionality review, the general principles of EU law are at risk of being reduced to mere economic considerations without an adequate substantive reference to fundamental rights or other constitutional safeguards for the interests of private individuals under EU law.[123] This means that EU citizenship appears as a 'transitory status' which primarily assists the nationals of the Member State in striving for the more equal and privileged status of a Union worker.

In sum, the weak comparability in the case of 'needy' EU citizens indicates that the independence of the EU principle of equal treatment is often illusionary. This lack of independence undermines the credibility of the right to equal treatment as a fundamental right and EU citizenship as the 'fundamental status of all Member State nationals'. It is important to bear in mind that the concept of citizenship can usually be seen as affirming comparability between those who are otherwise different.[124] Despite the launch of EU citizenship as a new standard of comparability, the structural Equality Problem emerges from the following circularity in the discrimination analysis:

1) The *de facto* scope of EU citizens' fundamental right to non-discrimination and equal treatment depends on the proportionality analysis which is exercised in the context of another Treaty-based right.
2) The exercise of the right to equal treatment may lead to the termination of the same right from which it derives its existence in the first place (at least if the right to residence is based on national law and not EU law).

2.3 THE LIMITATIONS ON THE RIGHT: RELEVANT DIFFERENCES BETWEEN EU CITIZENS

2.3.1 Unlawful Discrimination or Legitimate Differential Treatment?

The previous section demonstrated how the comparability between EU citizens is qualified when it comes to 'needy' migrant EU citizens and how this state of affairs leads to the structural equality problem because EU citizens' fundamental right to non-discrimination and equal treatment under EU law has *de facto* no independent scope. This section moves on to examine a more substantive question: Under

[123] See more about this at the end of Section 2.3, p 86.

[124] For instance, Ulrich Preuß has articulated this by stating that citizenship entails the idea of 'free and equal individuals who are not "naturally" free and equal and whose rights are not inborn'. Ulirch Preuß, 'Citizenship and Identity: Aspects of a Political Theory of Citizenship' in Richard Bellamy and Vittorio Butacchi and Dario Castiglione (eds), *Democracy and Constitutional Culture in the Union of Europe* (Lothian Foundation Press, 1995) 111. It has also been noted that the idea of citizenship normally includes 'the reversal of inequality presumptions deeply held by human beings, putting individuals with this status on equal footing in a number of respects by ignoring any *objective* or *subjective* differences between them'. Dimitry Kochenov, 'Citizenship without Respect: The EU's Troubled Equality Ideal' Jean Monnet Working Paper No 8/10 http://jeanmonnetprogram.org/paper/citizenship-without-respect-the-eus-troubled-equality-ideal/, 18.

which circumstances is differential treatment legitimate between EU citizens? In those cases in which comparability is taken to be 'implicit', rather than 'explicit', the discrimination analysis becomes more 'contingent' by definition because the right to similar treatment is materialised 'if no sufficient reason exists for different treatment'.[125] Similarly, the leap from the explicit incomparability between economically inactive and dependent Union citizens and nationals of the host Member State towards their implicit comparability has placed an increasing importance on the assessment of reasonableness criteria and objective justifications as part of the discrimination analysis in EU law. This section will show that the EU equality problem also has a substantive dimension which is rooted in the lack of independence of those criteria under which differential treatment between EU citizens is justified.

The analysis of justificatory criteria for legitimate differential treatment between EU citizens will demonstrate that adopting EU citizenship as a standard of comparability has created new categories of objective justifications which restrict or even prevent the transformation of EU law from 'non-discrimination on the grounds of nationality' towards 'equal citizenship'. Zig Layton-Henry has examined the question of European identity by distinguishing between the following four categories: 'insiders who are really insiders', 'insiders who are really outsiders', 'outsiders who are accepted as insiders' and 'outsiders who are really outsiders'.[126] The reference to those EU citizens who are not treated as 'insiders' is based on the imbalance between those who seemingly fall into the scope of rights and those who can actually enjoy their rights. This imbalance is crystallised in the case of economically inactive and dependent migrant EU citizens who may fall into the personal scope of the residence-based right to equal treatment under Article 18 TFEU, but whose right is considerably limited as 'insiders who are really outsiders'.

Not all differential treatment constitutes prohibited discrimination. Drawing the line between 'legitimate differential treatment' and 'unlawful discrimination' therefore lies at the heart of the discrimination analysis. The situation is further complicated by the fact that treatment which fulfils the criteria of prohibited discrimination can sometimes be objectively justified.[127] The concept of objective justification in its simplest form is defined as a 'reason to be put forward in

[125] Kenneth W Simons, 'Equality as A Comparative Right' (1985) 65 *Boston University Law Review* 387, 424. Cf An 'explicit' use of comparability analysis defines which parameters are relevant for two situations to be relevantly similar for the application of the non-discrimination principle. Ibid.

[126] Zig Layton-Henry, 'Insiders and Outsiders in the European Union: The Search for a European Identity and Citizenship' in Elizabeth Guild (ed), *The Legal Framework and Social Consequences of Free Movement of Persons in the European Union* (Kluwer, 1999) 52–54.

[127] It is contested whether direct discrimination can be justified under any circumstances. Most commentators agree that direct discrimination should only be possible under explicit statutory exemptions. For more about this see eg Fredman (n 2) 190 and 196. However, this has not always been self-evident in the case law of the European Court of Human Rights, as discussed in Chapter 1 in Section 1.2.4, p 21. Moreover, it has also been explored in academic commentary whether objective justifications could be used to justify preferential treatment on protected grounds in the name of substantive equality and positive action. See eg Evelyn Ellis and Philippa Watson, *EU Anti-Discrimination Law* (Oxford University Press, 2012) 91 and 112–13.

order to defend the differentiation made'.[128] In EU law, the recourse to objective justifications is accepted in the context of indirect discrimination where disparate impact will establish a claim of *prima facie* discrimination which can then be justified by relying on objective justifications.[129] The concept of objective justification opens the more fundamental question of what is meant by 'discrimination' and whether objectively justified behaviour still falls within the scope of the term 'discrimination'.[130] The definition of justified differential treatment either as 'lawful discrimination' or 'non-discrimination' is not just of mainly theoretical interest but can arguably constitute 'a difference in the threshold of justifiability, which reflects itself in different notions of proportionality'.[131] The way in which legitimate differential treatment between EU citizens is conceptualised under the objective justification test has significant implications for EU citizenship as an equal status.

Despite the relatively uniform definition of direct discrimination[132] on the grounds of nationality, it is less clear on which basis *prima facie* indirect discrimination[133] may be justified under EU law. In the *O'Flynn* case, the Court of Justice clarified the concept of indirect nationality discrimination by stating that national law can be indirectly discriminatory if 'it is intrinsically liable to affect migrant workers more than national workers and if there is a consequent risk that it will place the former at a particular disadvantage'.[134] In the *Sotgiu* case, the Court confirmed that prohibited nationality discrimination covers both 'overt' and 'covert' forms of discrimination. However, the prohibited forms of discrimination would not cover cases 'which took account of objective differences'.[135] The Court of Justice later clarified the notion of objective justifications for indirect nationality discrimination by stating that legitimate justifications 'were objective

[128] See eg IP Asscher-Vonk, 'Towards One Concept of Objective Justification?' in Titia Loenen and Peter Rodrigues (eds), *Non-Discrimination Law: Comparative Perspectives* (Kluwer, 1999) 39.

[129] Titia Loenen, 'Indirect Discrimination: Oscillating between Containment and Revolution' in Loenen and Rodrigues (n 128) 203.

[130] Nicholas Bamforth, 'Setting the Limits of Anti-Discrimination Law: Some Legal and Social Concepts' in Dine and Watt (n 119) 58.

[131] See Nicolas Bernard, 'What are the Purposes of EC Discrimination Law?' in Dine and Watt (n 119) 85.

[132] The term 'direct discrimination' refers to nationality requirements under which differential treatment is based on the nationality of the host Member State or on other conditions which only non-nationals have to meet. EU law does not prohibit all instances of direct discrimination on the grounds of nationality within the Member States. Firstly, the Member States can favour their own nationals in those situations that fall outside the scope of EU law and, thus, outside the scope of application of the non-discrimination principle. Secondly, Article 45(3)–(4) TFEU includes the so-called public service and public policy exceptions which allow the Member States to exercise differential treatment in certain cases. The Court has, nonetheless, interpreted both of these two exceptions strictly. See eg Case 36/75 *Roland Rutili and the Minister for the Interior* [1975] ECR 1219, para 27 and Case C-348/96 *Criminal proceedings against Donatella Calfa* [1999] ECR I-11, para 23.

[133] The term 'indirect discrimination' refers to situations in which criteria other than nationality are more easily satisfied by the nationals of the host Member State. Unlike in the case of direct discrimination, the Member States are allowed to provide objective justifications for provisions that would constitute *prima facie* indirect discrimination by affecting non-nationals more than nationals.

[134] *O'Flynn* (n 34) para 20.

[135] Case 152/73 *Giovanni Maria Sotgiu v Deutsche Bundespost* [1974] ECR 153, paras 11–12.

considerations independent of the nationality of the persons concerned and were proportionate to the legitimate aim of the national provision'.[136]

In the light of Articles 24 and 7 of Directive 2004/38, the migrant Union citizens' right to equal treatment seems to be secured once they lawfully reside in the area of another Member State for more than three months, and as long as their right to residence is not determined on the basis of becoming an 'unreasonable burden' and they do not seek social assistance as migrant students or work-seekers. The right to equal treatment is not absolute, however. Although EU citizens now enjoy a 'prima facie entitlement'[137] to residence and equal treatment, it is legitimate for the Member States to require a real and effective link either with the territory or the society of the State in which access to social benefits is being claimed. The 'de-nationalisation' of welfare states by the prohibition of nationality criteria as conditions for access to social benefits[138] has not led to the 'de-territorialisation' of welfare states.[139] Direct discrimination in the form of explicit nationality clauses has become rare, but the focus of discrimination analysis has shifted to covert and indirect discrimination.[140] This means that objective justifications play a central role in the discrimination analysis in regard to economically inactive EU citizens.

One way to address the question of legitimate differential treatment is to argue that the acceptance of justificatory criteria necessarily implies non-comparability between EU citizens. This line of argument suggests that Member States could justify the use of a 'differentiating criterion' by claiming that 'it merely takes note of situations that are actually not comparable' when EU citizens from other Member States are placed at a disadvantage.[141] This approach would ensure that such justificatory criteria could no longer be based on arbitrary grounds, such as nationality.[142] However, it would also ignore the idea of EU citizenship as an equal (and comparable) status between all those who hold it. The analysis of the 'real link' case law in Sections 2.3.2 and 2.3.3 approaches the question of legitimate differential treatment from the perspective that justificatory criteria, whether statutory exceptions or exceptions based on the objective justification test, must not deface the idea of

[136] Case C-274/96 *Criminal proceedings against Horst Otto Bickel and Ulrich Franz* [1998] ECR I-7637, para 27; Case C-224/98 *Marie-Nathalie D'Hoop v Office national de l'emploi* [2002] ECR I-6212, para 36; Case C-224/02 *Heikki Antero Pusa v Osuuspankkien Keskinäinen Vakuutusyhtiö* [2004] ECR I-5763, para 20.

[137] Síofra O'Leary, 'Solidarity and Citizenship Rights in the Charter of Fundamental Rights of the European Union' in Graínne de Búrca (ed), *EU Law and the Welfare State: In Search of Solidarity* (Oxford University Press, 2005) 71.

[138] With certain exceptions in the case of war veterans and military service personnel. Eg Case C-315/94 *Peter de Vos v Stadt Bielefeld* [1996] ECR I-1417, para 23.

[139] See eg Anne Pieter Van der Mei, 'Union Citizenship and the "De-Nationalisation" of the Territorial Welfare State' (2005) 7 *European Journal of Migration and Law* 203, 207.

[140] Matthias Malmstedt, 'From Employee to EU Citizen—A Development from Equal Treatment as a Means to Equal Treatment as a Goal?' in Ann Numhauser-Henning (ed), *Legal Perspectives on Equal Treatment and Non-Discrimination* (Kluwer, 2001) 97.

[141] Koenraad Lenaerts, 'Union Citizenship and the Principle of Non-Discrimination on Grounds of Nationality' http://ecas.org/file_uploads/1095.pdf, 17–18.

[142] Ibid.

EU citizenship as a fundamental status of all Union citizens who fall within the scope of the EU Treaties.

2.3.2 A 'Real Link' with the Geographical Employment Market: A Story of *de jure* Economic Criteria

This section explores the lack of a 'real link' with the geographic employment market as an objective justification for legitimate differential treatment under EU law. The analysis builds upon three landmark cases, which illustrate the development of the 'real link' test in the case of work-seekers. The focus of these cases is economic. The Court approaches the requirement of a 'real link' with the geographic employment market primarily as a restriction on the right to free movement of workers under Article 45 TFEU and only secondarily as a restriction on Union citizens' right to free movement under Article 21 TFEU. The principle of equal treatment is therefore seen as an instrument to secure the full enjoyment of the right to (economic) free movement. This means that the 'real link' test fails to provide independent criteria for legitimate differential treatment between EU citizens in so far as its use is limited to the establishment of a link with the geographic employment market. Instead, it will only provide a means of extending the boundaries of what economic activity means in the case of EU citizens.

D'Hoop: Introducing the Economic 'Real Link' Test

The Court laid down the idea of a 'real link' as a legitimate condition for differential treatment between Union citizens in the *D'Hoop* case. The claimant, Ms D'Hoop was a Belgian national who had completed her secondary education in France and was therefore refused the Belgian tide-over allowance which is given to young people seeking their first employment. Ms D'Hoop was not regarded as a 'worker' under what is now Article 45 TFEU because she was looking for her first employment. However, the Court concluded that, as a citizen of the Union, her exercise of free movement fell within the scope of Article 18 EC (now Article 21 TFEU) despite the fact that the provisions of Union citizenship entered into force only subsequently. And it would not be compatible with a Union citizen's freedom of movement to receive less favourable treatment from his or her own Member State than what he/she would have enjoyed, had he/she not exercised the right to free movement.[143] The Court clarified this statement further by pointing out that '[s]uch inequality of treatment is contrary to the principles which underpin the status of citizen of the Union, that is, the guarantee of the same treatment in law in the exercise of the citizen's freedom to move'.[144]

[143] *D'Hoop* (n 136), para 30.
[144] Ibid, para 35.

However, the Court qualified its own statement of equal treatment as one of the principles that underpin the status of EU citizenship, by noting that the inequality of treatment could be justified if it is based on 'objective considerations independent of the nationality of the persons concerned and were proportionate to the legitimate aim of the national provisions'.[145] According to the Court, the limitation in question was 'too general and exclusive in nature' because it 'unduly favours an element which is not necessarily representative of the real and effective degree of connection between the applicant for the tide-over allowance and the geographical employment market, to the exclusion of all other representative elements'.[146] The Court's reference to the 'real and effective degree of connection' is here limited to the 'geographic employment market' and, thus, it provides little substance for equality as one of the principles underpinning the non-economic status of EU citizenship.

Collins: Constitutionalising the Economic 'Real Link' Test?

In the *D'Hoop* case, the requirement of a 'real link' appeared between an EU citizen and her state of origin. In the later *Collins* case, the Court applied the same logic to migrant EU citizens in their host Member States. In this case, the claimant was an Irish national who was lawfully resident in the United Kingdom with the intention of seeking employment and applied for Jobseeker's Allowance there. After concluding that the right to equal treatment for persons seeking employment could also cover benefits of a financial nature under Articles 48 and 6 of the EEC Treaty (now Articles 45 and 18 TFEU), the Court proceeded to answer the question of whether the EU principle of equal treatment prohibits national legislation which makes entitlement to Jobseeker's Allowance conditional on habitual residence.

With regard to the existence of indirect discrimination, the Court reiterated its statement in the *D'Hoop* case that

> it is legitimate for the national legislature to wish to ensure that there is a genuine link between an applicant for an allowance in the nature of a social advantage within the meaning of Article 7(2) of Regulation No 1612/68 and the geographic employment market in question.[147]

According to the Court, 'while a residence requirement is, in principle, appropriate for the purpose of ensuring such a connection, if it is to be proportionate it cannot go beyond what is necessary in order to attain that objective'.[148] Moreover, the Court amplified this by noting that a required period of residence may not exceed what is necessary for the national authorities to 'satisfy themselves that the

[145] Ibid, para 36. This was confirmed in the *Pusa* case which reiterated this wording. Case C-224/02 *Heikki Antero Pusa v Osuuspankkien Keskinäinen Vakuutusyhtiö* [2004] ECR I-5763, para 20.
[146] *D'Hoop* (n 136), para 39.
[147] *Collins* (n 82), para 67.
[148] Ibid, para 72.

person concerned is genuinely seeking work in the employment market of the host Member State'.[149]

In the earlier case law, the Court had maintained that work-seekers were entitled to equal treatment in relation to access to employment but not in relation to social advantages.[150] In the *Collins* case, the principle of non-discrimination was extended to cover work-seekers 'in its full scope' by interpreting Article 39 EC (now Article 45 TFEU) and Regulation 1612/68 in the light of EU citizenship.[151] It has been argued that the *Collins* case confirmed that EU citizenship is not just a 'safety net' for those individuals who could not rely on the traditional free movement provisions of the Treaty, but that EU citizenship has become a 'genuine constitutional tool' for interpreting the rights to free movement and residence regardless of which status those EU citizens would otherwise hold under EU law.[152] However, these comments conceal the fact that EU citizenship and EU citizens' right to equal treatment is here seen as an instrument to expand the economic right to equal treatment in the case of those EU citizens who do not (yet) hold the status of a Union worker but who, nonetheless, strive for that status.

Vatsouras and Koupatantze: The Combined Application of Directive 2004/38 and Article 45 TFEU—Still More Economic than Constitutional

In the *Vatsouras and Koupatantze* case, the referring national court wanted to know whether Article 24(2) of Directive 2004/38 is compatible with Article 18 TFEU, 'read in conjunction' with Article 45 TFEU.[153] The Court, first, reiterated its earlier conclusions in *Collins* that nationals of a Member State seeking employment in another Member State enjoy the right to equal treatment under what is now paragraph 2 of Article 45 TFEU and that, after the establishment of EU citizenship, it is no longer possible to exclude financial benefits from the scope of that Article.[154] However, the right to equal treatment can be legitimately limited by the requirement that the jobseeker has established a 'real link' with the labour market of that State. This, says the Court, could be done 'in particular, by establishing that the person concerned has, for a reasonable period, in fact genuinely sought work in the Member State in question'.[155]

The Court then declared that the derogations in Article 24(2) of Directive 2004/38 must be interpreted in the light of what is now Article 45(2) TFEU, noting that '[b]enefits of a financial nature which, independently of their status under national law, are intended to facilitate access to the labour market'

[149] Ibid.
[150] See eg *Lebon* (n 28) paras 26–27.
[151] See eg Oxana Golynker, 'Jobseekers' rights in the European Union: Challenges of Changing the Paradigm of Social Solidarity' (2005) 30 *European Law Review* 111, 112.
[152] Ibid 116.
[153] *Vatsouras and Koupatantze* (n 82) para 33.
[154] Ibid, paras 36–37.
[155] Ibid, paras 38–39.

could not be classified as 'social assistance' within the meaning of Article 24(2) of Directive 2004/38.[156] But the Court concluded that its examination on these grounds had not challenged the 'validity' of Article 24(2) of Directive 2004/38 in these cases.[157] The derogation from equal treatment in regard to benefits paid to jobseekers under Article 24(2) of Directive 2004/38 was therefore regarded as 'compatible with Article 12 EC [now Article 18 TFEU], read in conjunction with Article 39 EC [now Article 45 TFEU]'.[158] However, in the later *LN* case, which was about the definition of the 'worker' status under Article 45 TFEU, the Court concluded that Articles 7(1) and 24(2) of Directive 2004/38/EC may not prevent an EU citizen from receiving maintenance aid for studies if he or she at the same time pursues effective and genuine employment activities in the host Member State.[159]

The main focus of the Court's examination in these cases was on the relationship between the derogation clause in Article 24(2) of Directive 2004/38 and Article 45 TFEU. Despite its seemingly positive outcome, the *LN* case only confirms the privileged position of the economic status of a Union worker if compared to the status of an EU citizen. This case law emphasises that, unlike the status of EU citizenship, the 'objective status' of a Union worker will 'in principle' establish a 'sufficient link of integration' with the host Member State and will thus allow the holders of that status to benefit from the principle of equal treatment as regards social benefits.[160] Moreover, in *Vatsouras and Koupatantze*, this approach gives the 'real link' test an inherently economic tone, regardless of the reference to EU citizens' general right to non-discrimination and equal treatment under Article 18 TFEU. After all, the Court focused on studying the limitations on EU citizens' right to equal treatment 'in conjunction with' Article 45 TFEU.

The requirement of belonging to the employment market implies a highly instrumental view of equal treatment between EU citizens. It is therefore important to consider whether the Court might have reached a different conclusion in terms of the justifiability of the restriction on equal treatment, had it more explicitly considered the establishment of a 'real link' against the general Treaty-right to equal treatment. The Court's choice to interpret Article 24(2) of Directive 2004/38 in the light of Article 45 TFEU may be defended by noting that, unlike the general prohibition of nationality discrimination, the prohibition of nationality discrimination of workers under Article 45 TFEU is not subject to conditions or limitations, except for the statutory exceptions in Article 45(3) TFEU.[161] This, however, sounds less convincing if the general prohibition of nationality discrimination in

[156] Ibid, paras 44–45.

[157] Ibid, para 46.

[158] Ibid, para 21.

[159] Case C-46/12 *LN v Styrelsen for Videregående Uddannelser og Uddannelsesstøtte*, 21 February 2013.

[160] Case C-542/09 *European Commission v Kingdom of the Netherlands*, 14 June 2012, para 64. See also Opinion of AG Sharpston in Case C-542/09, delivered on 16 February 2012, paras 91 and 95.

[161] The Court also holds the view that the application of specific free movement provisions, such as Article 45 TFEU, is given priority in regard to the general provisions, such as Article 18 TFEU (*lex specialis derogat legi generali*).

Article 18 TFEU is seen as an expression of the EU principle of equality as a constitutional principle and a fundamental right of all EU citizens who fall within the scope of application of the EU Treaties.

2.3.3 A 'Real Link' Based on Other Social and Economic Factors: A Story of *de facto* Economic Criteria

This section examines how the Court has been willing to expand the 'real link' test beyond the purely economic assessment of a 'link with the geographic employment market' or a 'substantial occupation to the national labour market'. It will be seen that the 'real link' test is nonetheless reduced to an economic assessment because the Court has merged it with the so-called 'unreasonable burden' test. This convergence between the 'real link' test and the 'unreasonable burden test' was introduced in the *Bidar* case and its consequences were further clarified in the *Förster* case. These two cases will be compared with the later *Commission v Austria* and *Prinz and Seeberger* judgments in which the Court addressed some of the problems that followed from a strictly durational interpretation of a 'real link'. However, it will also be seen that these judgments do not challenge the connection between the 'economic objective' and the 'integration objective' and, thus, fail to recognise a more independent 'equality objective' in assessing the integration requirements. Finally, this argument about the economic bias in integration requirements will be discussed in the light of the recent *Brey* and *Dano* judgments.

Bidar: Towards a Non-economic 'Real Link' Test

Mr Bidar was a French national who was lawfully resident in the United Kingdom and had received a substantial part of his secondary education there. After starting a university course in the host Member State, he applied for assistance to cover his maintenance costs in the form of a student loan, but his application was rejected on the basis that he was not 'settled' in the United Kingdom. The Court reversed its earlier decisions in the *Lair* and *Brown* cases that the payment of student grants would fall outside the competences of the Union by stating that, in the light of the establishment of EU citizenship, assistance with maintenance costs for students could fall within the scope of application of the Treaties and thus within the scope of the right to equal treatment.[162] The Court, then, proceeded to consider the claim that the scope of application of the Treaty within the meaning of what is now Article 18 TFEU can be restricted by the limitations and conditions of the Union citizens' right to move and reside under what is now Article 21 TFEU.

[162] *Bidar* (n 82) paras 38–39 and 42. For the earlier case law, see Case 39/86 *Sylvie Lair v Universität Hannover* [1988] ECR 3161, para 15 and Case 197/86 *Steven Malcolm Brown v The Secretary of State for Scotland* [1988] 3205, para 18.

The *Bidar* case resembles the above-mentioned cases on work-seekers in the sense that the applicant's right to residence was not contested. Rather, the question was about the right of the host Member State to limit the 'fundamental principle of equal treatment' on the basis of 'objective considerations independent of nationality'. The Court first stated that the definition of who is 'settled' in the United Kingdom for the purposes of national law on the basis of 'certain residence conditions' would 'risk placing at a disadvantage primarily nationals of other Member States'.[163] After this, the Court turned to assess the question of whether such a difference in treatment is 'based on objective considerations independent of the nationality of the persons concerned and is proportionate to the legitimate aim of the national provisions'.[164] What is noteworthy is the way in which the Court derived the rationale of the 'real link' test from the 'unreasonable burden' test.

First, the Court pointed out that 'it is permissible for a Member State to ensure that the grant of assistance to cover the maintenance cost of students from other Member States does not become an unreasonable burden which could have consequences for the overall level of assistance which may be granted by that State'.[165] And, only then, the Court outlined that 'it is *thus* [italics added] legitimate for a Member State to grant such assistance to students who have demonstrated a certain degree of integration into the society of that State'.[166] Thus, although the Court in *Bidar* held that a certain period of residence in the host Member State can indicate the establishment of a 'real link' without any connection with the geographical employment market, it still failed to provide a genuinely non-economic criterion for legitimate differential treatment between EU citizens.[167] It is also important to bear in mind that this case preceded the transposition of Directive 2004/38, although the Court itself still frequently refers to it.

In the *Bidar* case, the Court rejected the national rules which 'preclude any possibility of a national of another Member State obtaining settled status as a student—whatever his actual degree of integration into the society of the host Member State'.[168] In other words, the Court declared that such requirements cannot be objectively justified if they make it impossible for the applicant to satisfy those conditions whatever his actual degree of integration into the society of the host Member State is. It has been noted that the Court, thus, refused to view solidarity as 'a mechanism that only involves those who contribute to the society in economic terms' and opened the door for a 'larger notion of solidarity' under which EU citizens can demonstrate integration on the basis of mere residence.[169] However, in so far as the 'actual degree' of integration as a criterion for equal treatment has its origins in the idea that the applicant must not establish an

[163] *Bidar* (n 82), paras 52–53.
[164] Ibid, para 54.
[165] Ibid, para 56.
[166] Ibid, para 57.
[167] Ibid, paras 58–59.
[168] Ibid, para 61.
[169] Lenaerts (n 141) 16.

unreasonable (economic) burden to the society of the host Member State, this idea of solidarity appears rather limited.

Förster: A Formalistic Interpretation of the 'Real Link' Test

The complex issue of what integration means under the 'real link' test was developed further in the *Förster* judgment.[170] Ms Förster was a German national who moved to the Netherlands, first to train as a primary school teacher and then to pursue a university degree in educational theory. During her studies, she had 'various kinds of paid employment' and, on this basis, she was considered to be a worker under Article 39 EC [now Article 45 TFEU] and Article 7(2) of Regulation 1612/68 as it was then and was, thus, awarded a maintenance grant under the same conditions as a student of Dutch nationality. However, Ms Förster did not take any employment during the final year of her studies and, on this basis, the Dutch authorities decided that she was no longer a 'worker' and the decision concerning her maintenance grant was annulled for a period of five months beginning from the month following the end of her last employment.

In this case, the Court concluded that, as the applicant had ceased her employment without giving up her plan to continue her career in the Netherlands, where she also maintained her residence, she could not be regarded as a worker who has ceased his or her employment activity in the sense of Article 7 of Regulation 1251/70 and would not come under Article 7(2) of Regulation 1612/68 on this basis.[171] The Court, then, proceeded to examine the question of when a Union citizen who travels to another Member State as a student can rely on what is now Article 18 TFEU in order to obtain a maintenance grant in the host Member State.[172] The Court referred to the *Bidar* case in order to draw a distinction between those situations in which an economically inactive Union citizen can rely on what is now Article 18 TFEU based on the fact that she or he has already been lawfully resident in the host Member State 'for a certain time' and those situations in which '[a] student who travels to another Member State to start or pursue education' could benefit from a right of residence on the basis of what are now Article 21 TFEU and Directive 2004/38.[173]

The Court's reasoning was rather cryptic in this case. It first stated that the fact that a student falls within the scope of Article 18 TFEU 'for the purposes of obtaining a maintenance grant' through lawful residence in the *Bidar* case 'does not establish any entitlement to the payment of maintenance grant by the host

[170] *Förster* (n 82).

[171] Ibid, para 31. The Court hold that Regulation (EEC) No 1251/70 of the Commission of 29 June 1970 on the right of workers to remain in the territory of a Member State after having been employed in that State [1970] OJ L 142, which was later repealed by Commission Regulation (EC) No 635/2006 of 25 April 2006 repealing Regulation (EEC) No 1251/70 on the right of workers to remain in the territory of a Member State after having been employed in that State OJ L 112/9, did not apply to the applicant's situation.

[172] Ibid, para 34.

[173] Ibid, paras 39–40.

Member State on the part of students benefiting from the right of residence'.[174] However, the Court then pointed out that none of this would prevent the student who is lawfully resident in the Member State under Article 21 TFEU 'from relying during that residence on the *fundamental principle* of equal treatment enshrined in the first paragraph of Article 12 EC [now 18 TFEU]'.[175] The Court clarified this statement further by pointing out that '[f]or that purpose, the fact that Ms Förster came to the Netherlands principally in order to study there is irrelevant'.[176] But the actual implications of this distinction between the right to non-discrimination and equal treatment as expressed in Article 18 TFEU and the 'fundamental principle of equal treatment' that is enshrined in that Article, but that can be relied on in other cases too, remain obscure in this judgment.

The Court simply moved on to consider the question of whether the fact that the requirement of minimum residence of five years prior to the application for a maintenance grant did not concern Dutch students could be considered discriminatory under what is now Article 18 TFEU.[177] Without giving any further explanations, the Court concluded that the requirement of uninterrupted residence of five years was 'appropriate for the purpose of guaranteeing that the applicant for the maintenance grant at issue is integrated into the society of the host Member State'.[178] With regard to the proportionality of this requirement, the Court decided that neither could it be held to be 'excessive having regard, inter alia, to the requirements put forward with respect to the degree of integration of non-nationals in the host Member State'.[179] In practice, this approach would mean that Union citizens' fundamental right to equal treatment in those cases which fall into the scope of the derogations in Article 24(2) of Directive 2004/38 is only actualised once the conditions for permanent residence under Article 16 of Directive 2004/38 have been met.

The *Förster* judgment represents a purely formal approach to a 'real link' on the basis of a length of residence, whereas, in the *Bidar* case,[180] the criterion of a length of residence was introduced as one possible way to prove a sufficient degree of integration on a more circumstantial basis. By choosing a strictly formalistic approach in *Förster*, the Court ignored the question of whether 'other factors' could indicate a 'substantial degree' of integration into the society of the host Member State, as Advocate General Mazák mused.[181] It has been suggested in academic commentary that the Court could have analysed in more detail whether the residence requirement and the derogation clause were compatible

[174] Ibid, paras 41–42.
[175] Ibid, para 43 (emphasis added).
[176] Ibid, para 44.
[177] Ibid, para 45.
[178] Ibid, para 52.
[179] Ibid, para 54.
[180] *Bidar* (n 82).
[181] Opinion of AG Mazák in *Förster* (n 82) para 41.

with the previous interpretation of Articles 18 and 21 TFEU.[182] This view has been juxtaposed with the fact that, in the earlier *Bidar* and *Grzelczyk* cases,[183] the Court's reasoning had suggested that its interpretation of the Residence Directives was 'mandated'[184] by EU primary law.

A more substantive approach to what is meant by a real and effective link was also discussed by Advocate General Mazák who would have accepted 'general conditions which require no further individual assessment' only in so far as they are 'indicative of the degree of integration into society'.[185] According to the Advocate General, the fact that Directive 2004/38 does not place Member States under any obligation to award a maintenance grant for students prior to their acquisition of permanent residence, cannot 'detract' the analysis from the 'requirements flowing from' Article 18 TFEU and the general principle of proportionality.[186] The Advocate General further suggested that a period of five years of continuous residence in the host Member State should only mark the 'outer limit' for claiming that a migrant student has not established a 'sufficient degree' of integration 'to qualify for equal treatment' in the host Member State.[187] This argument was based on the view that formalistic residence conditions might prevent applicants, such as Ms Förster, 'from benefiting from their right to equal treatment as citizens of the Union—regardless of the actual link they may have established with the society of the host Member State'.[188]

Commission v Austria *and* Prinz and Seeberger*: A More Substantive, but still Economic, Version of the 'Real Link' Test*

A critique of strictly durational residence requirements has now been accepted by the Court of Justice. The Court has always held that the requirement of a 'real link' must be regarded as 'too general and exclusive in nature' if it 'unduly favours an element which is not necessarily representative of the real and effective degree of connection—to the exclusion of all other representative elements'.[189] However, this approach has been given more substance in later case law. In the *Commission v Austria* case, the Court decided that it would be against the EU principle of equal treatment to grant reduced transport fares to only those students whose parents received Austrian family allowances 'to the exclusion of all other representative elements' of a genuine link.[190] Following Advocate General Kokott's analysis, the

[182] Síofra O'Leary, 'Equal Treatment and EU Citizens: A New Chapter on Cross-Border Educational Mobility and Access to Student Financial Assistance' (2009) 34 *European Law Review* 612, 622–23.
[183] *Bidar* (n 82); *Grzelczyk* (n 8).
[184] O'Leary (n 182) 623.
[185] Opinion of AG Mazák in *Förster* (n 82), para 129.
[186] Ibid, para 131.
[187] Ibid, para 132.
[188] Ibid, para 130.
[189] *D'Hoop* (n 136), para 39.
[190] Case C-75/11 *European Commission v Republic of Austria*, 4 October 2012, para 62.

Court underlined that the definition of a link should not 'be fixed in a uniform manner' but it should depend on 'the constitutive elements of the benefit in question'.[191]

The Court thus seemed to follow its reasoning in the earlier *Tas-Hagen* case in which it had already confirmed that a residence requirement could not be considered as a 'satisfactory indicator' of the degree of connection between the applicant and his/her own Member State if it led to differential treatment in the case of 'persons resident abroad whose degree of integration into the society of the Member State granting the benefit is in all respects comparable'.[192] Similarly, in the more recent *Prinz and Seeberger* cases, the Court of Justice was asked to assess a residence requirement which was imposed on the nationals of the Member State in question. In both of these joined cases, the applicants had been refused an educational grant for their studies abroad on the basis that they did not fulfil the requirement of a three-year uninterrupted residence in their state of origin before commencing their studies abroad.[193]

Following Advocate General Sharpston's Opinion, the Court held in *Prinz and Seeberger* that a 'sole condition of uninterrupted residence' was 'too general and too exclusive' to be proportionate under Article 21 TFEU.[194] Notably, the judgment provided a more detailed analysis of those economic and social factors which may count for 'other representative elements' when the Court needs to assess whether the applicant is 'sufficiently connected' to the Member State in question even in the absence of required residence. The list of relevant factors presented both by the Advocate General and the Court included nationality, prior education, family ties, employment, and language skills. However, the list is open-ended and 'other social and economic factors' may also gain relevance in the assessment. The Court also noted that these factors must be examined in the light of other provisions of the national legislation.[195]

This discussion on 'other economic and social factors' is important because it gives more substance to the Court's earlier rulings on the legitimacy of social integration requirements. Moreover, it can be asked whether this analysis would also lay the ground for a more flexible approach to the requirement of a 'real link' as part of the discrimination analysis under Article 18 TFEU. The list of relevant factors must nonetheless be read in the overall context of the Court's reasoning. In *Prinz and Seeberger*, the Court's interpretation of the 'real link' test was still based on the rationale that economically inactive and dependent EU citizens must not

[191] Ibid, para 63.

[192] Case C-192/05 *K Tas-Hagen and RA Tas v Raadskamer WUBO van de Pensioen- en Uitkeringsraad* [2006] ECR I-10451, para 38. See also Opinion of AG Kokott in Case C-192/05 of 30 March 2006, paras 67 and 68.

[193] C-523/11 and C-585/11 *Laurence Prinz v Region Hannover* and *Philipp Seeberger v Studentenwerk Heidelberg*, 18 July 2013.

[194] Ibid, para 40 and Opinion of AG Sharpston in joined cases C-523/11 and C-585/11 of 21 February 2013.

[195] *Prinz and Seeberger* (n 193), para 38.

become an unreasonable financial burden on the welfare system in the Member State which awards the funding.[196] In the words of Advocate General Sharpston, the Member States can 'limit the range of beneficiaries in order to achieve the economic objective; and it is acceptable for that purpose to use a criterion that establishes evidence of a degree of integration'.[197] It is noteworthy that both the Court and Advocate General Sharpston took it for granted that the requirement of a minimum level of integration provides a legitimate way for the Member State to avoid an unreasonable financial burden.[198]

However, the Advocate General did point out the 'false logic' under which the requirement of a 'real link' is often derived from the 'economic objective', while their proportionality is justified merely by referring to the 'integration objective'.[199] By this, the Advocate General referred to the fact that the proportionality of the residence requirement cannot be justified by simply claiming that 'the required degree of connection is invariably demonstrated by residence for a certain numbers of years'.[200] This criticism led her to assess the proportionality of the residence requirement both in the light of the 'economic objective' and in the light of the 'integration objective', as well as to conclude that a 'single criterion' cannot, therefore, be proportionate in relation to the integration objective.[201] However, neither the Advocate General nor the Court developed further the analysis of what implications the definition of a 'real link' under these different objectives would have for the status of EU citizenship.

In *Prinz and Seeberger*, both applicants were applying for a study grant for studies abroad from their own Member State. This meant that Article 24(2) of Directive 2004/38 did not apply to the applicants' situations and both cases were assessed under Article 21 TFEU. It therefore remains unclear whether a similar approach to the 'real link' test would now be adopted in those cases which concern 'needy' migrant EU citizens who apply for social benefits in their host Member State and not in their State of origin. In general, the Court's case law tends to apply a similar logic to integration requirements in both of these two contexts. Moreover, the Court has underlined elsewhere that Article 24 of Directive 2004/38 is 'merely a specific expression' of the principle of equal treatment provided for in Article 18 TFEU and that derogations included in Article 24(2) must be interpreted 'narrowly and in accordance with the provisions of the Treaty, including those relating to citizenship of the Union and the free movement of workers'.[202] It therefore seems possible that the same logic of a more substantive analysis could also apply to integration requirements when they are used as justifications for differential treatment between EU citizens under Article 18 TFEU and Article 24(2)

[196] Ibid, para 36.
[197] Opinion of AG Sharpston (n 194), para 70.
[198] *Prinz and Seeberger* (n 193), para 36.
[199] Opinion of AG Sharpston (n 194), para 77.
[200] Ibid, para 88.
[201] Ibid, para 90.
[202] *LN* (n 159).

of Directive 2004/38. However, the role given to individual circumstances in assessing integration requirements seems more ambiguous in the light of the recent *Brey* and *Dano* judgments.[203]

From Brey *to* Dano*: The Contested Role of Individual Circumstances in Defining Relevant Integration*

It has been seen in Section 2.2.3 that, in the *Dano* judgment,[204] the reason for entering the host Member State and the lack of sufficient resources were used to demonstrate the lack of sufficient integration into the society of the host Member State. It followed from this that the applicant, who was an economically inactive EU citizen, was considered as an unreasonable burden, meaning that she did not fill the conditions for the right to residence under Article 7(1)(b) of Directive 2004/38 and, thus, did not enjoy the right to equal treatment under Article 24 of the same Directive. The Court also confirmed in this case that a general criterion which is able to demonstrate the lack of 'sufficient integration' according to the above (narrow and economic) definition of sufficient integration can be legitimate under EU law. It can be asked whether these considerations about what constitutes sufficient integration also apply to the requirement of a 'real link' when it is applied as part of the objective justification test, as discussed in this section. This question is relevant despite the fact that, in *Dano*, the objective justifications for legitimate differential treatment were not even discussed because the Court held that, in the absence of lawful residence under Directive 2004/38, the applicant did not enjoy the right to equal treatment under that Directive.

It is important to bear in mind that the proportionality analysis, in the form of integration requirements, can play a dual role in defining EU citizens' access to equal treatment. Firstly, the lack of sufficient integration can indicate the establishment of an unreasonable burden which entitles the host Member State to terminate an economically inactive EU citizen's right to residence. This assessment is primarily economic, although the termination of residence must not become an automatic consequence of recourse to the host Member State's social assistance system, as discussed in Section 2.2.3. Secondly, as part of the discrimination analysis, the lack of sufficient integration can also provide an objective justification for differential treatment which would otherwise amount to prohibited discrimination under EU law, as discussed in this section. The Court's reasoning in *Dano* focused on the first of these two uses of integration requirements. However, it has been noted in the literature that 'in concrete cases the equal treatment test and the end of residence test might blend into one inquiry'.[205]

[203] *Brey* (n 84); *Dano* (n 76).

[204] *Dano* (n 76).

[205] Alexander Somek, *Individualism: An Essay on the Authority of the European Union* (Oxford University Press, 2008) 209. Note that Somek has distinguished between the two roles of proportionality analysis in the interpretation of Union citizens' right to equal treatment as follows: 'It is one question, hence, whether there is a non-discriminatory reason to treat non-nationals differently; and quite

It is therefore important to consider what implications the generic definition of the absence of sufficient integration in the context of the 'unreasonable burden' test may have for the application of integration requirements as part of the discrimination analysis. This is also where the *Dano* judgment can be compared with the Court's reasoning in the earlier *Brey* judgment.

One of the central questions arising from the *Dano* judgment is which criteria are actually capable of demonstrating the absence of a genuine link with the host Member State. Answering this question depends on how the relationship between the 'unreasonable burden' test and the 'real link' test is defined and whether this assessment happens as part of the discrimination analysis or not. In *Dano*, the Advocate General suggested that using 'a general criterion, such as the reason for entering the territory of the host Member State, which is capable of demonstrating the absence of a genuine link with that State, in order to prevent an unreasonable burden on its social assistance system' to exclude nationals of other Member States from entitlement to special non-contributory cash benefits is not precluded by Directive 2004/38.[206] The Advocate General also noted that it would be paradoxical if jobseekers could be refused to access social benefits on the basis of the derogation clause in Article 24(2) of Directive 2004/38, whereas those EU citizens who have exercised their right to free movement and residence without intending to integrate themselves into the labour market of the host Member State could be refused access to social benefits 'only on the basis of a thorough examination of his personal situation'.[207]

But there is no such paradox in so far as the personal proportionality assessment is also required in relation to short-term residents, students, and work-seekers under the derogation clause of Article 24(2) of Directive 2004/38. It is therefore striking that, in defining what constitutes a 'real link', the Advocate General himself referred to such cases as *Bidar* and *Förster*, in which the lack of a 'genuine link' or a 'certain degree of integration' was used to balance the requirement of 'a certain degree of financial solidarity' in regard to students who claimed for maintenance allowance in their host Member State[208] By looking at these two cases, one can see how the personal assessment under the 'real link' test can justify both an extensive and a restrictive interpretation of EU citizens' right to equal treatment. However, in *Dano*, the Court did not discuss the legitimacy of general exclusions from the perspective of equal treatment, but simply held that, in so far as the applicants do not fulfil the conditions for the right to residence under Article 7(1)(b) of Directive 2004/38, they do not enjoy the right to equal treatment under Article 24

another question how much weight is to be accorded to the interest of a European citizen to reside in another Member State in contrast to the countervailing interest of this state not to be "unreasonably burdened" with having to pay out benefits to whoever happens to have successfully crossed the stateline.'

206 eg Opinion of AG Wathelet in *Dano* (n 74) para 139.

207 Ibid, para 116.

208 Ibid, para 127–28. Refers to *Bidar* (n 82) paras 56–57; *Förster* (n 82) paras 48–49; *Collins* (n 82) 67; and *Vatsouras and Koupatantze* (n 82) 38.

of that same Directive.[209] This means that the assessment of the accepted sources of EU citizens' unequal treatment never reached the stage in which it would be discussed in the light of more equality-based arguments.

The Court's understanding of 'sufficient integration' in *Dano* can be compared with the earlier *Brey* judgment in which the Court had emphasised the importance of individual circumstances in deciding what constitutes sufficient integration between the applicant and the Member State in question.[210] The applicant, Mr Brey, was a German national who was residing in Austria and applied for a compensatory supplement to his German retirement pension under Austrian law. The national authorities refused to grant this benefit to him on the grounds that, despite holding a certificate of residence, he could not be regarded as having 'sufficient resources' to lawfully reside in Austria and because the granting of the compensatory supplement in question was made conditional upon fulfilling the requirements for the right to residence under national law. The national court wanted to know whether this benefit could be regarded as 'social assistance' under Article 7(1)(b) of Directive 2004/38.[211] However, the Court of Justice reformulated this question as to whether EU law precludes national legislation which does not grant the benefit in question to economically inactive migrant EU citizens on the grounds that he/she does not meet the requirements for obtaining the right to reside in the host Member State.[212]

In *Brey*, the Court held that granting social benefits to economically inactive EU citizens can be made dependent on lawful residence, but the requirements for the right to residence must nonetheless be 'themselves consistent with EU law'.[213] The Court confirmed that it is in line with Directive 2004/38 to impose restrictions on granting such benefits to EU citizens on the basis that they must not 'become an unreasonable burden on the social assistance system of that Member State'.[214] What is noteworthy, however, is that the Court underlined that

> the competent national authorities cannot draw such conclusions without first carrying an overall assessment of the specific burden which granting that benefit would place on the national social assistance system as a whole, by reference to the personal circumstances characterising the individual situation of the person concerned.[215]

According to the Court, national authorities should, in particular, examine 'whether the person concerned is experiencing temporal difficulties and take into account the duration of residence of the person concerned, his personal circumstances, and the amount of aid which has been granted to him'.[216] Moreover, the

[209] *Dano* (n 76) para 78.
[210] *Brey* (n 84).
[211] Ibid, para 25.
[212] Ibid, para 32.
[213] Ibid, paras 44–45.
[214] Ibid, para 57.
[215] Ibid, para 64.
[216] Ibid, para 69.

Court pointed out that the conditions included in Article 7(1)(b) of Directive 2004/38 'must be construed narrowly'.[217]

In *Brey*, the Court suggested that the national authorities can take into account 'a range of factors in the light of the principle of proportionality' in assessing whether an economically inactive EU citizen would place a burden on the social assistance system as a whole.[218] The Court also explicitly mentioned that Directive 2004/38 'recognises a certain degree of financial solidarity between nationals of a host Member State and nationals of other Member States, particularly if the difficulties with a beneficiary of the right of residence encounters are temporary'.[219] This statement had its origins in the *Grzelczyk* judgment, in which the Court famously articulated the idea of 'a certain degree of financial solidarity' between the Member States.[220] The mere fact that an economically inactive EU citizen would receive social assistance in the host Member State would therefore not suffice to demonstrate an unreasonable burden in this sense.[221] These references to the importance of individual circumstances in assessing whether an economically inactive migrant EU citizen would place an unreasonable burden on the social assistance system appear in a different light in the *Dano* judgment.

The Opinion of Advocate General Wathelet in *Dano* defended the view that 'the grant of a social assistance benefit is necessarily a burden on the social assistance system'.[222] The Advocate General also found the *Brey* and *Dano* cases factually different. He acknowledged that it would be contrary to Articles 8(4) and 14(3) of Directive 2004/38 to 'authorise automatic exclusion from entitlement to a social benefit by a general and abstract reference to the lawfulness of the residence', as was the case in *Brey*.[223] In his view, the situation was different in *Dano* because the relevant national provisions did not directly concern 'the lawfulness of the applicant's residence' but, rather, refused to grant access to social assistance benefits to 'persons whose right of residence is based on the sole objective of seeking employment or obtaining social assistance'.[224] However, he also acknowledged that this distinction was 'at the very least tenuous' because it would be 'likely' that the applicant's residence would be 'jeopardised' if she was not granted the basic provision benefits in question.[225]

The above considerations led Advocate General Wathelet to conclude in the *Dano* case that the 'final analysis' must therefore 'be carried out in the light of the

[217] Ibid, para 70. For a similar approach in relation to the rights of third-country nationals and the principles of family reunification, see Case C-571/10 *Servet Kamberaj v Istituto per l'Edilizia sociale della Provincia autonoma di Bolzano (IPES) and* Others, 24 April 2012, para 86; and Case C-578/08 *Rhimou Chakroun v Minister van Buitenlandse Zaken* [2010] ECR I-1839, para 43.

[218] *Brey* (n 84) para 72.

[219] Ibid.

[220] *Grzelczyk* (n 8) para 44.

[221] *Brey* (n 84).

[222] Opinion of AG Wathelet in *Dano* (n 74) para 117.

[223] Ibid, para 122.

[224] Ibid, para 123.

[225] Ibid, para 125.

principle of proportionality'.[226] For him, this meant examining the relationship between the general criterion used in national legislation and the existence of a 'genuine' link between the applicant and the host Member State.[227] In practice, however, the way in which the relationships between the 'unreasonable burden' test and the 'real link' test was defined in this case leads to a narrow view of relevant integration in the case of economically inactive EU citizens. The Court did not discuss what different sources can indicate 'relevant integration' in the case of economically inactive EU citizens beyond economic factors or the original reason to enter into the host Member State. Defining the lack of sufficient integration in a generic way may seem understandable in the light of the 'unreasonable burden' test under Article 7(1)(b) of Directive 2004/38. However, a similar approach to sufficient integration would seem more problematic in relation to the objective justification test. Thus, replacing the individual assessment under the objective justification test with the individual assessment under the 'unreasonable burden' test is likely to curtail EU citizens' access to equal treatment in the relevant Member State.

It has been noted that the proportionality assessment more often functions in favour of the individual in the context of equal treatment, whereas individual considerations in assessing the conditions for lawful residence under Article 7(1)(b) of Article 2004/38 often rely on more 'systemic' reasoning for why the individual has become a 'burden' which could have negative consequences for the overall level of social assistance in the host Member State.[228] In particular, the fact that national law can now categorically exclude groups of citizens from access to social benefits may hinder 'the option of assessing or even asking the relevant questions in individual cases'.[229] It would therefore be desirable that the narrow economic interpretation of what constitutes the absence of a 'real link' does not become the prominent approach to the social integration requirements as part of the objective justification test under Article 18 TFEU. But, whether or not this is the case, it is clear that the *Dano* judgment has far-reaching indirect implications for EU citizens' right to equal treatment through the structural equality problem, as discussed in Section 2.2.3.

2.3.4 The Lack of Non-economic Criteria for Legitimate Differential Treatment: The Substantive Equality Problem

Objectively justified differential treatment between EU citizens must involve 'objective considerations independent of the nationality of the persons concerned' and 'proportionate to the legitimate aim'. The absence of a 'real link' with the territory

[226] Ibid, para 126.
[227] Ibid.
[228] Daniel Thym, 'The Elusive Limits of Solidarity: Residence Rights of and Social Benefits for Economically Inactive Union Citizens' (2015) 52 *Common Market Law Review* 17, 30 and 32.
[229] Nic Shuibhne (n 101) 912.

or society of the relevant Member State can constitute such a justification. It has been seen in Section 2.3.3 that the recent case law has moved beyond both the purely economic and the strictly formalistic definitions of what is meant by a 'real link'. However, it has also been seen that the case law still leaves the economic logic that underlies the 'real link' test unchallenged. This convergence between the 'real link' test and the 'unreasonable burden' test captures the substantive dimension of the EU equality problem: both the case law and the secondary legislation fall short of providing genuinely non-economic justificatory criteria for legitimate differential treatment between EU citizens, that is, they fail to recognise a horizontal 'equality objective' in EU law, as will be discussed in this section.

Academic commentary has widely criticised the 'real link' case law for a lack of substantive ambition. The core of this criticism is captured in the plea that 'there has to be room for considering other indications of integration, such as the individual circumstances of the applicant'.[230] The recent case law has responded to this criticism by confirming that a 'sole condition of uninterrupted residence' cannot usually be regarded as proportionate under EU law. Does this mean that the substantive equality problem is now solved? The answer is 'no' for the following two reasons: Firstly, the fact that the 'real link' test is still reduced to the directly and indirectly economic considerations means that its potential to provide genuinely independent criteria for the assessment of objective justifications for legitimate differential treatment between EU citizens is largely wasted. Secondly, it is not just the lack of substance that hampers the 'real link' case law. The more fundamental problem is that the 'real link' test has its focus on the vertical link between a Union citizen and the host Member State and it fails to adequately consider what implications these objective justifications may have for the equality of relationships between EU citizens and, thus, for the status of EU citizenship.

The Court has sometimes held that it is proportionate to exclude a Union citizen whose situation fell into the scope of Article 24(2) of Directive 2004/38 until the conditions for permanent residence under Article 16 of Directive 2004/38 have been met.[231] But the durational approach was later replaced with a more substantive approach to integration requirements at least in those cases which are assessed under Article 21 TFEU.[232] It is now clear that 'other social and economic' factors than the length of residence should also be taken into account in assessing what constitutes a 'sufficient degree of integration' between an EU citizen and the relevant Member State. The Court has also held that, although lawful residence does not establish the right to a maintenance grant in the case of short-term residents, students, and jobseekers, the derogation clause in Article 24(2) of Directive 2004/38 does not prevent those EU citizens who are lawfully resident in the host Member State 'from relying during that residence on the fundamental principle

[230] Koen Lenaerts and Tinne Heremans, 'Contours of a European Social Union in the Case-Law of the European Court of Justice' (2006) 2 *European Constitutional Law Review* 101, 114.

[231] *Förster* (n 82) para 52.

[232] *European Commission v Republic of Austria* (n 190); *Tas-Hagen* (n 192); and *Prinz and Seeberger* (n 193).

of equal treatment enshrined in the first paragraph of Article 12 EC [now 18 TFEU]'.[233] However, it seems that the recent case law on EU citizenship has moved away from this idea of a more independent 'equality objective' for EU law.[234]

To sum up, the 'real link' test as a criterion for legitimate differential treatment between EU citizens can justify multiple different and even conflicting outcomes depending on how the substance of a 'link' is defined, ie what constitutes sufficient/relevant integration for the purposes of equal treatment under EU law. In theory, the *establishment* of a 'real link' can provide a means of extending the right to residence and, thus, the right to equal treatment in the context of the 'unreasonable burden' test. In practice, the *absence* of a 'real link' test can provide a further limitation on EU citizens' right to residence and equal treatment: a functional criterion of belonging becomes more important than the shared status of EU citizenship. As noted above, different factors may amount to the establishment of a 'real link' and a more substantive approach has recently replaced the strictly formalistic definition of a 'real link' in the case law, at least in some cases. However, the 'real link' test is still based on the rationale that economically inactive EU citizens must not become an unreasonable financial burden on the welfare system in the host Member State. This means that the 'real link' test fails to provide any new insight into the question of what equal treatment means between EU citizens (the substantive equality problem).

The key to the 'real link' test and social integration requirements lies in the premise that only 'proportionate' justifications for unequal treatment between Union citizens can be accepted under EU law. It has been noted that the 'real link' test 'represents a more conceptual than material shift' because in its current form it simply implies a 'right to be assessed, but no more'.[235] It is therefore important to consider in more detail what proportionality means in the context of social integration requirements. In particular, it is important to consider under what conditions a more independent 'equality objective' could be given weight in assessing the requirement of a 'real link' under the 'objective justification' test. For instance, in her opinion in the *Commission v Austria* case, Advocate General Sharpston discussed in detail the difference between the 'economic objective' with reference to the *Bidar* judgment and the 'integration objective' with reference to the *Förster* judgment.[236] What is nonetheless missing from this case law is the analysis of the relationship between the 'integration objective' and what is here called the 'equality objective'.

[233] *Förster* (n 82) para 43.

[234] *Dano* (n 76).

[235] Charlotte O'Brien, 'Real Links, Abstract Rights and False Alarms: The Relationship between the ECJ's "Real Link" Case Law and National Solidarity' (2008) *European Law Review* 643, 644.

[236] Opinion of AG Sharpston in *European Commission v Republic of Austria* (n 190) paras 83–84. The AG has suggested that the 'integration objective' must be applied in compliance either (1) with the 'economic objective' which has its aim in ensuring that making a social benefit available does not unreasonably burden the stability of the public finances of the Member State in question or (2) with 'any other legitimate objective justified by overriding reasons of public interest'. Ibid, para 85.

Advocate General Wathelet argued in *Dano* that the Member States can refuse to grant social assistance benefits to citizens who do not have sufficient resources in so far as the 'validity' of Directive 2004/38 is not questioned on the basis of Articles 18, 20, and 21 TFEU.[237] The Court's ruling, for its part, stated that EU citizens' rights under Article 18, 20, and 21 TFEU are subject to further conditions and limitations as laid down in the EU Treaties and in the measures adopted to give them effect.[238] Moreover, the Court outlined that the principle of non-discrimination, 'laid down generally' in Article 18 TFEU, finds its 'specific expression' in Article 24 of Directive 2004/38 and Article 4 of Regulation No 883/2004.[239] The Court's silence over the different expressions of equality as a fundamental right, a Treaty right and a constitutional principle underlines the ambivalent hierarchy of norms in EU equality law. It is worth noting that the Court has stated elsewhere that the derogation clause in Article 24(2) of Directive 2004/38 must be 'interpreted narrowly' because it is '*merely* a specific expression' of Article 18 TFEU.[240] In other contexts, the Court has also recently highlighted the 'constitutional status' of the general principles of EU law.[241] This has inspired arguments that equality as a general principle of EU law could potentially act independently in relation to 'constitutionally prohibited forms of discrimination', including nationality discrimination.[242]

The important question is what role equality as a constitutional principle could play in identifying the accepted criteria for justifying differentiation between individual cases.[243] For instance, Niamh Nic Shuibhne writes that the Court's decision to only discuss Article 18 TFEU in conjunction with Article 24 of Directive 2004/38 'undercuts five decades of understanding equal treatment as a legal principle of autonomous *worth*'.[244] Some question whether the interpretation and application of concrete provisions of secondary legislation, above all Directive 2004/38, should at all fall within the more abstract general principles of Union law.[245] But others note that the notion of general principles will inherently carry over 'an abstract concept of law which cannot always be derived from the written rules laid down by

[237] Opinion of AG Wathelet in *Dano* (n 74) para 105.

[238] *Dano* (n 76), para 60.

[239] Ibid, para 61.

[240] *European Commission v Republic of Austria* (n 190) para 54 (emphasis added).

[241] eg *Audiolux* (n 6). For older case law, see eg Case C/46/93 and 48/93 *Brasserie du Pêcheur SA v Bundesrepublik Deutschland and The Queen v Secretary of State for Transport, ex parte: Factortame Ltd and others* [1996] ECR I-1029, para 25.

[242] Lenaerts and Gutiérrez-Fons (n 109) 1662.

[243] Ibid 1662.

[244] Nic Shuibhne (n 101) 935.

[245] See more about this argument in Michael Dougan, 'The Constitutional Dimension to the Case Law on Union Citizenship' (2006) 31 *European Law Review* 613, 616–17. Dougan observes that secondary legislation no longer offers definite conditions for Union citizens' rights to residence and equality but merely a 'framework' within which the lawfulness and proportionality of different conditions and limitations can be assessed 'having regard to their degree of integration into the host society' in the light of Article 21 TFEU (ex 18 EC). Ibid 621.

the Member States or institutions and is superior to those rules'.[246] Traditionally, the general principles of EU law have been seen as an aid for interpretation or as a ground for judicial review.[247] But recourse to the general principles and, above all, the incorporation of fundamental rights in these principles can arguably also provide a way of proceeding towards a more substantive conception of the rule of law in EU law, as well as a clearer hierarchy of norms in EU law.[248]

The general principles of EU law have a tendency to create 'positive obligations' in the context of the non-discrimination principle and in the context of the application of the proportionality principle more generally.[249] This indicates that the application of general principles will necessarily push the Court to exercise balancing.[250] It has been suggested that the balancing criteria can be 'enriched by different, albeit converging legal, moral, or political theories'.[251] Moreover, it has also been suggested that the general principles can play an independent role in providing criteria for balancing along with 'constitutional fundamental rights guarantees'.[252] In particular, the 'constitutional function' of the general principles of EU law is called on to give more substance to the 'common European values' which are already embedded in the EU Treaties.[253] These propositions support the argument that a more thorough analysis of the philosophical foundations of the EU principle of equality in the next chapter is necessary for a better understanding of whether EU law could develop towards a more independent non-economic 'equality objective' in the assessment of legitimate differential treatment between EU citizens.

The objective justification test in general and the assessment of social integration requirements in more particular would need to address the 'effect' of differential treatment on relationships between EU citizens if EU citizenship is considered as a fundamental status of all Member State nationals. The question is therefore not just how the right to equal treatment can be limited in an objectively justified manner, but also whether the principle of equality could become one of the

[246] AG Toth, 'Human Rights as General Principles of Law, in the Past and in the Future' in Ulf Bernitz and Joakim Nergelius (eds), *General Principles of European Community Law* (Kluwer, 2000) 78.

[247] Academic debate has usually focused on the question of when a situation falls within the scope of application of the general principles of EU law. It has been argued that, besides the situations in which the Union institutions exercise their conferred powers or the Member States implement EU law or derogate from their obligations under EU law, the general principles can also apply on the basis that the action of the Member State overlaps with 'some substantive measure of Union law'. See eg Editorial Comments, 'The Scope of Application of the General Principles of Union Law: An Ever Expanding Union?' (2010) 47 *Common Market Law Review* 1589, 1590 and 1594.

[248] Lenaerts and Gutiérrez-Fons (n 109) 1632 and 1636. On this basis, it has also been claimed that whether or not the general principles produce effects beyond the requirement of consistent interpretation is about the interpretation of primary EU law and, thus, falls within the jurisdiction of the Court of Justice. Ibid 1649.

[249] Sacha Prechal, 'Competence Creep and General Principles of Law' (2010) 3 *Review of European Administrative Law* 5, 14–15.

[250] Lenaerts and Gutiérrez-Fons (n 109) 1650.

[251] Ibid 1653.

[252] Prechal (n 249) 21.

[253] Lenaerts and Gutiérrez-Fons (n 109) 1667.

standards against which justificatory criteria for differential treatment between Union citizens must be reviewed (the 'equality objective'). If a more independent and horizontal equality objective could be given weight in assessing the requirement of a 'real link', it is problematic that the analysis of sufficient integration, or the lack of it, primarily happens in relation to the 'unreasonable burden' test and the right to residence, rather than in the context of discrimination analysis, where these questions would more naturally become part of the Court's reasoning.

At the moment, EU law could at most grant equal access to social assistance in the host Member State. The national legislature can always decide that these benefits should not be granted 'in the absence of any attempt at all to seek employment'. But it seems problematic if such qualification only applies to migrant EU citizens. In the *Dano* judgment, the Court made a substantive reference to the fundamental status of EU citizenship at the beginning of its judgment, but it did not engage with a substantive analysis of EU citizens' right to non-discrimination and equal treatment further than that. Instead, the judgment focused on the conditions for EU citizens' non-economic right to residence under Directive 2004/38. In the absence of a more nuanced theory of transnational justice, the Court perhaps chose the politically most realistic path in its ruling. However, for this very reason the Court's conclusion that EU citizens' right to equal treatment depends on the sufficient economic resources can also be read as an open invitation for EU law scholars to think harder about the issues of transnational justice and to provide more convincing arguments for how and why EU citizens' right to equal treatment should and could matter beyond the mere idea of economic self-sufficiency.

2.4 CONCLUSION

This chapter described the structural and substantive dimensions of the EU equality problem by exploring how the emergence of EU citizenship as a new standard of comparability, ie the definition of EU citizenship as a 'fundamental status' of all Member State nationals, has been compromised both structurally, in regard to the scope of EU citizens' general right to equal treatment, and substantively, in regard to the accepted justifications for legitimate differential treatment between EU citizens. The first part of the chapter argued that it is problematic that not just the limitations but also the *de facto* scope of the right to equal treatment are made dependent on the proportionality analysis in regard to the right to residence (the structural equality problem). The second part of the chapter engaged in a more substantive analysis of justificatory criteria for legitimate differential treatment between EU citizens both in the secondary law and in the case law of the Court of Justice of the EU. It concluded that the 'real link' case law has failed to provide a set of independent non-economic criteria for legitimate differential treatment, or to adequately consider what differential treatment means for the equality of relationships between EU citizens (the substantive equality problem).

The legal analysis of EU citizens' general right to equal treatment in this chapter illustrated that economically inactive EU citizens now enjoy a 'fundamental' right to equal treatment which derives its existence from other rights and whose exercise may lead to the termination of those very rights from which it derives its existence. These qualifications to EU citizens' general right to equal treatment leave us with a set of puzzling questions: What does the word 'fundamental' mean in relation to the EU principle of equality when it is applied to economically inactive and dependent migrant EU citizens? Is it just about judicial rhetoric? Or, is there indeed something fundamental in the EU principle of equality when it is also applied to economically inactive EU citizens? If so, what is it? Above all, under what conditions could EU law develop towards a more independent and horizontal 'equality objective' in its assessment of legitimate differential treatment between EU citizens? The remaining chapters of this book will provide a more theoretical account of equality between EU citizens in order to address these questions.

3

EU Citizens' Responsibility to be Active and its Alternatives

3.1 INTRODUCTION

THE FIRST TWO chapters of this book discussed the EU equality problem as a matter of individual rights, by looking at the scope and limits of EU citizens' general right to equal treatment. This chapter finishes the analysis of the 'Equality Problem' with a more theoretical argument which shows that both the structural and the substantive indeterminacy of EU citizens' access to equal treatment as EU citizens point towards a deeper philosophical problem. The way in which legitimate differential treatment is justified between EU citizens indicates that EU citizenship as an equal status is still conditioned on the ideals of individual responsibility and activity. From this starting point, the chapter argues that (1) the current interpretation of the EU principle of equality fails to recognise equality as a 'normative ideal of human relationships'[1] and (2) an unfortunately narrow and individualistic view of agency underlies the EU principle of equality. In order to solve the EU equality problem, it is important to consider what alternatives can be provided to the current activity-oriented understanding of when EU citizens deserve to be treated equally under EU law.

A more detailed analysis of the EU principle of equality as a matter of distributive justice is needed to assist the Court of Justice and the EU legislature in the difficult task of defining the substance of EU citizenship in the realm of non-discrimination and equal treatment. In order to extract a relevant theoretical synthesis for this purpose, the chapter discusses both the responsibility-sensitive and the democratic theories of egalitarian social justice to demonstrate why the current account of equality in EU law is problematic and how it could be changed. This insight into philosophical egalitarianism also clarifies that the mere reference to comparability between EU citizens is not helpful in justifying more equal treatment between EU citizens. Instead, a more 'relational' understanding of equality is needed to replace the current activity-based account of equality in EU law. However, this argument

[1] Samuel Scheffler, *Equality and Tradition Questions of Value in Moral and Political Theory* (Oxford University Press, 2007) 234.

in favour of relational equality leaves us with the hard question of what constitutes a meaningful relationship for the purposes of equal treatment and non-discrimination between EU citizens. In other words, can the relational account of egalitarian social justice be justified in a transnational context?

Sections 3.2 and 3.3 develop the argument of the EU equality problem further by showing how an activity-based conception of equality underlies the current interpretation of EU citizens' general right to non-discrimination and equal treatment. The chapter then moves on to explore the EU principle of equality within the theoretical framework of contemporary philosophical egalitarianism. Section 3.4 suggests that EU equality law is vulnerable to similar criticism as the liberal theories of equal opportunities on the basis that the central role given to the individual choice and responsibility in these theories fail to recognise equality as a relational ideal. It will be argued that the 'lack of relationality' as the core of the EU equality problem has its roots in a narrow and individualistic view of human agency in EU law. The key to addressing the EU equality problem is therefore how the relational account of social justice can be justified transnationally. Section 3.5 will conclude the chapter by considering two possible answers to this question. It will first be seen that the mere argument of more comparability between EU citizens does not provide an adequate solution to the EU equality problem. It will then be suggested that recognising the connection between EU citizens' agency and their sense of subjectivity as EU citizens can provide a more plausible way forward.

3.2 EQUAL CITIZENSHIP AS A PROBLEM OF BELONGING

Integration requirements in the form of the 'real link' test now provide a legitimate means of justifying differential treatment between EU citizens. In practice, the requirement of sufficient integration provides one possible answer to the question of what kind of belonging is a pre-condition for access to social equality in a polity. The term 'belonging' can have a dual meaning: (1) as being a member or part of something and (2) as a relationship of affinity. Integration requirements promise to bring these two dimensions of belonging together by deriving the membership of a polity from a demonstrated relationship of affinity. To the extent that the enjoyment of EU citizens' right to equal treatment depends on the establishment of sufficient economic or social integration, it is important to understand why the idea of belonging has been considered as relevant for equal social citizenship. This section begins the theoretical analysis of the EU principle of equality by briefly discussing the role that 'belonging' has traditionally been given in the context of social equality and how EU citizenship has challenged that role.

In social security law, the right to social benefits has traditionally been based on the bond of belonging between the private individual and the polity. What is noteworthy, however, is that the evidence for relevant belonging can be derived from many different sources, such as factual contributions, habitual residence, or citizenship.[2] The increasing movement of people across Europe has presented a compelling challenge to the definition of relevant belonging in the context of social equality. It has been noted that the idea of limited (national) solidarity appears to be in conflict with a new principle of equality, according to which 'all who belong to a greater community are treated in an equal manner'.[3] The fundamental question of EU law in the context of social welfare benefits is therefore when and where migrants should have access to social benefits outside their countries of origin and who should pay the bill—the host State or the home State. The EU-wide co-ordination of social security schemes under Regulation 883/2004 focuses on the more 'technical' questions about what constitutes relevant belonging under EU law, whereas the accepted derogations from EU citizens' rights to free movement and residence under Directive 2004/38 give a more 'normative' definition for what relevant belonging means under EU law.[4] It is this second dimension of belonging which is relevant for the analysis of EU citizenship in this section.

The principle of territoriality of social assistance is often closely linked with immigration policy: States may use the need for social assistance as a reason for not granting residence in their territory.[5] However, later becoming in need of social assistance can no longer lead to the termination of the right to residence in the same way as before. Moreover, even those residence or integration requirements which apply to both nationals and non-nationals can be indirectly discriminatory because it may be more difficult for non-nationals to meet them.[6] There is no unconditional right to equal treatment until the attainment of permanent residency under Article 16 of Directive 2004/38 and even this right can be terminated

[2] Anna Christensen and Mattias Malmstedt, 'Lex Loci Laboris versus Lex Loci Domicilii—an Inquiry into the Normative Foundations of European Social Security Law' (2000) 2 *European Journal of Social Security* 69, 73.

[3] Ibid 74.

[4] Ibid 75. Regulation (EC) No 883/2004 of the European Parliament and of the Council of 29 April 2004 on the coordination of social security systems [2004] OJ L166/1; Directive 2004/38 on the right of citizens of the Union and their family members to move and reside freely within the territory of the Member States [2004] OJ L158/77.

[5] No 'clear' or 'fixed' concept either of domicile or of residence exists in private international law to the extent which would be useful for the analysis of EU law. It has been argued that 'domicile' generally provides a more precise legal concept, whereas 'residence' is often factual, ie 'founded more solidly in reality given that it is the place with which a person actually possesses personal and occupational ties'. Marie-José Garot, 'A New Basis for European Citizenship: Residence' in Massimo La Torre (ed), *European Citizenship: An Institutional Challenge* (Kluwer, 1998) 237–38. Moreover, residence is often qualified with the term 'habitual' which can be derived from 'the length of stay' of from 'other facts of a personal or professional nature which point to durable ties between a person and his residence'. This means that the notion of residence can be defined either by virtue of 'qualitative' or 'quantitative' elements. In determining the relevant indicators for residence, the priority can be given either for 'occupational' or for 'personal' ties. Even an 'intention to establish residence' could, arguably, have relevance as a qualitative element of residence. Ibid 240–42 and 247.

[6] Access to social assistance can depend both on lawful residence and on the fulfilment of a minimum period of residence. See more about this eg in Anne Pieter Van der Mei, *Free Movement of Persons within the European Community—Cross-Border Access to Public Benefits* (Hart Publishing, 2003) 120–21.

under Article 28 of the same Directive.[7] But the need for social assistance must not lead to the automatic loss of the right to reside under EU law before the acquisition of the right to permanent residence. Some authors speak in this context of the 'spatial challenges' of EU law towards national welfare systems.[8] By this, they mean that European integration has led to the opening of the traditional boundaries of social citizenship.[9]

In practice, EU rules have challenged both the 'territorial' and the 'membership' boundaries of the national welfare systems.[10] First, the Member States may be obliged to provide social benefits to their own nationals extra-territorially, in order not to prevent them from exercising their right to free movement as EU citizens. Secondly, they may be obliged to grant access to social assistance in their territory to EU citizens who are non-nationals. The 'territorial' and 'membership' boundaries are thought to enforce 'affiliation to a sharing community'.[11] The worst-case scenario is, therefore, that the fragmented welfare experience in the transnational context leads to a 'diminished sense of a link', first with private individuals and then with the national welfare state.[12] Moreover, the potential of legal rules to create a 'sense of shared life' at the transnational level has been called into question.[13] For many commentators, the concern is that the common market has led to a 'tendency to deconstruct' the protective welfare regimes at the national level.[14]

[7] See eg Case C-145/09 *Land Baden-Württemberg v Panagiotis Tsakouridis* [2010] ECR I-11979 and Case C-400/12 *Secretary of State for the Home Department v MG*, 16 January 2014.

[8] Maurizio Ferrera, 'Towards an "Open" Social Citizenship? The New Boundaries of Welfare in the European Union' in Graínne de Búrca (ed), *EU Law and the Welfare State: In Search of Solidarity* (Oxford University Press, 2005) 12.

[9] Ibid.

[10] Maurizio Ferrera, 'European Integration and National Citizenship: Changing Boundaries, New Structuring?' (2003) 36 *Comparative Political Studies* 611, 619.

[11] Ferrera (n 8) 20. This same idea has been summarised by Síofra O'Leary as follows: 'the more redistributive and therefore morally demanding the nature of the social right or policy concerned, the more necessary it is thought for the basis of entitlement to be reflected in reciprocal ties of citizenship or some other form of diffuse solidarity'. Síofra O'Leary, 'Solidarity and Citizenship Rights in the Charter of Fundamental Rights of the European Union' in de Búrca (n 8) 57.

[12] Gareth Davies, 'The Process and Side-Effects of Harmonisation of European Welfare States' Jean Monnet Working Paper No 02/2006 http://jeanmonnetprogram.org/paper/the-process-and-side-effects-of-harmonisation-of-european-welfare-states/, 49. For further discussion, see Alexander Somek, 'Solidarity Decomposed: Being and Time in European Citizenship' (2007) 32 *European Law Review* 787.

[13] Davies (n 12) 62.

[14] See eg Manfred Weiss, 'Fundamental Social Rights for the European Union' (1997) 18 *Industrial Law Journal* 417, 420. Similarly, Gareth Davies argues that the fact that the Court's decision in *Kranemann* (C-109/04) held that 'purely economic' reasons cannot justify a restriction of free movement is 'devastating for welfare structures'. Davies (n 12) 30 and Case C-109/04 *Karl Robert Kranemann v Land Nordrhein-Westfalen* [2005] ECR I-2421, para 34. Erica Szyszczak has formulated the same concern by noting that 'the process of creating an integrated European economy is one of de-regulatory re-regulation of national law' and that the Member States' competence 'has been negated, if not lost'. Erika Szyszczak, 'The New Paradigm for Social Policy: A Virtuous Circle?' (2001) 38 *Common Market Law Review* 1125, 1128. It has also been argued that the 'legal constraints' of European integration mean in practice that, if the Member States wish to accommodate their welfare systems, they must lower their tax burdens or further deregulation or drive down labour conditions. Fritz W Scharpf, 'The European Social Model: Coping with the Challenges of Diversity' (2002) 40 *Journal of*

These concerns illustrate why the quest for equal citizenship across the borders of the Member States must not be examined as a mere individual rights issue but also as a matter of (transnational) justice.[15]

In the context of EU law, the instances of positive harmonisation are still rare and the main impacts on national welfare systems have emerged in the realm of negative harmonisation.[16] The Member States are free to organise their welfare systems but, in doing so, they have to respect the Treaty provisions of free movement and non-discrimination. It has been noted that this means that the legitimacy of national preferences is determined 'within the context of justification rather than within the context of applicability'.[17] The edge of this criticism is captured in Gareth Davies' argument that the Court of Justice uses 'functional justifications' for limitations on free movement and competition in so far as the protection of 'solidarity-based' welfare systems is concerned.[18] His claim is directed against the requirement to justify the boundaries of national welfare systems against transnational interventions in the first place. But it is equally important to consider what justifications can be accepted for selective solidarity claims under EU law. In other words, what reasons can the Member States present for limiting access to social benefits to some EU citizens, while other holders of EU citizenship have no access to the same benefits at all?

As a response to this latter question, it has been suggested that it is not sufficient to invoke the political or social goals of European integration without first addressing the even deeper question of whether these non-economic rationales only arise from a 'functional necessity deriving from economic integration', or whether they can provide an 'independent political claim' for solidarity in Europe.[19] The concern is that, at the level of European integration, social rights are 'narrowly defined' as mere 'derogations from economic rights'.[20] More optimistic authors talk about the redistributive dimension of the internal market rules

Common Market Studies 645, 649. A more theoretical articulation of the same problem is that the process of European integration in its current form 'drastically reduces the effectiveness of democratic self-determination at the national level'. Ibid 650 and Fritz W Scharpf, 'Economic Integration, Democracy and the Welfare State' (1997) 4 *Journal of European Public Policy* 18, 26.

[15] See more about this in Section 3.4.3, p 112.

[16] The mechanism by which the rules of competition and free movement have an impact on national welfare systems is two-fold. It can either be based on positive harmonisation, ie 'replacement of national legislation by European', or on negative harmonisation, ie 'the application of more general principles of EU law'. See eg Davies (n 12) 12–13.

[17] Ibid 25–26.

[18] Gareth Davies, 'The Price of Letting Courts Value Solidarity' in Yuri Borgmann-Prebil and Malcolm Ross (eds), *Promoting Solidarity in the European Union* (Oxford University Press, 2010) 107.

[19] Miguel Poiares Maduro, 'Europe's Social Self: "The Sickness Unto Death"' in Jo Shaw (ed), *Social Law and Policy in an Evolving European Union* (Hart Pubishing, 2000) 326. For more recent analysis on these questions, see Floris De Witte, *Justice in the EU: The Emergence of Transnational Solidarity* (Oxford University Press, 2015).

[20] Sandra Fredman, 'Transformation or Dilution: Fundamental Rights in the EU Social Space' (2006) 12 *European Law Journal* 41, 42.

'through the recognition of specific rights to determined categories of persons'.[21] In practice, however, social rights at the EU level often appear like a side product of regulatory/economic policies rather than an independent goal of redistributive policies.[22] In academic commentary, this state of affairs has been framed by claiming that EU citizenship still has 'no real social content'.[23] It is thus understandable that the problem of belonging manifests itself in the different concepts of 'social citizenship'[24] which have been used to advance EU citizens' access to equal treatment outside the State of origin. But it is also clear that EU citizenship's momentum for advancing the development of a more social Europe remains vague if the principles of equal treatment and non-discrimination are not seen as integrative beyond the economic objectives of European integration.

It was recognised early in EU law scholarship that the structural inequalities originating from the limitations on freedom of movement and residence may 'constitute a pervasion of Community principles' in so far as the fundamental idea of justice penetrates the process of European integration.[25] In practice, these structural inequalities may lead to a situation in which 'discrimination attaches to those very precepts that purport to advance human rights'.[26] The first two chapters of this book demonstrated how the development of EU citizenship has shed light on a new equality problem: understanding EU citizenship as a fundamental status of all Member State nationals requires a clearer answer to the question of what 'equal citizenship' means for economically inactive and needy EU citizens. This problem is captured in the parameters, sometimes termed 'new generation imperative requirements',[27] which define when a migrant EU citizen does not deserve to be treated as equal to the nationals of the host Member State because of an insufficient degree of integration. However, this question of how unlawful discrimination differs from legitimate differential treatment under EU law cannot be separated from a more theoretical question of what philosophical ideals of equality and social justice underlie the EU principle of equality. On the contrary,

[21] Vassilis Hatzopoulos, 'A (More) Social Europe: A Political Crossroad or a Legal One-Way? Dialogues between Luxembourg and Lisbon' (2005) 42 *Common Market Law Review* 1599, 1602.

[22] Oxana Golynker, 'Jobseekers' Rights in the European Union: Challenges of Changing the Paradigm of Social Solidarity' (2005) 20 *European Law Review* 111, 114.

[23] Maduro (n 19) 340.

[24] See eg Mark Bell, *Anti-Discrimination Law and the European Union* (Oxford University Press, 2002) 32.

[25] See eg T Hoogenboom, 'Free Movement and Integration of Non-EC Nationals and the Logic of the Internal Market' in Schermers, Flinterman, Kellermann, Haersolte and van de Meent (eds), *Free Movement of Persons in Europe: Legal Problems and Experiences* (Martinus Nijhoff Publishers, 1993) 498–99 and 511.

[26] Andrew Williams, *EU Human Rights Policies: A Study in Irony* (Oxford University Press, 2004) 202. See further Andrew Williams, *The Ethos of Europe: Values, Law and Justice in the EU* (Cambridge University Press, 2010) 263 and 277 where the author argues that 'whatever else the ECJ may have done, particularly through its development of general principles, it has singularly failed to countenance "justice" as a clear ethical commitment in its own rights'.

[27] See more about the relationship between the traditional market access theory and Union citizenship eg in Eleanora Spaventa, 'From Gebhard to Carpenter: Towards a (Non-) Economic European Constitution' (2004) 41 *Common Market Law Review* 743, 743–73.

these philosophical propositions of equality must be clarified and must, then, be critically examined in the light of the objectives of European integration.

It is clear that the element of external exclusion between citizens and non-citizens is usually compensated with a strong commitment to equal treatment between citizens within a democratic national state.[28] But even when the definition of relevant difference no longer happens on the axis of workers and non-workers in EU law, it still happens between those EU citizens who belong and those who do not belong. The remaining sections of this chapter will therefore examine what it means for the EU principle of equality that the duty to establish sufficient economic or social integration has become the main parameter for EU citizens' general right to equal treatment and, thus, for their agency as EU citizens. It is important to recognise that relevant belonging for the purposes of social equality has traditionally been derived from 'nationality' and 'territoriality',[29] as has been discussed in this section. At the same time, however, it is important to consider whether and to what extent the parameters for EU citizens' agency under EU law can and should be independent of the parallel concept of *ex ante* 'belonging'. As part of this analysis, it will be seen that the potential of EU citizenship to transform what constitutes a 'meaningful relationship' for the purposes of non-discrimination and equal treatment is a decisive factor in response to these questions.

3.3 PROVING BELONGING OR 'HOW ECONOMIC AND SOCIAL ACTIVITY TRUMP EU CITIZENSHIP'

The insight into the case law of the CJEU in Chapter two showed that the requirement of sufficient integration has become the main tool for deciding whether there exists a legitimate and proportionate reason for differential treatment between EU citizens, their implicit comparability notwithstanding. The crucial question is therefore what type of belonging constitutes sufficient integration in the case of economically inactive EU citizens and what this tells us about the status of EU citizenship. This section uses the notion of individual activity to further theorise the EU equality problem in regard to economically inactive EU citizens. It is important to note that here the term 'activity' does not refer to the mere cross-border activity, as the mainstream EU law scholarship might give a reason to assume, but to the individual responsibility to be active and prove belonging in the host Member State. The activity-based conception of equality reveals that the EU principle of equality is deontologically biased because it ultimately places 'responsibility through individual action' over the status of EU citizenship.

[28] See more about this in Chapter one, Section 1.4, p 33.

[29] See eg Neil Walker, 'Denizenship and Deterritorialisation in the European Union' in Hans Lindahl (ed), *A Right to Inclusion and Exclusion* (Hart Publishing, 2009) and Michael Dougan, 'Expanding the Frontiers of European Union Citizenship by Dismantling the Territorial Boundaries of the National Welfare States?' in Catherine Barnard and Okeoghene Odudu (eds), *The Outer Limits of European Union Law* (Hart Publishing, 2009) 119–20.

The spirit of the Court's case law has been captured in many of the recent commentaries on EU citizenship. It has been noted that at the heart of the 'judicial construction' of EU citizenship lies 'the will to facilitate movement if migration contributes to the realization of the individual's personal potential'.[30] Similarly, it has been argued that EU citizenship rights 'encourage individuals to pursue their own interpretation of a "good life", wherever that may lie'.[31] Or, that the Court of Justice has adopted the notion of citizenship which affirms 'individual needs'.[32] On this basis, it has been suggested that the Treaty provisions on EU citizenship can be referred to as an 'important source of rights for all those willing to use them'.[33] Despite this optimism in the relevant academic literature, it seems more realistic to view EU citizenship as an important source of rights for all those *able* to use them. This argument emerges from the fact that proving belonging in the form of sufficient integration is accepted as a precondition for the enjoyment of EU citizenship rights and, thus, for the meaningful exercise of agency on the basis of EU citizenship, as discussed below in Sections 3.3.1 and 3.3.2.

3.3.1 Equal Treatment Based on the Individual Responsibility to be Active

The requirement to prove sufficient integration under the 'real link' test arguably adds an 'element of transaction' to the citizen-state relationships.[34] Firstly, the 'real link' test is based on the assumption that access to welfare benefits requires more than a mere 'physical presence' even in the case of EU citizens.[35] Secondly, it promises to rank residents according to the 'strength of their affiliation'.[36] On this basis, it has been suggested that EU citizenship together with a 'tangible shared experience between the individual and his/her host society' has now become a 'legitimate gateway' to national welfare communities.[37] However, the problem of belonging which underlies the 'real link' case law cannot be solved so easily. In contrast, it is important to consider what type of integration can be regarded as relevant for equal treatment between EU citizens and what the requirement of

[30] Anastasia Iliopoulou Penot, 'The Transnational Character of Union Citizenship' in Michael Dougan, Niamh Nic Shuibhne and Eleanora Spaventa (eds), *Empowerment and Disempowerment of the European Citizen* (Hart Publishing, 2012) 17.

[31] Floris de Witte, 'The End of EU Citizenship and the Means of Non-Discrimination' (2011) 18 *Maastricht Journal of European and Comparative Law* 86.

[32] Michelle Everson, 'A Very Cosmopolitan Citizenship: But Who Pays the Price?' in Dougan, Nic Shuibhne and Spaventa (n 30) 147.

[33] Dimitry Kochenov, '*Ius Tractum* of Many Faces: European Citizenship and the Difficult Relationship between Status and Rights' (2009) 15 *Columbia Journal of European Law* 169, 214.

[34] Gareth Davies, 'Comment: The High Water Point of Free Movement of Persons: Ending Benefit Tourism and Rescuing Welfare' (2004) 26 *Journal of Social Welfare and Family Law* 211, 214.

[35] Charlotte O'Brien, 'Real Links, Abstract Rights and False Alarms: The Relationship between the ECJ's "Real Link" Case Law and National Solidarity' (2008) 33 *European Law Review* 643, 643.

[36] Golynker (n 22) 119.

[37] Dougan (n 29) 158.

sufficient integration says about the EU principle of equality and, thus, about the status of EU citizenship as an equal status.

Integration requirements, such as residence conditions, can be seen as essential for maintaining national social assistance schemes.[38] It has been noted that the requirement of a 'real link' emerges from the fact that, while 'nationally defined exclusions' are still necessary, they must now be based on something other than nationality.[39] The introduction of the 'real link' test by the Court of Justice has been welcomed by those authors who argue that transnational citizenship rights should depend on habitual residence.[40] Some even describe the reliance on residence conditions as a means of 'completion of non-discrimination' because these conditions can be applied to all non-residents and not just to foreigners.[41] The establishment of a real link has also been optimistically viewed as a sign of 'citizenship specificity' which 'both triggers and justifies equal treatment of migrant citizens'.[42] However, others describe the 'real link' test as a way to allow the Member States to rely on 'potentially indirectly discriminatory precondition[s]' in limiting EU citizens' access to social assistance.[43] Several authors have therefore probed a clearer articulation of the legitimacy of such conditions.[44]

A number of different 'economic and social factors' can contribute to the process of establishing a 'real link' in the light of the Court's case law. However, what combines these different factors is the fact that the rights attached to the status of EU citizenship can only be enjoyed by those EU citizens who have already proved their active presence in the host Member State. Thus, even if the right to non-discrimination and equal treatment under EU law is now disconnected from the individual's direct economic activity in the internal market, it has not been disconnected from the individual duty to prove value by being economically or socially active in a more general sense. On the contrary, the common denominator for the different justifications for legitimate differential treatment is the strong reliance on the individual's responsibility to reach a sufficient level of economic or social integration to qualify for equal treatment. Or, as Charlotte O'Brien has put it, the 'real link' case-law approaches integration 'as the duty of the migrant, whether economically active or not'.[45] It is important to consider further what this focus

[38] Van der Mei (n 6) 75.

[39] O'Brien (n 35) 646.

[40] See eg Bruno Nascimbene, 'Towards a European Law on Citizenship and Nationality?' in Síofra O'Leary and Teija Tiilikainen (eds), *Citizenship and Nationality Status in the New Europe* (Sweet & Maxwell, 1998) 72 and 78.

[41] Gareth Davies, 'Any Place I Hang My Hat? Or: Residence is the New Nationality' (2005) 11 *European Law Journal* 43, 49 and 53.

[42] Yuri Borgmann-Prebil, 'The Rule of Reason in European Citizenship' (2008) 14 *European Law Journal* 328, 345.

[43] O'Brien (n 35) 646.

[44] For instance, S O'Leary writes: 'Vague references to Member States' legitimate concerns or to nebulous concepts centred on real and effective links with the host Member State are insufficient to justify, or even explain, a departure from the principles held dear by the Court when dealing with the rights to free movement and non-discrimination of the economically active'. O'Leary (n 11) 73.

[45] O'Brien (n 35) 663.

on the individual responsibility to be economically or socially active tells us about EU citizens' agency.

Chapter two concluded that the economic considerations often prevail over other forms of social and political integration and the case law falls short of articulating adequate non-economic criteria for legitimate differential treatment between EU citizens. However, the Court's recent case law on the right to permanent residence under Article 16 of Directive 2004/38 has added an entirely new strand to the requirement of integration between migrant EU citizens and their host Member States. Namely, the integration requirements no longer focus on 'economic requirements' but also on 'a normative attitude of respect towards the host society and its particular values', as Stephen Coutts has put it.[46] It follows from this that the mere 'factual integration' is not considered relevant but the Court's focus is on 'compliance with the structure and values of the host society'.[47] In practice, this could mean that 'an attachment to society as a space of values' becomes a precondition for EU citizens' treatment as equals.[48] This approach to the permanent right to residence has also been described as 'a communitarian vision of Union citizenship' because it places more weight on the individual 'responsibility of integration' towards the community.[49]

The argument that the Court might at the moment 're-engineer'[50] its view on what constitutes relevant integration between the individual and the host Member State is based on the judgments in the recent *Dias* and *Onuekwere* cases. In both of these cases, the Court faced the question of which time periods contribute to acquiring the right to permanent residence under Article 16 of Directive 2004/38. In the earlier *Lassal* case, the Court had already confirmed that the right to permanent residence under Article 16 of Directive 2004/38 relies on 'the integration-based reasoning'.[51] In *Lassal*, the Court decided that a continuous period of residence of five years which was completed before the transposition of Directive 2004/38 must be taken into account for the purposes of acquiring the right to permanent residence under that Directive and that absence from the host Member State for less than two years, following a continuous period of five years, does not affect the right to permanent residence even if that absence occurred before the date of the transposition of Directive 2004/38.[52] In the *Dias* judgment, the Court also outlined that, although Article 16(4) only refers to the absence from the host Member State for more than two consecutive years as a valid reason for losing the right to permanent residence, the 'integration link' between an EU

[46] Stephen Coutts, 'Union Citizenship as Probationary Citizenship: *Onuekwere*' (2015) 52 *Common Market Law Review* 531, 538.

[47] Loïc Azoulai, 'Transfiguring European Citizenship: From Member State Territory to Union Territory' in 'The (Mis)Construction of the European Individual Two Essays on Union Citizenship Law', EUI Working Papers LAW 2014/14, 7.

[48] Ibid 7.

[49] Coutts (n 46) 536.

[50] Ibid 538.

[51] Case C-162/09 *Secretary of State for Work and Pensions v Taous Lassal* [2010] ECR I-9217, para 37.

[52] Ibid, paras 53 and 57–58.

citizen and the host Member State may be called into question if an EU citizen, after having first resided in the host Member State legally for five years, later stays in that same Member State without a legal right to residence.[53]

In *Dias*, the Court held that the 'integration objective' in Article 16 of Directive 2004/38 'is based not only on territorial and time factors but also on qualitative elements, relating to the level of integration in the host Member State'.[54] The Court thus agreed with Advocate General Trstenjak who had suggested in her opinion that 'unlawful conduct of a Union citizen may diminish his integration in the host State from a qualitative point of view'.[55] In the *Onuekwere* judgment, the Court also first emphasised that the right to permanent residence under Article 16 of Directive 2004/38 is 'a key element in promoting social cohesion' and that it was included in the Directive 'in order to strengthen the feeling of Union citizenship'.[56] However, the Court then referred to its conclusion in *Dias* that the link between the EU citizen and the host Member State can be undermined 'even outside the circumstances mentioned in Article 16(4) of Directive 2004/38.[57] The Court also clarified that, in addition to 'territorial and temporal factors', this assessment may also involve 'qualitative elements'.[58] On this basis, it was concluded that periods of imprisonment 'show the non-compliance by the person concerned with the values expressed by the society of the host Member State' to such extent that taking these periods into account in establishing the permanent right to residence 'would be contrary to the aim pursued' by Article 16 of Directive 2004/38.[59]

The Court's reasoning in *Onuekwere* was in line with Advocate General Bot's statement that not just the right to permanent residence, but also the 'system set up by Directive 2004/38' in more general, is based on the view that 'it must have an effect of strengthening the feeling of belonging to the society of the host Member State'.[60] Advocate General Bot also discussed the idea of 'social cohesion' in his Opinion in the joined *Ziolkowski* and *Szeja* cases, both of which concerned the acquisition of the right to permanent residence on the basis of a five-year period of residence that was completed before the State of origin of the applicants had acceded to the EU. The Advocate General suggested that the purpose of Directive 2004/38, in the light of Recitals 3 and 17 of its preamble, is 'to achieve a system focussing on strengthening social cohesion, in which the right of permanent residence appears as a key factor, being an element of the citizenship of the

[53] Case C-325/09 *Secretary of State for Work and Pensions v Maria Dias* [2011] ECR I-6387, para 63.

[54] Ibid para 64.

[55] Opinion of AG Trstenjak in *Secretary of State for Work and Pensions v Maria Dias* (C-325/09) 17 February 2011, para 106.

[56] Case C-378/12 *Nnamdi Onuekwere v Secretary of State for the Home Department*, 16 January 2014, para 24.

[57] Ibid para 25.

[58] Ibid para 25.

[59] Ibid para 26.

[60] Opinion of AG Bot in *Nnamdi Onuekwere v Secretary of State for the Home Department* (C-378/12) 3 October 2013, para 47.

Union'.[61] In his view, the fact that an EU citizen who enjoys the right to permanent residence under Article 16 of Directive 2004/38 'should have in almost all respects equal treatment with nationals of the Member States' presumes that 'after a sufficiently long period of residence in the host Member State, the Union citizen has developed close links with that Member State and become an integral part of its society'.[62]

The meaning of 'social cohesion' in this context has been debated in academic commentary from different perspectives. Some ponder whether the Court recognises that EU citizens can also 'represent themselves as being part of Europe as a whole' in addition to being 'parts of home and host societies'.[63] However, in the light of the Court's emphasis on 'the particular value system of the host Member State', it has been noted that the meaning of 'social cohesion' seems to move away from 'the possibility of creating bonds and promoting new forms of solidarity in Europe'.[64] Others distinguish between the expressions of solidarity based on 'territorial presence', on the one hand, and 'social cohesion', on the other.[65] In the latter approach, relevant integration is conceived as a process in which the individual will 'actively pursue incorporation into societal structures'.[66] Although rights can in theory be seen as 'a means of securing integration', the Court's interpretation of the acquisition of the right to permanent residence underlines that rights only follow from integration.[67] For instance, Loïc Azoulai concludes on this basis that '[t]o the broadened agency resulting from Union's citizenship is added a particular sense of obligation and duty'.[68] This tendency to emphasise individual responsibility in regard to the acquisition of EU citizens' permanent right to residence, is also captured in the statement that the Court's case law 'transposes the ambition of integration to a discourse of obligation and responsibility'.[69]

It has been suggested that integration requirements reflect the view that social cohesion, understood as 'a sense of shared identity', is 'a precondition for democratic allegiance'.[70] However, it is important not to confuse the democratic and communitarian justifications for integration requirements with one another.[71] It has also been argued that, in so far as this case law focuses on the right to permanent residence, its overall impact should not be 'overestimated'.[72] At the same

[61] Opinion of AG Bot in *Tomasz Ziolkowski* (C-425/10) *and Barbara Szeja and others* (C-425/10) *v Land Berlin*, 14 September 2011, para 50.

[62] Ibid para 51.

[63] Azoulai (n 47) 15.

[64] Ibid 16.

[65] Daniel Thym, 'The Elusive Limits of Solidarity: Residence Rights of and Social Benefits for Economically Inactive Union Citizens' (2015) 52 *Common Market Law Review* 17, 17.

[66] Ibid 36.

[67] Coutts (n 46) 537.

[68] Azoulai (n 47) 17.

[69] Niamh Nic Shuibhne, 'Limits Rising, Duties Ascending: The Changing Legal Shape of Union Citizenship' (2015) 52 *Common Market Law Review* 889, 917.

[70] Thym (n 65) 36.

[71] See more about this in Section 3.4, p 103.

[72] Thym (n 65) 37.

time, however, it has been noted that these developments reflect 'a conceptual shift away from equal rights as a means for integration, towards an output-oriented assessment'.[73] A similar tendency to focus on individual responsibility to be active and prove belonging is emerging from the 'real link' case law in regard to EU citizens' right to equal treatment prior to the acquisition of the right to permanent residence, as discussed above in this section. These developments are significant because they increasingly call into question EU citizenship's ability to live up to its potential as a fundamental status of all Member Sate nationals. EU law scholars speak of 'status convergence'[74] as something inherent to the expression of EU citizenship as a fundamental status. It is clear that access to equal treatment would have a central role in this process of 'convergence' and integration requirements restrict that role.

3.3.2 Theorising the Requirement of *ex ante* Integration

The requirement of *ex ante* integration as a condition for equal treatment between EU citizens means that the status of EU citizenship becomes functional rather than constitutive. In order to enjoy their right to non-discrimination and equality, EU citizens must be active agents: they must, first, establish a 'connecting factor' with EU law and, then, a 'real link' with the society of the Member State in which citizenship rights are being claimed. The normative indeterminacy of the EU principle of equality follows from the fact that, at the same time, the right to equal treatment is rhetorically based on the 'fundamental status' of EU citizenship. It is, therefore, important to consider whether this normative indeterminacy between 'activity' and 'status' is necessarily embedded in the EU principle of equality or whether it can be overcome by re-interpreting the EU principle of equality in the light of the objectives of European integration. Following Alexander Somek's critique of EU equality law, this section will conceptualise the imbalance between 'activity' and 'status' as an argument that the EU principle of equality is deontologically biased. From this argument emerges a further claim that the mere reference to more status-based rights for EU citizens remains largely meaningless if the underlying parameters for EU citizens' agency are not first rethought in the light of a more developed ideal of transnational political and social justice.[75]

The concern that the legal discourse on equality often 'places overwhelming emphasis upon the legal subject'[76] directs attention to what is the legitimate sphere of the agent's own responsibility in qualifying for equal treatment and non-discrimination. The tension between equality and balancing which lies at

[73] Ibid 38.
[74] See eg Nic Shuibhne (n 69) 890 and Thym (n 65) 18.
[75] For a similar argument see eg Thym (n 65) 49.
[76] Jan Broekman, 'Justice as Equilibrium' (1986) 5 *Law and Philosophy* 369, 376 and 379.

the heart of discrimination analysis can arguably be addressed by exploring the extent to which the 'norm-addressees' are required to 'adjust their behaviour to circumstances in order to obtain a benefit or avoid a burden'.[77] The way in which this question is currently answered in EU law seems to place the requirement of individual responsibility for demonstrating relevant integration above the idea of EU citizenship as an equal status. Firstly, the enjoyment of EU citizens' general right to equal treatment depends on *ex ante* integration. Secondly, the establishment of a sufficient degree of integration for equal treatment under EU law is currently approached as an individual responsibility rather than a positive aim of political and legal integration. This means that the Court of Justice still interprets EU citizenship in the light of its old activity-based notion of equality, instead of genuinely engaging in the debate on how EU citizenship must transform what is meant by equality in the context of EU law.

In his essay *Engineering Equality*, Alexander Somek argues that European anti-discrimination law is 'normatively deficient' because it is a project that 'tries to accomplish redistributive objectives by deontological means', ie by focusing on 'agents, their responsibilities, their failures, and intentions'.[78] For Somek, 'the translation of distribution into deontology systematically invites misreading the law's redistributive thrust', ie its promise to provide a tool for social engineering.[79] Somek concludes his analysis of EU anti-discrimination law, suggesting that giving 'accommodation' a more central role in anti-discrimination law 'reverses the deontological twist and *fully* reveals why discrimination is wrong'.[80] By analogy, it is important to consider under what conditions the 'deontological twist' of EU equality law in the case of needy EU citizens can be reversed by demonstrating that equal treatment could be integrative even in the absence of *ex ante* belonging/integration.[81] One way to answer this question is to argue for EU citizenship as a proxy for relevant comparability between all those who hold that status and

[77] Alexander Somek, 'A Constitution for Antidiscrimination: Exploring the Vanguard Moment of Community Law' (1999) 5 *European Law Journal* 243, 254.

[78] Alexander Somek, *Engineering Equality: An Essay on European Anti-Discrimination Law* (Oxford University Press, 2011) 93 and 117.

[79] Ibid 93. This claim is based on the view that, even in the case of direct discrimination, the necessary failure of the 'extensional interpretation' to 'isolate normative intent ('x ought to count as y') leads to the 'intentional interpretation' which 'examines conceivable reasons for action and thereby has to open the door to the consideration of pre-normative intent'. This means that, for Somek, even 'direct discrimination is in fact best understood to be a special case of indirect discrimination'. Ibid 113. On this basis, Somek argues that 'a self-repairing anti-discrimination law would have to be more self-consciously political in the sense that the choice of the threshold standard need not be left to the regulatory market'. He also argues that a 'truly self-repairing' anti-discrimination law 'would lift disadvantages also from those who may well seem "undeserving" from a deontological point of view' and, in this sense, it 'would eventually merely be a misnormer for an alternative social model that promises to make social relations more hospitable to equality broadly understood'.

[80] Ibid 185. Somek wants to explain why 'protection from discrimination without accommodation is empty'. He also envisions how '[t]he relation between the redistributive perspective and decommodification alters' and '[t]he latter takes precedence over the former'. Ibid 182.

[81] Note that Alexander Somek might not agree on this connection, though. See how he discusses EU citizenship in Somek (n 12).

fall into the material scope of EU law. But justifying EU citizens' access to social equality in the host Member State with a mere reference to the EU citizenship status appears somewhat hollow because, as discussed in Chapter one, the status of transnational citizenship is in many ways different from the status of national democratic citizenship.

Moreover, it is clearly not enough to claim that the principle of equal treatment must now be regarded as a goal of European integration in itself. One must also reply to the question of why this is the case. What normative justifications, other than economic rationales, can be provided for the principle of equal treatment in European Union law? And why should the ideas of 'substantive equality' or 'redistributive social justice' have anything to do with EU citizenship? Again, it is not enough to merely refer to the concept of EU citizenship itself. One should also be able to articulate why a concept of transnational citizenship will increase the 'substantial meaning'[82] of the EU principle of equality and will, thus, grant the right to equal treatment in relation to social rights in national welfare systems, even in the case of economically inactive EU citizens. That is, what would legitimise the view of EU citizenship as a 'social citizenship'? Last but not least, is it possible to answer these questions in a way which goes beyond the mere goal of promoting cross-border individual rights and opportunities? These are the questions that underlie the activity-based conception of equality in EU law and they will direct the philosophical analysis of the EU principle of equality in the next section.

3.4 WHAT IS WRONG WITH THE ACTIVITY-BASED ACCOUNT OF EQUALITY IN EU LAW?

The EU principle of equality is 'deontologically biased' in so far as it focuses on EU citizens' individual responsibility to actively integrate themselves as a condition for equal treatment under EU law. It is therefore important to explore the philosophical foundations which underlie the justificatory criteria for legitimate differential treatment between EU citizens. It was claimed more than 20 years ago that: 'The fact remains that there is no jurisprudential tradition in European law. Both constitutionally and jurisprudentially Europe is as yet "silent"'.[83] This 'silence' over the jurisprudential foundations of EU law is poignant in the field of equality law where the choice between different conceptions of equality and distributive justice imposes a great normative force both on the rights of private individuals and on the potential of EU citizenship to become a fundamental status of all Member State nationals. The idea of equality can be described and justified in a variety of ways. The theoretical analysis of equality can therefore provide us with a better understanding of the way in which the EU principle of equality is currently

[82] Catherine Jacqueson, 'Union Citizenship and the Court of Justice: Something New under the Sun? Towards Social Citizenship (2002) 27 *European Law Review* 260, 273.

[83] Ian Ward, 'Identity and Difference: The European Union and Postmodernism' in Jo Shaw and Gillian More (eds), *New Legal Dynamics of European Union* (Clarendon Press, 1995) 27.

applied between EU citizens, as well as to what alternatives it could have within the existing constitutional framework of the EU.

In particular, the EU principle of equality can benefit from how the role of individual responsibility has been debated in different egalitarian accounts of distributive justice.[84] A philosophical analysis of egalitarian social justice gives substance to the argument that the bias in favour of individual responsibility and self-sufficiency is detrimental to EU citizenship because it fails to recognise the importance of just and equal relationships between EU citizens. Firstly, a brief overview of the liberal theories of equal opportunities will show that the role of responsibility is contested within philosophical egalitarianism (Section 3.4.1). Secondly, it will be seen how an alternative account of equality as a 'normative ideal of human relationships'[85] emerges from the democratic critique of liberal egalitarianism (Section 3.4.2). Finally, the core of the EU equality problem will be conceptualised as the question of whether a more relational account of egalitarian social justice can be justified transnationally (Section 3.4.3).

3.4.1 Egalitarian Justice as a Liberal Ideal of Equal Opportunities

The assumption of basic moral equality is accepted by most major political theories, whether egalitarian or not.[86] What is distinctively egalitarian is the idea that social and distributive equality has not just instrumental but also intrinsic value. Philosophical egalitarianism can therefore be described as a belief that equality makes an outcome intrinsically better 'above and beyond whatever impact this might have on levels of well-being'.[87] However, most contemporary egalitarians are ready to accept a certain form of pluralism under which equality is integrated with other values, such as 'choice', 'desert', or 'responsibility'. In order to better understand the EU principle of equality, it is important to consider what these 'other values' are in EU law and how they are weighted against EU citizens' right to equal treatment. This section will engage in this task by discussing the convergence between the activity-based conception of equality in EU law and the liberal egalitarian theories of equal opportunities. It will be seen that they share a strong emphasis on the exercise of individual responsibility and choice.

[84] The following terminological distinctions are important for understanding different types of justice claims: (1) It is possible to distinguish between 'procedural' and 'substantive' accounts of justice. (2) Substantive accounts of justice often distinguish between 'political justice' and 'social justice', although these two are closely connected. (3) Social justice can be distributive or non-distributive. (4) Distributive justice can be egalitarian or non-egalitarian.

[85] Scheffler (n 1) 444.

[86] See eg Nils Holtug and Kasper Lippert-Rasmussen, 'An Introduction to Contemporary Egalitarianism' in Nils Holtug and Kasper Lippert-Rasmussen (eds), *Egalitarianism: New Essays on the Nature and Value of Equality* (Clarendon Press, 2007) 1–2

[87] Shelley Kagan, 'Equality and Desert' in Louis P Pojman and Owen McLeod (eds), *What Do We Deserve? A Reader on Justice and Desert* (Oxford University Press, 1999) 298.

The basic definition of egalitarian justice is derived from the claim that 'how much one person ought to receive of some important good can only be ascertained relative to what others can receive'.[88] This definition is based on two further principles: (1) the assumption of 'equal status of the persons' holds that there is something about that person in virtue of which one owes it to that person to treat them equally; and (2) the assumption of the 'absence of relevant differences' takes into account other considerations, such as the above-mentioned 'choice', 'desert', and 'responsibility'.[89] Thus, the egalitarian principles of social and distributive justice presuppose that the limits of equal treatment depend on how the balance is struck between the assumption of 'equal status', on the one hand, and that of the absence of 'relevant differences', on the other. These analytical principles can also be applied to the critique of EU citizenship as a fundamental status of all Member State nationals. As seen in Chapter two, the emergence of EU citizenship as an 'equal status' has been qualified by shifting the focus of discrimination analysis to the definition of 'relevant differences' under the objective justification test. In practice, the lack of sufficient economic or social integration has become a relevant difference in EU equality law.

A common point of criticism in regard to egalitarian accounts of social justice is that they fail to pay enough attention to the more fundamental question of whether equality is 'desirable' in the first place.[90] However, one must first understand what equality means in order to decide whether or not it is a legitimate goal.[91] Similarly, the question of when equal treatment between EU citizens is desirable can only be answered if we first gain a more thorough understanding of those philosophical ideas that underlie the EU principle of equality. In so far as EU citizens' access to social equality as EU citizens is concerned, the EU principle of equality can potentially rely on multiple different understandings of social and distributive justice. These accounts of justice can in principle be either egalitarian or non-egalitarian. However, one thing is clear: EU citizens' general right to equal treatment provides an important expression of the theory of social justice within the EU and more attention must therefore be paid to how access to social equality is justified in EU law. In particular, it is informative to examine the EU principle of equality in the light of how the balance between distributive equality and the ideal of individual responsibility is struck in the contemporary liberal theories of equal opportunities.

[88] Thomas Christiano, *The Constitution of Equality: Democratic Authority and its Limits* (Oxford University Press, 2007) 52–53.

[89] Ibid 49 and 55.

[90] Holtug and Lippert-Rasmussen (n 86) 15. See also J-S Gordon, 'Justice or Equality?' (2006) 7 *Zeitschrift für Wirtschafts- und Unternehmensethik (zfwu)* 183, 183. A common argument against egalitarianism is the so-called 'levelling down' objection, ie the claim that egalitarians would need to accept levelling down of human welfare if it increases equality. One way to respond to this objection is to argue that many inequalities are unjust, 'but not all equalities are fully just' and that 'Pareto superior equalities are more just than Pareto inferior equalities'. See eg Thomas Christiano, 'A Foundation for Egalitarianism' in Holtug and Lippert-Rasmussen (n 86) 42.

[91] Holtug and Lippert-Rasmussen (n 86) 15.

Contemporary philosophical egalitarianism has its primary focus on the question of 'equality of what', ie on the question of what it is that needs to be equally distributed.[92] However, egalitarians also need to answer the question of 'equality of whom' which requests a decision on 'who should stand in this relation of equality—in the favoured currency—to each other'.[93] This question entails a further question of whether the ideal of egalitarian social justice applies only within politically unified societies (such as states) or also between them.[94] This latter question is particularly relevant for EU citizens' access to equal treatment as EU citizens, as will be seen in Section 3.4.3. There is no need to go into the technical details of different liberal egalitarian theories here. However, a brief overview of the main strands of these theories is useful for understanding what their main problems are according to those egalitarians who emphasise the value of equal relationships and what makes this criticism relevant to EU citizenship.

In brief, many contemporary liberal egalitarians want to challenge the idea of 'desert'[95] as the basis of the principle of justice without compromising the idea of individual responsibility.[96] What is common to these so-called responsibility-sensitive theories of egalitarian justice and equal opportunities is the claim that John Rawls's famous rejection of the idea of desert does not pay enough attention to the question of what is not under one's control versus what is one's genuine

[92] See more about this set of questions eg in Amartya Sen, *Inequality Reexamined* (Clarendon Press, 1992). Competing suggestions for the 'currency' of egalitarian justice include welfare, resources and capacities. GA Cohen, 'On the Currency of Egalitarian Justice' (1989) 99 *Ethics* 906. Richard Arneson's theory of equality of welfare can be contrasted with Ronald Dworkin's theory of equality of resources which is based on the ideas of an 'envy test' and a 'hypothetical auction' on the basis of which people can be made responsible for their 'option luck' but not for their 'brute luck'. Amartya Sen's approach to equality can be seen as a form of welfare egalitarianism, but it emphasises the capacities under which welfare becomes possible. See more about these theories below in this section.

[93] Holtug and Lippert-Rasmussen (n 86) 5.

[94] Ibid 7.

[95] The question of legitimate 'desert bases' is crucial for the notion of desert. The academic commentary usually distinguishes between the following four major 'desert-bases': (1) 'effort'; (2) 'achievement'; (3) 'virtue'; and (4) 'compensation'. See eg Jonathan Wolf, 'The Dilemma of Desert' in Serena Olsaretti (ed), *Desert and Justice* (Clarendon Press, 2003) 220–21. It has been noted that 'desert-claims' differ from 'rights' or 'entitlements' because there are situations in which desert-claims can only find their justification in the fact that 'there is value in the deserving party's having what he deserves'. See eg George Sher, *Desert* (Cambridge University Press, 1987) 195. This same idea has been expressed by claiming that, in order to deserve something, 'one must satisfy certain conditions of worthiness'. See eg Joel Feinberg, 'Justice and Personal Desert' in Pojman and McLeod (n 87) 71.

[96] The relationship between the concepts of 'equality' and 'desert' arguably depends on whether 'desert' is seen as a 'comparative' or 'non-comparative' concept. The traditional 'non-comparative' approach to desert holds that equality is 'important simply as a part of the theory of desert' and that 'it would simply be that in some ways (though not in others) people are equally deserving'. See eg Kagan (n 87) 312. The notion of 'comparative desert' as an idea that it is not possible to say what each person should get independently of what others get, has been developed to prove that the idea of desert and the responsibility sensitive egalitarianism are not always mutually conflicting. As Serena Olsaretti has noted, the crucial question is 'whether comparisons are relevant for determining what each person's due is in the first place'. Serena Olsaretti, 'Distributive Justice and Compensatory Desert' in Olsaretti (n 95) 19.

choice.[97] These theories are called 'responsibility-sensitive' because they derive the 'egalitarian intuition' from the responsibility principle which can be summarised as follows: '[i]f ... it is objectionable for some to suffer a harm or loss through no fault of their own, then it follows ... that it is objectionable to suffer an inequality through no fault of their own'.[98] It remains, nonetheless, problematic what sort of responsibility should matter and why. This lack of clarity over when and why individual responsibility should matter also penetrates the EU principle of equality in so far as it is based on the ideas of individual activity and self-sufficiency.

Most contemporary versions of liberal egalitarianism are concerned with neutralising the effect of what is called 'brute luck' and not with the equality of outcomes as such.[99] This view is rooted in the argument that equal concern requires treating people as equals and not necessarily treating them equally.[100] In order to reach this goal of equal opportunities, liberal egalitarians distinguish between 'preferences' and 'resources', between 'persons' and 'circumstances', and between 'option luck' and 'brute luck'.[101] Despite this common starting point, liberal egalitarians differ in their views on whether equal opportunities should be assessed in terms of 'resources' or in terms of 'welfare'.[102] Moreover, some frame their answer to the 'equality of what' question by emphasising the capability to achieve functionings and the 'agency aspect',[103] while others see a conflict between the individual 'personal motivation' and 'egalitarian justification' primarily as a 'problem of moral psychology' which needs to recognise both 'agent-relative' and 'agent-neutral' grounds.[104]

On the basis of this brief summary, it can be seen that the responsibility-sensitive idea of equal opportunities promises to define the appropriate role of individual responsibility within the egalitarian theory by distinguishing between unchosen circumstances for which people cannot be regarded to be responsible

[97] In *A Theory of Justice*, Rawls argues that 'no one deserves his place in the distribution of native endowments' and that 'claims of desert are always dependent on a prior conception of justice'. From this starting point, Rawls' theory of justice conditions equal citizenship on the basic structure of society, ie 'the way in which the major social institutions distribute fundamental rights and duties and determine the division of advantages from social cooperation'. Rawls formulates this as the two principles of justice which regulate how the distribution of basic social goods should be organised. As long as the principles of equal liberty and equal opportunity are satisfied, the Rawlsian difference principle rules out any inequalities which do not benefit the worst-off group. John Rawls, *A Theory of Justice* (Harvard University Press, 1971).

[98] Christopher Lake, *Equality and Responsibility* (Oxford University Press, 2001) 1 and 14.

[99] Peter Vallentyne, 'Brute Luck Equality and Desert' in Olsaretti (n 95) 169.

[100] Ronald Dworkin, *Taking Rights Seriously* (Duckworth, 1977).

[101] Ronald Dworkin, *Sovereign Virtue: The Theory and Practice of Equality* (Harvard University Press, 2000).

[102] Richard Arneson, 'Equality and Equal Opportunity for Welfare' (1989) 56 *Philosophical Studies* 77 and Richard Arneson, 'Equality of Opportunity for Welfare Defended and Recanted' (1999) 7 *The Journal of Political Philosophy* 488. Arneson has moved from welfare egalitarianism towards prioritarianism in his latter writings. See eg Richard Arneson, 'Luck Egalitarianism and Prioritanism' (2000) *Ethics* 110 339.

[103] Sen (n 92).

[104] Thomas Nagel, *Equality and Partiality* (Oxford University Press, 1991).

and genuine choices for which people should bear full responsibility.[105] However, this position has been criticised for adopting a view of responsibility which is 'narrowly economistic, focusing on the responsibility to refrain from making demands on the resources of the state'.[106] It has also been noted that the 'inherently normative character' of the idea of responsibility raises 'other political possibilities'.[107] Thus, somewhat ironically, the responsibility-sensitive theories of equality which are firmly rooted in John Rawls' work are now criticised for ignoring the dimensions of political equality between citizens.[108] It is important to understand that this tension between the ideal of equal citizenship, on the one hand, and the requirement of individual responsibility, on the other, also defines the interpretation of the principle of equality under EU law.

In sum, holding individual responsibility for economic or social integration as a precondition for the full enjoyment of EU citizens' right to equal treatment does not just protect the national welfare sovereignty, but it also takes the EU principle of equality into the realm of some difficult philosophical and normative choices. The analysis of the responsibility-sensitive theories of equal opportunities in this section has demonstrated that the ideal of individual responsibility as the basis of egalitarianism remains ambiguous and normatively vague. In practice, this means, as will be discussed in the next section, that the current interpretative bias in favour of EU citizens' responsibility to be active at the expense of their status as EU citizens, cannot avoid the criticism which has been directed against the responsibility-sensitive theories of equality on the basis that they fail to pay sufficient attention to the democratic value of just and equal relationships between citizens.

3.4.2 Egalitarian Justice as a Democratic Ideal of Human Relations

The critics of responsibility-sensitive egalitarianism suggest that it is not enough for an account of egalitarian citizenship to deal with mere economic inequalities, but that various types of social hierarchies and forms of oppression should also

[105] The fundamental distinction between 'choice' and 'luck' was introduced as an alternative to Ronald Dworkin's original position which focused on distinguishing between 'preferences' and 'luck'. Cohen (n 92) See also GA Cohen, 'Where the Action is: On the Site of Distributive Justice' (1997) 26 *Philosophy & Public Affairs* 3.

[106] Chris Armstrong, *Rethinking Equality: The Challenge of Equal Citizenship* (Manchester University Press, 2006) 98.

[107] Ibid 98. Armstrong argues that '... our ideas about responsibility will be unavoidably normative. They will reflect back to us dominant views on the boundaries of personhood, on the nature of citizenship, and dominant conceptions of rationality' and that 'the distinction is at the heart of our moral conception of what it means to be a person, and what the relation between individuals, and between individuals and the state, should be'. Ibid 106–07.

[108] It has been suggested that Rawls' theory of justice can be understood as an attempt to make the ideal of equal status of citizens more concrete. See eg Samuel Scheffler, 'Equality as the Virtue of Sovereign: A Reply to Ronald Dworkin' (2003) 3 *Philosophy & Public Affairs* 199. Rawls' theory of justice has

be addressed. Moreover, according to the critics, the liberal egalitarian ideal of equal opportunities relies on a 'broadly neoliberal sensibility'.[109] By this, they refer to the way in which the liberal egalitarian notions of choice and responsibility cement the dichotomy between 'the (bad) "dependent" and the good "independent" citizen', defining dependency 'as failure to support yourself economically' and independence as the ability of 'being economically self-supporting and suitably ambitious', as Chris Armstrong has put it.[110] It is obvious that this criticism has a strong echo in EU law which, as discussed in Section 3.3, conditions the right to equal treatment on the individual responsibility to be active and prove sufficient *ex ante* integration.

The neoliberal view of active citizenship, which is arguably embedded in the responsibility-sensitive egalitarianism, has been described as follows:

> [It] is overwhelmingly an economic category, rather than a political, social, cultural or ecological one. It is also an overwhelmingly personal, as opposed to interpersonal category: it primarily specifies vertical responsibilities vis-à-vis the state, not horizontal responsibilities towards fellow citizens.[111]

It has been noted that this way of defining equal citizenship fails to adequately address the question of 'what equality means for the way we relate to each other'.[112] The attempt to shift the focus of philosophical egalitarianism to relationships builds on the claim that the 'presence of equal opportunity' does not indicate the 'presence of agency'.[113] On this basis, it has been suggested that the idea of individual choice-making as a 'sociologically and economically naïve ideal of self-sufficiency' should be replaced by the concepts of 'self-direction' and 'political voice' within philosophical egalitarianism.[114] This quest for more diverse parameters for agency is also important when looking for alternatives to the activity-based conception of equality in EU law.[115]

also been described as a theory of equal citizenship with the intention 'to model the relations between such citizens, and to identify the social and distributive preconditions necessary to sustain this ideal'. See eg Armstrong (n 106) 27–28 and 49.

[109] Armstrong (n 106) 3.

[110] Ibid 86.

[111] Ibid 99.

[112] Lake (n 98) 87. Lake has also noted that '[t]he fact that social institutions serve to enforce the relevant principles of mutual respect ought not to distract from us recognizing these principles to operate primarily between one individual and the next rather than between each individual and the state'. Ibid 38.

[113] Ibid 89.

[114] See Iris Marion Young's arguments as discussed in Armstrong (n 106) 87. However, some have expressed the concern that the idea of political equality has surpassed the idea of economic equality when the focus of egalitarian debate has shifted to the (cultural) recognition of social groups in the work of such authors as Nancy Fraser, Iris Marion Young and Martha Minow. See eg Anne Phillips, *Which Equalities Matter* (Polity Press, 1999) 13 and 20. Phillips notes that '[p]olitical reforms cannot substitute entirely for economic and social ones'. In her view, the politics of recognition will, thus, 'draw us back … into unfinished business around the nature of equal citizenship'. Ibid 27 and 355.

[115] See more about this in Section 3.5, p 122.

It has also been noted that even if the responsibility-sensitive theories of equality were able to curtail injustice, they might still 'sacrifice other egalitarian values'.[116] The core of this criticism is that the ideal of individual responsibility as the 'centre of an egalitarian theory of justice' must be more explicitly weighted against 'other egalitarian values', such as respect.[117] Similarly, it needs to be asked what those 'other egalitarian values' are, which are compromised under the activity-based and responsibility-oriented conception of equality in EU law and whether the individual responsibility to prove belonging should be more explicitly weighted against these other values. Thus, the theory of democratic equality which forms the basis of my critique of the EU principle of equality in this section can be seen as an attempt to define what these 'other egalitarian values' must entail. Its critical edge is based on the idea of citizenship as a central principle for egalitarian politics.

The underlying theme in the relational accounts of egalitarian social justice is the concern that the commitment to distributive equality is not seen as an 'inherently democratic project' even if it produces a 'defence of formal democracy'.[118] This view is articulated in Elizabeth Anderson's famous article 'What is the Point of Equality', which argues that the mainstream egalitarianism 'fails the most fundamental test any egalitarian theory must meet: that is its principles express equal respect and concern for all citizens'.[119] From this starting point, equality can be defined as follows:

> The proper negative aim of egalitarian justice is not to eliminate the impact of brute luck from human affairs, but to end oppression which by definition is socially imposed. Its proper positive aim is not to ensure that everyone gets what they morally deserve, but to create a community in which people stand in relations of equality to others.[120]

[116] Jonathan Wolff, 'Fairness, Respect, and the Egalitarian Ethos' (1998) 27 *Philosophy and Public Affairs* 97, 102.

[117] Ibid. On this basis, Wolff argues that it may be that 'finding the fairest principle of equality' is not the most important task of philosophical egalitarianism. This idea is developed further in Wolff's own work which examines the extent to which 'fairness' and 'respect' can be in tension with each other. Wolff speaks of 'failures of trust' and claims that 'there are certain areas such that, if I feel I am not trusted in those areas I will also feel I am not respected'. Ibid 102, 106 and 108. However, it has been suggested that this conflict disappears if 'fairness is understood to consist of equality of status, which is concerned primarily with the moral attributes of the social and economic relations in which people stand'. See eg Thomas Hinton, 'Must Egalitarians Choose between Fairness and Respect?' (2001) 30 *Philosophy and Public Affairs* 72, 73.

[118] Armstrong (n 106) 3.

[119] Elizabeth Anderson, 'What is the Point of Equality' (1999) 109 *Ethics* 287, 289. Anderson insists that equality is not opposed to luck, as the responsibility-sensitive theories of equality suggest, but to oppression and heritable hierarchies of social status and the undemocratic distribution of power. Anderson also distinguishes between 'oppressive social relations' and '[l]ess extreme forms of group inequality'. For her, the former are unjust 'because they deprive members of the disadvantaged group of their basic human rights', whereas the latter are unjust 'because they violate a fundamental norm of democracy, which is social equality'. Elizabeth Anderson, *The Imperative of Integration* (Princeton University Press, 2010) 21. For further discussion, see also Elizabeth Anderson, 'The Fundamental Disagreement between Luck Egalitarians and Relational Egalitarians' (2010) 40 *Canadian Journal of Philosophy* 1.

[120] Anderson, 'What Is the Point of Equality' (n 119) 289.

This theory is called democratic because it claims that the 'construction of a community of equals' must integrate the principles of economic distribution with the 'expressive demands of equal respect'.[121] A central idea in the theory of democratic equality is that citizens are entitled to make claims 'in virtue of their equality, not their inferiority, to others'.[122]

The reference to the citizens' right to make claims 'in virtue of their equality' can also be contrasted with EU citizens' right to make claims on the basis of their activity and *ex ante* belonging. It is therefore important to examine further how the democratic egalitarians would solve the problem of 'rugged individualism' of contemporary philosophical egalitarianism by means of a more relational view of equality.[123] Viewing egalitarian justice as an 'ideal of social and political relations', indicates that the egalitarian concept of justice must defend distributive principles, which, above all, are 'appropriate to a society of equals'.[124] This principle of 'equality of relationships' has been crystallised by Samuel Scheffler who argues that the fundamental egalitarian question is not 'what it is for a government to treat people with equal concern', as Ronald Dworkin holds, but 'what it is for people to relate to one another as equals'.[125] From this starting point follows Scheffler's central claim of equality as a 'normative ideal of human relations'.[126]

For Scheffler, the relational understanding of equality includes: (1) a *moral* idea 'that all people are of equal worth and that there are some claims that people are entitled to make on one another simply by virtue of their status as persons; (2) a *social* idea of a human society as 'a cooperative arrangement among equals, each of whom enjoys the same social standing'; and (3) a *political* idea of 'claims that citizens are entitled to make on one another by virtue of their status as citizens, without any need for a moralized accounting of the details of their particular circumstances'.[127] Scheffler has summarised this account of relational equality

[121] Ibid.

[122] Ibid. Anderson defines democratic citizenship by stating that it 'entails not only equality of legal rights, but public standing as fit for association with fellow citizens' and that '[e]quality is thus a cultural norm, not only a legal status'. Anderson, *The Imperative of Integration* (n 119) 102. Anderson also underlines that 'democratic equality guarantees not effective access to equal levels of functioning but effective access to levels of functioning sufficient to stand as an equal in society', although '[f]or some functionings, equal citizenship requires equal levels'. Elizabeth Anderson, 'What is the Point of Equality' (n 119) 318. For Anderson, '[w]hat counts as "enough" varies with cultural norms, the natural environment, and individual circumstances'. Ibid 320.

[123] Anderson, 'What Is the Point of Equality' (n 119) 313.

[124] Scheffler (n 1) 7.

[125] Scheffler (n 108) 204–05. However, Scheffler acknowledges that 'Dworkin is exceptional among luck-egalitarian authors because he does seek to anchor his egalitarian distributive principles in a more general ideal of equality'. Ibid 203.

[126] Scheffler (n 1) 234. It is important to recognise different implications of the word 'relational'. According to Scheffler, it is one thing to state that 'equality is an intrinsically relational notion; the fact that two people have equal amounts of some good constitutes a kind of relation between them' and another thing to see it as an 'ideal that governs the terms on which independently existing human relationships should be conducted: it is not the "relationship" that consists in two people's having the same amount of something'. Ibid 229, fn 26.

[127] Ibid 191.

by pointing out that 'it insists on the very great importance of the right to be viewed simply as a citizen'.[128] Thus, according to the democratic theory of equality, affirming the status of citizenship goes hand in hand with placing more emphasis on just and equal relationships between citizens. This is also a central point of the critique of EU citizenship in this section. Namely, the bias in favour of individual responsibility under the activity-based conception of equality seems to neglect the importance of just and equal relationships for the status of EU citizenship.

Despite its emphasis on the value of equal citizenship, the democratic ideal of egalitarian social justice does not aim at rejecting the distributive implications of equality altogether. On the contrary, it has been underlined that adopting the principle of equal relationships will necessarily have 'distributive implications'.[129] More attention should therefore be directed at how the distributive principles are related to equal social relationships.[130] What is clear is that distributive principles may be 'instrumental to securing such relationships, follow from them, or even be constitutive of them'.[131] Similarly, it is important to consider how the importance of just and equal relationships between citizens could be accommodated within the EU principle of equality in so far as EU law interacts with the principles of distributive social justice. The next section will assess the relevance of these critical democratic claims for the EU equality problem—bearing in mind that EU citizenship in its current form falls short of the ideal of *democratic* citizenship in many ways.

3.4.3 Justifying a More Relational Account of Justice Transnationally: The Crux of the EU Equality Problem

The democratic critique of egalitarian social justice claims that the liberal theories of equal opportunities focus on the ideas of individual choice and responsibility at the expense of just and equal relationships between citizens. The connection between the EU principle of equality and this critique becomes obvious if relational equality is defined as a view that inequality arises when 'individuals or groups exist in relations of hierarchy, or are prevented from standing together as peers'.[132] The crux of the EU equality problem can now be defined as follows: the EU principle of equality suffers from a bias in favour of individual responsibility at the expense of just and equal relationships between EU citizens. What is still clearly lacking in EU equality law is the conviction that an independent standard

[128] Ibid.
[129] Ibid.
[130] Ibid 228. For Scheffler, this means that the 'differing contingencies of individuals' situations' must be abstracted in so far as they 'claim equal rights as citizens' but that the 'interpretation and application of those rights will often depend on features of their individual circumstances'. Ibid 191–92.
[131] Anderson (n 119) 314. For further discussion, see Christian Schemmel, 'Why Relational Egalitarians Should Care about Distributions' (2011) 37 *Social Theory and Practice* 365 and 'Distributive and Relational Equality' (2011) 11 *Politics, Philosophy & Economics* 123.
[132] Armstrong (n 106) 5.

for justifying equal treatment between EU citizens could be derived from 'the aim of enabling people to be fully cooperating members of society'.[133] The crucial question for the study of EU citizenship is therefore whether the relevance of just and equal relationships between citizens can only be rooted in an already existing democratic structure at a national level, or whether the relational account of egalitarian social justice can also be justified in a transnational polity, such as the EU.

The democratic theory of egalitarian justice fails to give an unequivocal answer to the question of its transnational or international application. It has been acknowledged amongst democratic egalitarians that the question of the relations between people who are not citizens in the same country or in the same political society is an 'important interpretative issue, about which there is no general consensus'.[134] Some commentators have expressed the concern that the critical potential of democratic equality is undermined if democratic egalitarians extend their definition of relevant capabilities to cover many of those capabilities which we need 'as a human being' rather than as citizens.[135] This ambiguity over the scope of democratic equality indicates that, although the relational ideal of egalitarian social justice provides a helpful critical tool for challenging the activity-based conceptions of egalitarian justice in general, it alone cannot provide a sufficient normative justification for a more relational account of equality within the EU. What is important, however, is that the relational critique of the EU principle of equality shows that, in order to overcome the EU equality problem, EU citizenship must be examined as a matter of transnational justice.

The important question for the analysis of EU citizenship is whether the substantive justice claims are only meaningful within a 'closed community of shared citizenship'.[136] David Miller is one of those authors who argue that the principles of social justice cannot be widened beyond the boundaries of national political

[133] Scheffler (n 1) 198.

[134] Ibid 192, fn 42. For instance, Elizabeth Anderson only states in one of her footnotes that it is not possible to consider the 'international implications' of democratic equality within the scope of her current work. Anderson, 'What Is the Point of Equality' (n 119) 321. Anderson also speaks of an approach which 'narrows our focus to social relations within the borders of a democratic state but expands the demands of justice inside those borders'. She claims that '[t]he distinctive normative feature of democratic societies is social equality'. This, for its part, leads her to conclude that '[a]ll of the members of a democratic society have a just claim to stand in relations of equality with their fellow citizens'. Anderson, *The Imperative of Integration* (n 119) 18.

[135] Jonathan Wolff, 'Fairness, Respect and the Egalitarian *Ethos* Revisited' (2010) 14 *The Journal of Ethics* 335, 349. Anderson herself ackonwledges that citizenship 'involves functioning not only as a political agent ... but participating as an equal in civil society' and that 'functioning these ways presupposes functioning as a human being'. Anderson, 'What Is the Point of Equality' (n 119) 317. But some argue that luck egalitarianism is, nonetheless, more cosmopolitan than any version of 'social interactionist' theories of equality which 'apply only among people who interact or are socially related in significant ways such as being members of a single political community'. See eg Richard Arneson, 'Luck Egalitarianims—A Primer' in Carl Knight and Zofia Stemplowska (eds), *Responsibility and Distributive Justice* (Oxford University Press, 2011) 49.

[136] See eg Andrew Williams, 'The Problem(s) of Justice in the European Union' in D Kochenov, G de Búrca and A Williams (eds), *Europe's Justice Deficit?* (Hart Publishing, 2015) 35.

communities.[137] However, Miller acknowledges that it is difficult to distinguish 'what is actually implicit in the idea of citizenship' from those claims which people are entitled to make on the basis of their membership in a national community.[138] As an example, he notes that, although welfare rights were originally seen as 'expression of national solidarity', they have now become an essential part of citizenship in the sense that 'someone whose welfare rights are not respected can claim with *justice* [italics added] that he or she is not being treated as an equal citizen'.[139] This challenge of distinguishing the relevant social relationships embedded in citizenship as citizenship from the relevant social relationships embedded in the membership of a national community is central to the relational critique of EU citizenship. At the heart of this enquiry lies the question of whether meaningful relationships for the purposes of equal treatment of EU citizens can be independent of proving *ex ante* integration and belonging in the host Member State, as discussed above in this chapter.

The critique of EU citizenship in this book builds on the premise that EU law lacks clarity in what equal treatment means relationally, that is, between EU citizens. It is now time to re-conceptualise this critique by suggesting that the EU equality problem is fundamentally a problem about which relationships are meaningful for the purposes of non-discrimination and equal treatment under EU law. The emphasis on meaningful relationships finds an expression in Erwin Chemirensky's statement that equality is not only the 'concept that tells us that different treatment of people does matter' but it is also the 'concept that forces us to consider how society treats people in relationship to one another'.[140] This leads us to the hard question of whether a 'society of equals' can be transnational and to what extent it must be politically constructed. Underlining this question is an even deeper philosophical question of why and how just and equal relationships between citizens gain value in the first place and why they would gain value in a transnational context. It is this question of 'meaningful relationships' which informs the attempt to re-interpret EU citizenship as an equal status in Part II of this book.

[137] David Miller, *Principles of Social Justice* (Harvard University Press, 2001) 19. Miller bases this view on the claim that 'the idea of social justice makes sense only if we assume there is a broad consensus about the social value of a range of goods, services, and opportunities, some disagreement in private values notwithstanding'. Ibid 8.

[138] Ibid 31.

[139] Ibid.

[140] Erwin Chemirensky, 'In Defense of Equality: A Reply to Professor Westen' (1983) 81 *Michigan Law Review* 575, 585. Similar thoughts in regard to (political) equality can also be found from other authors. Jeremy Waldron claims that equality 'is a useful term here all the same, rebutting as it does from the outset any suggestion that what matters in politics is the ranking or differentiation of human knowledge and intelligence'. Jeremy Waldron, 'The Substance of Equality' (1991) 89 *Michigan Law Review* 1350, 1362 and 1364. Kenneth Karst notes that equal treatment protects against 'derogation' or the 'imposition of stigma' and that 'the ideal of equal membership in the community' is, therefore, implicit in the values of citizenship and respect. Kenneth Karst, 'Why Equality Matters' (1983) 17 *Georgia Law Review* 245, 247—48.

The relational account of egalitarian social justice as discussed in Section 3.4.2 is firmly rooted in the idea of a 'society of equals'. It has rightly been noted that a mere reference to the higher importance of some relationships fails to recognise that a non-egalitarian theory of justice is needed to define what these relationships are.[141] In order to justify the EU principle of equality in relational terms, we must first understand 'what counts as "related" and why relationship matters as it does'.[142] The fact that EU citizenship is now regarded as a relevant 'comparison class' for the personal scope of equal treatment under EU law could potentially imply a change of perception regarding what relationships are meaningful from the perspective of EU law and European integration.[143] However, the structural and substantive equality problems illustrate that it remains highly controversial whether EU citizenship has actually shifted the focus of the EU principle of equality from the individual responsibility to be economically and socially active to just and equal relations between EU citizens. The central question to the relational critique of EU citizenship is how the project of European integration redefines a 'society of equals' and whether this definition is also politically sustainable.

Any reference to EU citizenship as a question of transnational justice will therefore face a set of difficult questions concerning the EU's existence as a polity, including its relationship with democracy and justice. The academic debates on the EU's legitimacy have traditionally centred around the question of whether European integration can be regarded as legitimate on the basis of its results ('output legitimacy'), or whether it also requires democratic legitimacy ('input legitimacy').[144] The so-called no-Demos thesis, first articulated by the German Constitutional Court in its Maastricht judgment, holds that the EU is not democratic because it lacks a demos, ie the common people which is able to decide collectively about its affairs. The EU has nevertheless been described as a 'new kind of democracy-in-the-making' which cannot be assessed against the idea of 'statehood'.[145] Thus, the question of 'what sort of polity' the EU is or may be

[141] Christopher Peters, 'Equality Revisited' (1997) 110 *Harvard Law Review* 1210, 1250. The so-called 'emptiness' of equality debate has its roots in this need to define what constitutes a relevant comparison class. Peter Westen has famously distinguished between 'descriptive equality' as the idea that two things are 'identical in all significant descriptive respects' and 'prescriptive equality' as the idea that two or more persons or things 'ought to be treated as equal (or unequal)'. On this basis, Westen has concluded that 'equality is nothing but a rhetorical device for talking about legal and moral rules on how people should be treated'. Peter Westen, 'The Meaning of Equality in Law, Science, Math, and Morals: A Reply' (1983) 81 *Michigan Law Review* 604, 611, 614, 618–19 and 629.

[142] Kent W Greenawalt, '"Prescriptive Equality": Two Steps Forward' (1997) 11 *Harvard Law Review* 1265, 1289.

[143] See more about this in Chapter two, Section 2.2, p 41.

[144] See eg Giandomenico Majone, 'Europe's "Democracy Deficit": The Question of Strandards' (1998) 4 *European Law Journal* 5.

[145] Kalypso Nicolaïdis, 'The New Constitution as European "Demoi-cracy"?' (2004) 7 *Critical Review of International Social and Political Philosophy* 76, 79. It has been suggested on this basis that the EU ought to be seen as a 'demoi-cracy', meaning that it values the 'plurality of its component peoples' rather than 'a common identity'. Ibid 84.

becoming is connected to the question of whether the EU can be seen as a 'political community'.[146] At the same time, the EU's existence as a polity is closely related to the question of whether the EU ought to 'promote or secure justice for and amongst its members and associates'.[147]

Some optimistically argue that a 'revised justification' for the EU can be derived from the fact that it provides 'renewed possibilities for democracy and social justice where Member States can no longer offer them'.[148] However, the desirability of 'majoritarian democracy' on the EU level has also been called into question both on practical and normative grounds.[149] A separate, although inter-connected, debate is whether justice-based arguments can play an independent role in legitimating European integration, or whether any claim for more justice at the EU level would only be meaningful in the context of political justice and representative democracy. The role of the EU as 'an actor of justice'[150] has accordingly become a topic of intense scholarly debate. The central theme in this discussion is that, while 'justice' cannot be assimilated with 'democracy' and 'legitimacy', a more just EU might still be able to provide new solutions to the EU's legitimacy crisis.[151] However, the actual content of these justice claims has remained controversial.

Jürgen Neyer is one of those authors who suggest that the appropriate standard for assessing the EU is 'justice, not democracy'.[152] Others, however, have responded to this that democracy 'is *the* political practice of justice'.[153] It has therefore been argued that the 'politicisation' of the EU's 'justice deficit' is a necessary precondition for its solution.[154] The term 'political justice' can refer to just government broadly understood.[155] But it is widely acknowledged that the emergence of political equality also depends on the distribution of resources.[156] This means that the issues of distributive and political justice are in many ways connected. The motivation for redistribution in the national context is often seen as a complex mix of 'belonging', 'collective political identity', and 'culturally embedded

[146] Michael A Wilkinson, 'Political Constitutionalism and the European Union' (2013) 76 *Modern Law Review* 191, 192.

[147] Neil Walker, 'Justice in and of the European Union' in Kochenov, de Búrca and Williams (n 136) 250.

[148] Miguel Poiares Maduro, 'A New Governance for the European Union and the Euro: Democracy and Justice', RSCAS Policy Papers 2012/11, 1.

[149] See eg Fritz Scharpf, 'After the Crash: A Perspective on Multilevel European Democracy' (2015) 21 *European Law Journal* 384, 394.

[150] Dimitry Kochenov, 'The Ought of Justice' in Kochenov, de Búrca and Williams (n 136) 21.

[151] Ibid 22.

[152] Jürgen Neyer, 'Justice, Not Democracy: Legitimacy in the European Union' (2010) 48 *Journal of Common Market Studies* 903, 903.

[153] Rainer Frost, 'Justice, Democracy and the Right to Justification: Reflections on Jürgen Neyer's Normative Theory of the European Union' in Kochenov, de Búrca and Williams (n 136) 227. For further discussion, see Rainer Frost, *Justification and Critique towards a Critical Theory of Politics* (Polity, 2014).

[154] Michael Wilkinson, 'Politicising Europe's Justice Deficit: Some Preliminaries' in Kochenov, de Búrca and Williams (n 136) 113–14.

[155] Williams (n 136) 42.

[156] Robert Dahl, *On Political Equality* (Yale University Press, 2006) iv.

reciprocity'.[157] These attributes for redistributive justice arguably underline the connection between 'democracy' and 'justice': democratic processes give legitimacy to redistributive justice within a bounded polity.[158] However, the motivation for transnational social justice cannot be based on a simple reference to EU citizenship as an expression of democratic belonging. It is therefore important to consider other *political* motivations for just and equal relationships between EU citizens.

Some suggest that the need for 'global background justice' could justify the principles of (egalitarian) distributive justice globally even in the absence of a 'politically constructed global basic structure'.[159] It has even been proposed that 'the sheer existence of national borders' provides a basis for demands of global justice because these borders prevent people 'from taking advantage of opportunities open to people born elsewhere'.[160] Philippe Van Parijs is one of those authors who argue that the competences of the EU should be increased in the field of distributive justice.[161] In his view, the principles of egalitarian distributive justice provide a moral basis for a democratic society, or, a 'demos-cracy' in the case of the EU, and they can therefore precede a fully functioning democratic regime.[162] This argument is based on the following reasoning:

> The key condition we thus end up with is not the factual one of the existence of a democratic regime, but a normative view about what relations should prevail between human beings. However, it must be conceded that such a normative view cannot make much sense unless some factual conditions are fulfilled, essentially that the people concerned should be able to picture their relations with one another as relations between individuals …[163]

Thus, Van Parijs, too, seems to acknowledge the need for what this book calls 'meaningful relationships' as a precondition for distributive social justice. What remains of this section will consider in more detail how the relationships that can provide a basis for the principles of distributive justice are constituted.

It has rightly been noted that the EU's claims for justice cannot be based on 'institutionalised collective agency' in the same way as is possible within a democratic state.[164] Moreover, justice in the national context focuses on (re)distribution, whereas transnational justice seems to have its focus on individual rights and opportunities in different cross-border situations.[165] These critical observations

157 Floris de Witte, 'Transnational Solidarity and the Mediation of Conflicts of Justice in Europe' (2012) 18 *European Law Journal* 649, 697.

158 Ibid 697.

159 For different approaches, see eg Thomas Pogge (ed), *Global Justice* (Blackwell, 2001).

160 Philippe Van Parijs, 'International Distributive Justice' in Robert Goodin, Philip Pettit and Thomas Pogge (eds), *A Companion to Contemporary Political Philosophy* (Blackwell, 2007).

161 Philippe Van Parijs 'Should the European Union Become More Democratic?' in Philip Van Parijs, *Just Democracy: The Rawls—Machiavelli Programme* (ECPR Press, 2011) 71.

162 Van Parijs (n 160).

163 Ibid.

164 de Witte (n 157) 698.

165 See eg de Witte (n 157), 696.

concerning the EU's quest for political and social justice have increased in the aftermath of the ongoing Europe-wide financial crisis. A common concern is that, while European integration has increased the availability of 'individual options', its focus on 'negative integration' has simultaneously increased 'social inequality' by decreasing 'the capacity of democratic politics to deal with the challenges of global capitalism'.[166] It has also been argued that 'placing the individual at the centre of political attention' within the EU means that '[s]ocial mobilization in Europe is at its strongest when the direct interest of the individual is at stake and at its weakest when it requires tending to the needs of the other'.[167] A similar observation in regard to the prohibition of nationality discrimination emerges from Alexander Somek's critique of what he calls 'cosmopolitan constitutionalism'.[168] The thrust of this criticism is that the cosmopolitan commitment to 'develop the rights of outsiders' is problematic if the principle of non-discrimination is also applied to those situations in which non-nationals are faced with 'obstacles to their economic activity that do not arise from discriminatory conduct but from the existence of different nations as such'.[169]

Here the concern is that the principle of non-discrimination may undermine 'the structures of reciprocity' that form the basis for 'welfare entitlements' in the national context.[170] These arguments concerning the transnational prohibition of nationality discrimination are highly relevant to the analysis of EU citizenship as an equal status. For instance, Somek argues that placing 'positive social rights' at the heart of EU citizenship rights 'render the European citizens as *bourgeois*'.[171] By this, he means that EU citizenship secures 'freedom of choice in the private sphere' and fails to see citizens as 'attached to a political community'.[172] A central theme in this discussion concerns citizens' ability to become part of 'the process of polity construction'.[173] More optimistic commentators argue that transnational citizenship is significant because it can create 'new relationships of rights between previously unconnected actors'.[174] From this perspective, EU citizenship could have 'a strong transformative influence both on our self-perceptions and our perceptions of others' in so far as the principle of non-discrimination and equal treatment brings forward 'another's point of view'.[175] This approach to EU citizenship is in line with the argument that the potential of non-discrimination to change

[166] Scharpf (n 149) 385.

[167] Joseph Weiler, 'The Political and Legal Culture of European Integration: An Exploratory Essay' (2011) 9 *International Journal of Constitutional Law* 678, 693.

[168] Alexander Somek, *The Cosmopolitan Constitution* (Oxford University Press, 2014).

[169] Ibid 260.

[170] de Witte (n 157) 703.

[171] Somek (n 168) 203.

[172] Ibid 204.

[173] Mark Dawson and Floris de Witte, 'Self-Determination in the Constitutional Future of the EU' (2015) 21 *European Law Journal* 371, 382.

[174] Justine Lacroix, 'Is Transnational Citizenship (Still) Enough?' in Kochenov, de Búrca and Williams (n 136) 178.

[175] Ibid 179.

'interpersonal relationships' indicates that EU equality law can function as 'a catalyst for a value driven transformation of society from *within* that society'.[176]

However, for instance, Somek argues that the very fact that the focus here is on 'equality' and 'social justice' means that 'social relations' have already become 'abstract'.[177] For him, political self-determination requires that one sees oneself 'as a part of a *place* that is shared with *concrete* others'.[178] It may be correct that we need to focus on the 'polis' as a spatial phenomenon, but 'spatial' does not need to mean territorial. On the contrary, it is important to consider more critically what it means that the other becomes 'concrete' in the sense that they deserve to be treated justly and equally with the members of the polity. In his recent monograph, Somek challenges Europeans to consider whether 'it is reasonable to have one's collective self-determination mediated by the judgment of an imaginary other'.[179] But he does not consider whether the 'imaginary other' can become a more concrete other through the process of European integration and as a consequence of transnational cooperation—not just *within* a single Member State but also *between* them.

The account of justice as a territorially-defined practice does not pay much attention to 'the "other" outside a society's borders'.[180] Moreover, it has also been noted that, in so far as distributive justice is based on the assumption of a 'common culture' or 'shared identity', it may happen sooner than we realise that these justice claims start to 'make as little sense on the domestic scale as they say it makes on the global scale'.[181] An alternative approach to justifying distributive justice claims is that just institutions and distributive policies can shape and maintain the sense of shared culture and belonging.[182] However, Somek also expresses the concern that EU anti-discrimination and equality law focuses on 'inclusion' at the expense of 'distribution'.[183] By this, he means that the EU advances an 'apolitical version of equality'.[184] In Somek's view, 'emancipatory political action' is needed to protect what he calls 'social freedom' which emerges from 'relationships with others in which people mutually support their aims'.[185] Here the term 'political' is understood as a substantive conception which refers to 'shaping, developing, and preserving a form of life that some share in a certain place of the earth'.[186]

[176] Elise Muir, 'The Transformative Function of EU Equality Law' (2013) 5&6 *European Review of Private Law* 1231, 1234 and 1238.

[177] Somek (n 168) 268.

[178] Ibid 161.

[179] Ibid 160.

[180] Williams (n 136) 316.

[181] Van Parijs (n 160).

[182] Ibid.

[183] Alexander Somek, 'The Preoccupation with Rights and the Embrace of Inclusion: A Critique' in Kochenov de Búrca and Williams (n 136) 308.

[184] Ibid 297.

[185] Somek (n 168) 165.

[186] Ibid.

However, it seems more correct to argue that the 'place' which may gain political relevance in this sense is a 'polis', rather than a 'territory' as such.

Moreover, viewing inclusion as 'apolitical' seems strange if one simultaneously adopts the view that the lack of 'emancipation' plays a central role in the EU's 'justice deficit'. Namely, it is important to bear in mind that, as Michael Wilkinson has put it, '[s]truggles for emancipation are now cross-cultural, transnational, plural and heterogeneous'.[187] It follows from this that advancing inclusion can also enrich the quest for emancipation within a polity. Somek's study on cosmopolitan constitutionalism underlines the need for 'sustaining *different* polities'.[188] However, he seems less concerned about what role difference should play within a polity.[189] If diversity is a central value not just between polities but also within them, it becomes clearer why the 'inclusion' of non-national EU citizens can increase, rather than decrease, the emancipatory goals within these societies/polities. It is therefore important to consider whether, following Lea Ypi's argument in the field of global justice, EU citizens can become 'avant-garde political agents'[190] who contribute to transforming the polis and its understanding of the 'other' for whom there exists a shared sense of responsibility. However, it would be absurd to argue for such transformative political potential in the absence of more just and equal relationships between EU citizens.

The critical analysis of EU citizenship in this book shares the now-common concern that the rhetoric of EU citizenship as a fundamental status of all Member State nationals conceals the economic and individualistic logic that underlies the EU principle of equality. It is a legitimate argument that reducing 'aggregate factors of social interaction' to 'individual experiences and opportunities' is harmful from a more emancipatory point of view.[191] A similar concern for narrow individualism will be discussed in more detail in regard to the accepted parameters for EU citizens' agency in the next section of this chapter. However, for instance, Somek criticises the idea of introducing migrant EU citizens as 'agents of change'.[192] In his view, their movement is not 'political', even if it could make 'societies more diverse and multicultural'.[193] But the transformative *political* potential of EU citizenship as an equal status becomes clearer if we consider it in terms of 'otherness' and 'diversity' within a polity. Namely, in so far as a 'society of equals' is defined

[187] Wilkinson (n 154) 134–35.

[188] Somek (n 168) 212.

[189] He said elsewhere that '[i]dentity is mediated by sustainable difference'. Alexander Somek, 'What is Political Union?' (2013) 13 *German Law Journal* 561, 569.

[190] Lea Ypi, *Global Justice and Avant-Garde Political Agency* (Oxford University Press, 2012) 166. These agents include 'all those individuals and social groups who appear distributively affected by current globalization processes and whose experience of conflict in particular societies forces us to rethink understandings of the function and purpose of existing political arrangements'. Ibid.

[191] Somek (n 168) 147.

[192] Ibid 211.

[193] Ibid. This is based on the view that 'it does not necessarily affect the basic structure of society in the sense of altering profoundly the allocation of the benefits and burdens of cooperation'. Ibid. This argument is based on a distinction between 'redistribution' and 'inclusion'. Ibid.

relationally, rather than through assimilation, it can be enriched by extending the scope within which the other is recognised as constitutive to the self and, thus, as a source of mutual responsibility.[194]

A more sceptical view holds that, in the case of post-national citizenship, '[a]ny association of citizenship with sharing responsibility and growing beyond oneself drops out of the picture'.[195] It is therefore important to consider more carefully why access to social resources matters in the case of EU citizens. As part of this analysis, it is also important to examine under what conditions European citizenship could develop beyond 'the type of subjectivity that is consistent with the private polity', as Somek has put it.[196] It has been noted that the idea of 'access' becomes important if we focus on 'the conditions for practising the relationship between citizen and community'.[197] Chapter one showed how EU citizenship is *inter alia* different from national citizenship in the sense that it has primarily defined the relationship between the individual and the relevant Member State rather than between the individual and the Union. The important question for justifying EU citizenship as an equal status is therefore whether those relationships which matter for the purposes of non-discrimination and equal treatment can be viewed more horizontally as relationships between EU citizens themselves.

It seems clear that the transformative potential of EU citizenship will not be actualised if the EU principle of equality fails to grow beyond its current individualistic ethos. The governing powers can be centralised or decentralised within the EU as a multi-level polity. But the important question remains: Can European integration transform that relationship to the other which lays the ground for any meaningful claim to political and social justice between citizens? If the answer to this question is negative, there is very little one can say about the EU equality problem. However, if the answer is positive, it seems increasingly important to consider what the conditions for that transformation would be, provided that the EU can overcome its current deep financial crisis and find a way forward as a polity which promotes diversity, rather than assimilation. Thus, the key to understanding the future of EU citizenship as an equal status is not about more (or less) equal treatment between EU citizens as such. Instead, it is crucial to rethink our answer to the question of *why* equal treatment between EU citizens matters and, above all, whether equal treatment between EU citizens can be justified in more relational terms, as has been discussed in this section.

The insight into the democratic account of relational egalitarian justice underlines the need to respect difference between citizens, while simultaneously advancing just and equal relations between citizens. The next section will conclude this chapter discussing these themes further by, firstly, explaining why the

[194] See more about this in Chapter 4, p 135.

[195] Somek (n 168) 210.

[196] Ibid.

[197] Antje Wiener, 'Constitution-Making and Citizenship Practice—Bridging the Democracy Gap in the EU?' (1997) 35 *Journal of Common Market Studies* 595. According to Wiener, the 'constitutive

mere reference to more comparability between EU citizens does not provide a firm basis for a more relational account of equality in EU law and, secondly, how a more balanced view of agency in the case of EU citizens as EU citizens can emerge from recognising the inherent connection between EU citizens' agency and their sense of subjectivity as EU citizens. Paradoxically, this means that more attention must be directed to the equal treatment of economically inactive and dependent EU citizens—despite the fact that that may simultaneously put more pressure on national 'social market democracies' than the equal treatment of economically active EU citizens alone would do.[198]

In sum, the core of the EU equality problem can be conceptualised as a lack of relationality. This lack of relationality is illustrated in the normative indeterminacy of EU citizens' general right to non-discrimination and equal treatment, as discussed in Chapter two. However, defining the EU equality problem in terms of just and equal relationships between EU citizens is clearly an argument for transnational justice rather than individual rights. For the purposes of this analysis, it is important to bear in mind that to value one's relationships 'non-instrumentally' can provide a way of seeing those relationships as 'sources of special responsibilities'.[199] On this basis, it has been suggested that citizens must accept 'some level of burdensome other-regarding behaviour'.[200] By analogy, justifying EU citizenship as an equal status of all Member State nationals depends on whether EU citizenship can provide a new source of meaningful relationships without collapsing into a cosmopolitan claim of the universal human condition. The remaining chapters of this book will explore whether and, if so why, just and equal relationships between EU citizens would matter, even in the absence of a single bounded democratic polity called the European Union.

3.5 FROM ASSIMILATION TO AGENCY: TWO POSSIBLE SOLUTIONS TO THE EU EQUALITY PROBLEM

Understanding equality as a 'normative ideal of human relations' challenges the current focus of the EU principle of equality. However, by approaching the EU equality problem from a more relational perspective we need to address the hard question of whether a more relational theory of egalitarian social justice can be justified in a transnational context. This question of what a 'society of equals' means transnationally underpins any credible attempt to solve the lack of relationality as the crux of the EU equality problem. This section will discuss two possible justifications for more just and equal relationships between EU citizens. First, it will be

elements' of citizenship practice consist of 'some broad acceptance of the terms of belonging, the rights conferred with that belonging and access to them'. Ibid 601.

[198] See more about this in Chapter 5, p 170.

[199] Samuel Scheffler, *Boundaries and Allegiances: Problems of Justice and Responsibility in Liberal Thought* (Oxford University Press, 2001) 6.

[200] Seana Valentine Shiffrin, 'Paternalism, Unconscionability Doctrine, and Accommodation' (2000) 29 *Philosophy & Public Affairs* 205, 239.

briefly explained why the argument for more comparability between EU citizens does not provide a helpful solution to the EU equality problem (Section 3.5.1). It will then be suggested that shifting the critical focus to EU citizens' agency can open up a more promising way forward for remedying the EU equality problem (Section 3.5.2). Lastly, EU citizens' agency is linked to their sense of subjectivity as EU citizens (Section 3.5.3).

3.5.1 More Comparability Between EU Citizens: A Cul-de-Sac

The requirement of comparability as part of the discrimination analysis means that access to equal treatment is connected to the question of who is relevantly similar to deserve equal treatment.[201] In those cases in which comparability is regarded as 'implicit', rather than 'explicit', the right to similar treatment materialises 'if no sufficient reason exists for different treatment'.[202] One way to address the EU equality problem would be to argue for more explicit comparability between EU citizens. In the Court's case law, the introduction of EU citizenship as a new standard for comparability has in practice shifted the focus of discrimination analysis towards the host Member State's ability to present objective justifications for discriminatory restrictions on access to public benefits.[203] Some authors therefore suggest that the welfare rights of migrant EU citizens should be approached from the perspective of comparability rather than through what is called 'the rather mechanical triptych "infringement-justification-proportionality"'.[204]

However, although citizenship is 'essentially an equality problem',[205] the mere reference to the comparability between different groups of EU citizens fails to provide an adequate solution to the current normative indeterminacy of EU citizenship. The problematic nature of making comparisons is widely recognised amongst anti-discrimination law scholars who examine non-discrimination as a universal human right—as opposed to non-discrimination as a citizenship right. The critics have pointed out that 'categories of morally alike people do not exist in nature'[206] and that the aspects which are weighted in the comparability analysis remain 'sociologically and culturally determined'.[207] Moreover, it has been noted

[201] See eg Gavin Barrett, 'Re-examining the Concept and Principle of Equality in EC Law' (2003) 22 *Yearbook of European Law* 117, 132.

[202] Kenneth W Simons, 'Equality as a Comparative Right' (1985) 65 *Boston University Law Review* 387, 424. Cf An 'explicit' use of comparability analysis defines which parameters are relevant for two situations to be relevantly similar for the application of the non-discrimination principle. Ibid.

[203] Michael Dougan, 'The Constitutional Dimension to the Case Law on Union Citizenship' (2006) 31 *European Law Review* 613, 631.

[204] de Witte (n 31).

[205] Andrew Evans, 'Union Citizenship and the Equality Principle' in Allan Rosas and Esko Antola (eds), *A Citizens' Europe: In Search of a New Order* (SAGE Publications, 1995) 86–87.

[206] Aileen McColgan, 'Cracking the Comparator Problem: Discrimination, "Equal" Treatment and the Role of Comparisons' (2006) 6 *European Human Rights Law Review* 650, 652.

[207] Sacha Prechal, 'Equality of Treatment, Non-Discrimination and Social Policy: Achievements in Three Themes' (2004) 41 *Common Market Law Review* 533, 543.

that the actual requirement of comparability is more often about 'proportionality, fairness, or balance'[208] than about similarity as such. In practice, the comparability analysis is often mixed up with the reasonableness analysis.[209] In theory, this may open up new possibilities for proving relevant comparability, but it may also mean that the reasonableness analysis is reduced to only considering whether situations are relevantly similar.[210]

A tendency to merge the comparability analysis with the reasonableness analysis can be tracked in EU equality law in so far as the scope of EU citizens' general right to equal treatment irrespective of nationality is conditioned on the proportionality analysis in regard to the right to residence. It has been seen in Chapter two how EU citizenship as a new standard of comparability has been qualified by a lenient application of the reasonableness test, both in relation to the scope of and the limitations on the right to equal treatment. In the context of nationality discrimination, the discrimination analysis focuses on similar treatment in relation to the nationals of the host Member State.[211] The comparability analysis therefore asks who should be treated equally to the nationals of the host Member State. In order to reply to this question, it is important to understand which aspects of agency are regarded to be relevant for the comparisons between the nationals of the Member State in question and nationals of other Member States in European Union law.

Placing more weight on the 'explicit' comparability between EU citizens would seemingly strengthen the status of EU citizenship as an equal status. However, it can be asked what kind of equality that would then be. Comparability between EU citizens presents a 'relative' claim for equal treatment between EU citizens; namely, it affirms similarity between EU citizens. The philosophical analysis of the EU principle of equality in this chapter depicted an alternative, more relational, justification for equal treatment in EU law. This approach to the EU equality problem suggests that the focus of discrimination analysis should move from similarity and assimilation to 'meaningful relationships' between the holders of EU citizenship. In practice, this would mean that the EU principle of equality is not confined to the mere Aristotelian concept of formal equality ('alike should be treated alike'), but can accommodate a more substantive ideal of equality as a means of protecting new 'meaningful relationships' between EU citizens.

In sum, the move from the explicit non-comparability between economically inactive and dependent Union citizens and nationals of the host Member State towards their implicit comparability has placed more weight on the assessment of

[208] Sandra Fredman, *Discrimination Law*, 2nd edn (Oxford University Press, 2011) 13.

[209] Jürgen Schwarze, *European Administrative Law* (Sweet & Maxwell, 1992), 584.

[210] For further discussion, see eg Suzanne B Goldberg, 'Discrimination By Comparison' (2010–2011) 120 *The Yale Law Journal* 728.

[211] Regarding the need for a comparator, A Evans writes: 'Persons from the various Member States will usually be alike in some respects and different in other respects. Hence, criteria are necessary to determine which similarities demand like treatment and which differences demand differential treatment.' Evans (n 205) 95. Similarly, Floris de Witte has noted that 'If it is accepted that Union citizenship only obliges Member States to treat economically inactive Union citizens equally when they find themselves in a comparable situation to nationals, we must describe which ties distinguish non-nationals from nationals'. de Witte (n 31).

reasonableness criteria and objective justifications as part of the discrimination analysis in EU law. A mere reference to the comparability between EU citizens can therefore easily hide the fact that the accepted parameters for EU citizens' agency remain contingent on the individual responsibility to prove sufficient economic or social integration, rather than on the status of EU citizenship. Moreover, solving the EU equality problem with affirming more explicit comparability between EU citizens would still lead to a narrow understanding of what constitutes relevant agency in the case of EU citizens. Namely, the idea of comparability underlines similarity and assimilation, rather than diversity or difference. This critique of comparability as a solution to the EU equality problem is particularly important if we recognise the potential of transnational citizenship to accommodate 'otherness' and, thus, to transform those relationships in which egalitarian social justice matters within the EU.

3.5.2 Revising the Reductionist View of Agency in EU Law: A Way Forward

The governments of the host Member States may easily find reasons for not showing equal concern for EU citizens because they do not belong to the group of their citizens. However, the integration requirements seem different if the analysis focuses on their impact on EU citizens' agency. The EU principle of equality is currently vulnerable to the criticism that it undermines the complexity of human agency beyond the capacity to make responsible and autonomous choices. In the case of EU citizens, this means that the enjoyment of their fundamental right to equal treatment is conditioned on individual responsibility to prove vertical belonging into the Member State in which access to social benefits is claimed. Academic commentary has noted that individual responsibility should matter for determining the boundaries of distributive justice and social equality only in so far as 'the capacities that are essential to the exercise of our responsible agency themselves matter for the standpoint of justice'.[212] Similarly, more attention must be paid to the question of whether individual responsibility and activity should be viewed as the primary parameters for agency in the case of EU citizens.[213]

[212] Lake (n 98) 30. The responsibility-sensitive theories of equality have been criticised by calling into question the idea of free will which seems to be embedded both in the notion of desert and that of responsibility. In response to this criticism, some authors argue for a 'political conception of human agency, taking this to be the agency of a citizens rather than that of a fully formed metaphysical person'. Ibid 51. Others suggest that the line between choice and circumstances can be understood as normative rather than metaphysical, along with the introduction of the 'reasonableness test'. See eg Arthur Ripstein, *Equality, Responsibility, and the Law* (Cambridge University Press, 1999) 292. Or, simply, that 'to treat someone as a responsible agent is to hold that person to a set of normative standards' Scheffler (n 1) 72.

[213] This argument is based on the view that EU citizens' access to equal treatment is intertwined with the accepted parameters for relevant agency in EU law. See more about this in Päivi Johanna Neuvonen, 'EU Citizens' Whimsical Status: Persons or Actors on their Way to Full Agency' in Nuno Ferreira and Dora Kostakopoulou (eds), *The Human Face of the European Union: Are EU Law and Policy Humane Enough?* (forthcoming by Cambridge University Press, 2016).

One approach to the 'transnational character' of European citizenship is to argue that the goal of EU citizenship is more about 'protecting the particular identity of the migrant' than about 'creating a European identity'.[214] This argument is correct in rejecting the assimilationist ideal of a single European identity. In practice, the 'logic of individual agency' is closely connected to the development of European economic constitution.[215] However, the individualistic view of agency does not come without costs. The costly side of things is captured, for instance, by Michelle Everson who has noted that 'the jurisprudence of the Court is founded within a particular personification of the European subject, that of the rationally confident and consuming individual'.[216] It is, therefore, important to explore what kind of theory of the person[217] underlies the EU principle of equality and under what conditions it could be replaced with a more balanced view of agency. A richer account of relevant agency is needed in EU law in order to transform EU citizenship from a transitory status to a source of moral, legal and political subjectivity.

The notion of 'agency' in its simplest form refers to 'the necessary pre-conditions for human activity rather than passivity'.[218] An agent is therefore a being with the capacity to act.[219] In practice, however, the idea of agency is contested both in social theory and in philosophy. The main line of demarcation has traditionally been drawn between (1) the Enlightenment view of rational and metaphysical individual, and (2) the constructivist accounts of agency as a social structure.[220] As an important methodological alternative, social realism[221] promises to bring together the metaphysical and constructivist dimensions of human agency by emphasising the continuity of self-consciousness as something 'which is prior to, and primitive to, our sociality' but which, nonetheless, 'derives from our embodied practices in the world'.[222] The social realist account of agency builds on the idea

[214] Anastasia Iliopoulou Penot, 'The Transnational Character of Union Citizenship' in Dougan, Nic Shuibhne and Spaventa (n 30) 26.

[215] De Witte (n 157) 699.

[216] Everson (n 32) 160. Everson also argues that this approach 'isolates and atomises the individual as a homo economicus'. Ibid 165.

[217] A similar question concerning EU citizens' personhood has recently been asked in Charlotte O'Brien, 'I Trade, Therefore I Am: Legal Personhood in the European Union' (2013) 50 *Common Market Law Review* 1643.

[218] Margaret Archer, *Being Human: The Problem of Agency* (Cambridge University Press, 2000) 2.

[219] 'Agency' in Stanford Encyclopedia of Philosophy. http://plato.standford.edu?entires/agency.

[220] Archer (n 218) 3–5. See also eg Anthony Giddens, *Central Problems in Social Theory: Action, Structure and Contradictions in Social Analysis* (The Macmillan Press Ltd, 1979) 49 and 54 who argues that a notion of human agency must be connected with 'structural explanations' and 'problems of institutional transformation'. For Giddens, '[s]tructure forms "personality" and "society" simultaneously'. Ibid 70. On this basis, he argues that '[i]nstitutions do indeed "result" from human agency: but they are the outcome of action only in so far as they are also involved recursively as the medium of its production'. Giddens, *Central Problems in Social Theory* 95.

[221] 'Realism' in its simplest form insists that 'none of the properties and powers of subjects are understandable in isolation from reality'. Archer (n 218) 154. This approach understands humanity as something 'which develops through practical action in the world'. For instance, Archer argues that agency is 'stratified', meaning that the 'properties' of the human being are neither 'pre-given nor as socially appropriated, but rather they are emergent from our relations with our environment'. Ibid 87.

[222] Ibid 7. For instance, Archer refers to the fact that 'it is only as embodied human beings that we experience the world and ourselves' (Ibid 145). On this basis, social realists argue for a 'stratified view

of 'human beings as the bearers of a continuous sense of self' and emphasises the 'active acquisition of a personal identity at maturity'.[223] But it also highlights 'embodied practices as the source of the sense of self' and, thus, the 'primacy of practice' in the development of subjectivity.[224] This methodological approach to EU citizens' agency is helpful because it directs our attention to the necessary connection between EU citizens' agency and their subjectivity.

The reference to 'self-consciousness' in explaining agency indicates that the idea of agency no longer refers to the mere capacity to act, but to the capacity to act consciously. The idea of human agency as 'self-conscious agency' is particularly important to those authors who base their theory of agency exclusively on individual autonomy and rationality.[225] Christine Korsgaard's Kantian theory of agency and identity provides a good example of this. As a moral philosopher, Korsgaard defines the struggle for moral integrity as 'the struggle to be, in the face of psychic complexity, a single unified agent'.[226] For her notion of agency as self-constitution, it is important that the agent is 'unified', so that action becomes 'an expression of myself as a whole'.[227] The argument for unity in the case of EU citizens is discussed from a more critical perspective in the next chapter. Moreover, Korsgaard holds the view that 'your identity is in a quite literal way constituted by your choices and actions'.[228] The liberal idea of individual autonomy will also be problematised in the next chapter. But approaching EU citizens' agency through the idea that 'the function of action is self-constitution'[229] can nonetheless lay the ground for the analysis of EU citizens' subjectivity in the next chapter.

What is also interesting for the study of EU citizenship is the way in which Korsgaard ties the 'practice of holding people responsible' to the integrity of their identity.[230] In her view, the judgments of responsibility will only 'make sense' if people as 'authors of their own actions' create themselves through their 'personal or practical identity'.[231] By analogy, this would mean that EU citizens' moral agency as EU citizens is dependent on their ability to see the status of EU citizenship as a source of 'practical identity'. The concept of 'practical identity' plays an important mediating role in Korsgaard's theory of agency.[232] As noted above, she

of "the subject"' whose 'properties and powers' emerge at the following levels: the 'self', the 'person', the 'agent' and the 'actor'. (Ibid 254) This allows them to claim that the emergence of our social selves is 'necessarily relational, and for it to be properly so, then independent properties and powers have to be granted to both "structures" and to "agents"' (Ibid 255).

223 Ibid 9.

224 Ibid 8.

225 Christine Korsgaard, *Self-Constitution Agency, Identity, and Integrity* (Oxford University Press, 2009) 26.

226 Ibid 7.

227 Ibid 18.

228 Ibid 19.

229 Ibid 32.

230 Ibid 20.

231 Ibid.

232 Ibid. Korsgaard defines the term 'practical identity' as 'a description under which you value yourself and find your life worth living and your actions to be worth taking'.

argues that 'we constitute our own identity in the course of action'.[233] A parallel argument is that '[o]ur conceptions of practical identity govern our choices of actions'.[234] These identities may include 'roles and relationships, citizenship, memberships in ethnic or religious groups, causes, vocations, professions and offices'.[235] Most practical identities are 'contingent'.[236] But, for Korsgaard, 'to be a person' is to have reason to act and these reasons are provided by our 'practical identities', that is, by a set of contingent principles with which we identify ourselves.[237]

Korsgaard also observes that, since every person may have several practical identities, 'we also face the task of uniting them into a coherent whole'.[238] For her, the 'value of our human identity' ultimately explains our different 'contingent forms of identity'.[239] If EU citizenship is seen as a practical identity, we would need to consider more carefully what in our human existence would give a reason for adopting such transnational practical identity. This is where it is fruitful to look for alternative accounts for human agency. It has been seen above in this section that the social realist account of agency also understands humanity as something 'which develops through practical action in the world'.[240] However, social realists argue that human agency is always 'stratified', meaning that the 'properties' of the human being are neither 'pre-given nor as socially appropriated, but rather they are emergent from our relations with our environment'.[241] Revising the reductionist view of EU citizens' agency can similarly gain more substance from recognising the relational and intersubjective dimensions of agency.

3.5.3 Linking EU Citizens' Agency to their Subjectivity: A Road-Map for a More Balanced View of Agency

The relational nature of social and political agency is captured in the work of such authors as Michael Sandel, Michael Walzer, Charles Taylor, and Alasdair MacIntyre whose arguments are often grouped together under the notion of communitarianism.[242] The common starting point for these authors is to claim that justifying rights must always presuppose a 'particular conception of the good'.[243] The communitarian critique will not provide a sufficient basis for

[233] Ibid 42.
[234] Ibid 20.
[235] Ibid.
[236] Ibid 23.
[237] Ibid.
[238] Ibid 21.
[239] Ibid 214.
[240] Archer (n 218) 87.
[241] Ibid.
[242] See eg Michael Sandel, *Liberalism and the Limits of Justice* (Cambridge University Press, 1982); Charles Taylor, *Sources of the Self: The Making of the Modern Identity* (Harvard University Press, 1989); Alasdair MacIntyre, *After Virtue: A Study in Moral Theory* (University of Notre Dame Press, 1981); and Michael Walzer, *Spheres of Justice: A Defense of Pluralism and Equality* (Basic Books, 1983).
[243] Sandel (n 242) x.

'equality of relationships' in the transnational context because of its tendency to define the relevant 'community' narrowly, but it, nonetheless, provides a helpful insight into what is problematic in the overly individualistic and reductionist conceptions of agency in EU law. The central theme in this criticism is that liberal theories presume the idea of the human subject as 'a sovereign agent of choice, a creature whose ends are chosen rather than given'.[244] On this basis, it has been suggested that the liberal account of justice fails to recognise 'intersubjective' forms of self-understanding.[245] In the context of distributive justice, this point has been developed further by noting that human agents depend on society in order to be able to make any contribution to it.[246] Charles Taylor has captured the essence of this argument in his statement that 'what man derives from society is not some aid in realizing his good, but the very possibility of being an agent'.[247]

What is central to these authors' ideas is their emphasis on the fact that full social and political agency is only possible 'intersubjectively', ie in relation to other agents. This critique lays the ground for the claim that every theory of justice must include 'a theory of the person, or more precisely, a theory of the moral subject'.[248] This insight into the communitarian ideals of agency directs our attention to the question of what kind of view of the human subject is embedded in the status of EU citizenship and the EU principle of equality. Is it correct that the parameters for EU citizens' agency are currently reduced to the individual responsibility to be an active agent who can prove economic or social belonging? Or, what must be true for a subject for whom activity is the first virtue? And, furthermore, is this really what EU citizenship is meant to be all about? This critique of the parameters for EU citizens' agency is in line with the social realist argument that the notions of agency and subjectivity are intertwined and that it is impossible to understand one without understanding the other. It follows from this that the activity-based conception of equality and its narrow and individualistic view of EU citizens' agency are harmful because they fail to recognise the inherent connection between EU citizens' agency and subjectivity and, thus, leave EU citizens deprived as equal subjects of EU law and European integration.

An alternative way of understanding EU citizens' agency is to examine the conditions under which EU citizens can become full and equal subjects of European integration. The term 'subject' refers to 'that which thinks or feels as opposed to

[244] Ibid 22.

[245] Ibid 62. However, Sandel also discusses what he calls '"intrasubjective" forms of self-understanding'. He suggests that 'to be capable of a more thoroughgoing reflection, we cannot be wholly unencumbered subjects of possession, individuated in advance and given prior to our ends, but must be subjects constituted in part by our central aspirations and attachments, always open, indeed vulnerable, to growth and transformation in the light of revised self-understanding'. Ibid 172. The connection between 'inter-subjective' and 'intra-subjective' subjectivity is discussed in more detail in the context of EU citizens' subjectivity in Chapter 4, p 135.

[246] Charles Taylor, *Philosophy and the Human Sciences—Philosophical Papers II* (Cambridge University Press, 1985) 314.

[247] Ibid 292.

[248] Sandel (n 242) 48.

the object of thinking; the self or the mind'. Subjectivity can accordingly be defined as 'a sense of self constituted and interpreted through conscious and unconscious experiences'.[249] Recognising EU citizens as subjects of EU law and European integration would mean that (1) they can be seen as constituting integration not just by acting and doing but also by 'having and being'[250] and that (2) they must not be treated as a thing or an object but as persons. The status of EU citizenship remains normatively indeterminate in so far as EU law both affirms and rejects EU citizens as subjects of European integration. This indeterminacy is at least partly due to the failure to discuss what 'equality between citizens' means in the context of transnational cooperation in general and that of European integration in particular. The liberal conceptions of equal (economic) opportunities and individual choices have too easily been accepted as a natural and indispensable interpretation of EU citizens' agency. This hides the need to explore more relational justifications for EU citizens' access to equal treatment as legitimate interpretations of the objectives and values of European integration.

The intellectual credibility of the (non-economic) constitution of the EU depends essentially on whether EU citizens can be recognised as full subjects of EU law and European integration—as opposed to being its mere objects.[251] This argument has its basis in the early case law and the Court's famous declaration of the European Economic Community as a new legal order, 'the subjects of which comprise not only Member States but also their nationals'.[252] However, both the philosophical foundations and the practical applications of transnational subjectivity are currently underdeveloped. In particular, it is important to find out whether the current bias in favour of individual interests and opportunities in justifying access to equal treatment under EU law (through individual rights some EU citizens can invoke against some Member States) could be replaced with a more relational understanding of what constitutes relevant agency within the EU. Part II of this book will discuss how recognising the connection between EU citizens' agency and their subjectivity as EU citizens can provide a relational justification for equal treatment between EU citizens. This approach to EU citizenship still has the individual at its centre, but this individual is no longer deemed to be an 'unencumbered Self', as will be seen in the next chapter.

The analysis of EU citizenship in terms of subjectivity must not be understood as an argument against the active nature of citizenship[253] as a whole, but rather,

[249] Shona Hunter, 'A Critical Analysis of Approaches to the Concept of Social Identity in Social Policy' (2003) 23 *Critical Social Policy* 322, 328.

[250] Gabriel Marcel, *Being and Having* (Dacre Press Westminster, 1949).

[251] See more about this in Chapters 4 and 5.

[252] 26/62 *NV Algemene Transport- en Expeditie Onderneming van Gend & Loos v Netherlands Inland Revenue Administration* [1963] ECR 3.

[253] See eg Bryan Turner, 'Outline of a Theory of Citizenship' (1990) 24 *Sociology* 189 about conceptualising citizenship on the passive/active and the public/private axes.

as an argument against the conceptualisation of EU citizenship through a narrow and individualistic view of agency, ie through the duty to be (economically or socially) active in order to exist in any meaningful way within the legal system of the EU. It has been shown in Section 3.4 that the focus on individual activity in the interpretation of the EU principle of equality fails to justify EU citizens' access to equal treatment in relational terms, that is, as a matter of political and social justice. It now becomes clear that this failure is significant because it neglects the intersubjective dimension of EU citizens' agency and, thus, leaves them deprived as full subjects of EU law and European integration. As the social realist account of agency indicates, and as will be discussed in more detail in Chapter four, a more balanced view of agency in the case of EU citizens can be based on the fact that human agents can be recognised as persons and subjects only in and through their social relationships with other agents. The next chapter will develop this argument further by examining the conditions under which EU citizenship could be (re)constructed as a source of subjectivity, instead of being a mere transitory status under which EU citizens can strive for the more privileged status of a 'Union worker'.

3.6 CONCLUSION

This chapter provided a theoretical account of the EU equality problem by asking what the conditions and limitations on EU citizens' general right to equal treatment, above all the requirement of sufficient economic or social integration in the form of a 'real link', tell us about the EU principle of equality and the status of EU citizenship. First, the chapter pointed out that the requirement of activity trumps the status of EU citizenship when it comes to the enjoyment of EU citizens' right to equal treatment because the enjoyment of EU citizens' right to equal treatment is dependent on individual responsibility to be active either economically or socially. Secondly, a more philosophical critique of the EU principle of equality demonstrated that the focus on individual responsibility is problematic because it fails to recognise equality as a 'normative ideal of human relationships', leaving unanswered the question of how EU citizenship transforms the idea of 'meaningful relationships' for the purpose of equal treatment within the EU. The common denominator underlying both the structural and the substantive Equality Problem is that the activity-based conception of equality fails to answer the relational question of what equality means between EU citizens.

The inquiry into philosophical egalitarianism helped us to frame the crux of the EU equality problem as follows: The responsibility-sensitive theories of equal opportunities focus on the conditions under which the agent is regarded to be responsible for his/her choices. A similar tendency to focus on the agent's individual responsibility to be active at the expense of 'other egalitarian values' is a distinctive feature of the EU principle of equality. First, it is questionable whether

EU citizens enjoy equal opportunities to integrate into the host Member State and, thus, to qualify for equal treatment under EU law. Secondly, even if that is the case, the current emphasis on the individual responsibility in defining the limits of EU citizens' right to equal treatment leads to a narrow and individualistic view of agency in EU law. This is problematic because the reductionist view of agency leaves EU citizens deprived as persons and as full and equal subjects of EU law. A more balanced view of EU citizens' agency will need to reconstruct EU citizenship as a source of political and legal subjectivity. The next chapter will develop this argument further.

Part II

EU Citizenship as a Source of Subjectivity

4

(Re)constructing EU Citizenship as a Source of Subjectivity

4.1 INTRODUCTION

THE CURRENT FOCUS on *ex ante* integration as a condition for equal treatment in EU law has its basis in a narrow and reductionist view of agency. It is widely accepted that social relationships are relevant for the development of personhood and human dignity. But it is less clear whether the political argument for more just and equal relationships between EU citizens can be justified independently of both the universalist ideal of shared humanity and the particularist claim of cultural or ethnic or democratic belonging. This chapter shows that shifting the focus to EU citizens' subjecthood can provide us with a mediating position between cosmopolitan universalism, on the one hand, and moral particularism, on the other, in justifying the equality of relationships between EU citizens. In other words, this chapter derives the normativity of just and equal relationships between EU citizens from EU citizens becoming subjects of European integration, rather than from ideas of personhood or human dignity as such. At the same time, however, it will be seen that treating EU citizens as persons is a necessary, even if not sufficient, precondition for their full subjectivity as EU citizens.

This chapter explores the conditions for EU citizens' subjectivity as EU citizens in the light of developmental psychology and phenomenological philosophy. First, Section 4.2 uses the feminist critique of citizenship to further explain the connection between EU citizens' agency and their subjectivity. The feminist emphasis on interdependent social relations in which citizens' subjectivity and agency are constituted lays the foundations for further analysis of EU citizens' subjectivity. Section 4.3 takes this approach further by considering what it would mean for EU citizenship that the psycho-dynamic constitution of subjectivity through the identification with the 'Other' at the early stages of human development is often reflected in the later constitution of political and legal subjectivity. This analysis is based on a brief overview of how subject-formation is explained in object-relations theory and structural psychoanalytic theory. It will be suggested on this basis that the analytic categories of a 'relational subject' and a 'subject-in-process' are helpful for understanding EU citizens as emergent subjects of European integration if the constitution of transnational subjectivity is a complex cognitive process which depends on the self's relation to the 'Other', both inter- and intra-subjectively.

Section 4.4 concludes the chapter by discussing in more detail what the subject's identification with the 'Other' could mean in the case of EU citizens. Section 4.4.1 argues that it is a necessary precondition for EU citizens' subjectivity to treat them as persons. This proposition will then be developed further by discussing Emmanuel Levinas' philosophical argument that the subjects as persons can come into existence only through a 'second-person perspective' when they accept responsibility for the 'Other' who is still a stranger to the self. Section 4.4.2 will further consider what ethical implications this argument of a 'second-person perspective' as a source of subjectivity can have for the EU principle of equality. It will be concluded that becoming EU citizens as full and equal subjects of European integration requires the adoption of a 'second-person perspective' which can create 'meaningful relationships' between EU citizens even in the absence of a full democratic pedigree and which can thus legitimise a more relational interpretation of the EU principle of equality. This analysis is based on the view that the experience of otherness is particularly pertinent in the transnational context and that interaction between EU citizens is likely to activate the inter- and intra-subjective complexities of the relationship between the Self and the Other.

4.2 SUBJECTIVITY IN AND THROUGH RELATIONSHIPS: A FEMINIST APPROACH TO EU CITIZENSHIP

The individualistic view of EU citizens' agency is problematic because it fails to do justice to the inherent connection between citizens' agency and their subjectivity. Feminist scholars are particularly concerned with the ideas of agency, subjectivity, and social practices and structures, and what their mutual connections are.[1] This section introduces the feminist critique of citizenship as the analytic framework within which the idea of EU citizens as full and equal subjects of EU law and European integration can be developed further. First, it will be seen how the feminist theory has conceptualised citizenship by emphasising (1) that agency essentially defines citizenship and (2) that citizens' agency is connected to their sense of subjectivity (Section 4.2.1). It will then be discussed in more detail how interdependent social relations are seen as a source of subjectivity and agency, and how these relationships shape our citizenship in a fundamental way (Section 4.2.2). The constructive potential of social relationships can provide a basis for rethinking EU citizens as subjects of EU law and European integration. At the same time, the feminist emphasis on human interdependence will provide a basis for a more substantive critique of EU citizens' agency in so far as the latter builds on the ideas of individual activity, responsibility, and self-sufficiency.

[1] See eg Philipa Rothfield, 'Feminism, Subjectivity, and Sexual Experience' in Sneja Gunew (ed), *Feminist Knowledge: Critique and Construct* (Routledge, 1990) 123.

4.2.1 Citizenship, Agency, and Subjectivity: A Triangle

The theoretical analysis of the EU principle of equality in the previous chapter conceptualised the crux of the EU equality problem as follows: the way in which the parameters for EU citizens' agency are defined in EU law ignores the fact that the development of citizens' social and political agency is connected to their sense of subjectivity and is therefore inherently relational.[2] The notions of agency which challenge the atomistic, individualised subject of liberal political philosophy can be derived from several different intellectual traditions, including social constructivism, communitarianism, feminist ethics of care, philosophical and political personalism, and developmental psychology. What is common to these different accounts is the idea that 'subjects come to understand themselves to an important degree through their relationships with others'.[3] In particular, feminism and communitarianism have a lot in common because both underline the importance of 'context, care, and community' and both adopt a critical stance towards many aspects of political liberalism.[4] However, there are also considerable differences in their conceptions of the self, social relations, and political community.[5] These differences have been sketched by noting that 'communitarians are concerned with the *loss* of "traditional boundaries", while feminists are concerned with the *costs* of those boundaries'.[6]

The feminist interest in the 'cost' of the traditional boundaries explains why feminism as a critical theory is so well suited for analysing the question of how EU citizenship transforms meaningful political and legal relationships and what this transformation means for the EU principle of equality. It has been seen in Chapters two and three that the issues of 'similarity vs. difference' and 'belonging vs. otherness' lie at the heart of the EU equality problem. But it has also been seen in these chapters that the mere reference to more explicit comparability between EU citizens is an analytical cul-de-sac if we want to affirm the value of diversity at the heart of EU citizenship. This section further explores the triangular relationship

[2] For instance, Margaret Archer argues that 'social agency' must always be viewed 'in terms of interrelations'. Margaret Archer, *Being Human: The Problem of Agency* (Cambridge University Press, 2000) 283–84. At the same time, however, she also claims that 'without personification no social identity derives from any role'. Ibid 294.

[3] Selma Sevenhuijsen, *Citizenship and the Ethics of Care* (Routledge, 1998) 61.

[4] Penny A Weiss, 'Feminism and Communitarianism' in Penny A Weiss and Marilyn Friedman (eds), *Feminism and Community* (Temple University Press, 1995) 161.

[5] Ibid 161–62. The ideal of community is not just a friend but also a foe for many feminist thinkers. It has been argued that instead of embracing a 'participatory democratic communitarianism' as the vision of the ideal society, feminists should argue for a 'politics of difference'. See eg Iris-Marion Young, 'The Ideal of Community and the Politics of Difference' in Linda J Nicholson (ed), *Feminism/Postmodernism* (Routledge, 1990) 301. At the core of Young's critique of community lies the claim that the ideal of community 'denies the difference between subjects'. Young, 'The Ideal of Community and the Politics of Difference' 302.

[6] Weiss (n 4) 167. See also Marilyn Friedman, 'Feminism and Modern Friendship: Dislocating the Community' in Cass R Sunstein (ed), *Feminism & Political Theory* (The University Chicago Press, 1982) 147 for a critique of the communitarian emphasis on the 'specific communities of family, neighbourhood, and nation' as 'troubling paradigms of social relationship'.

between citizenship, agency, and subjectivity in the light of a feminist critique of citizenship. For this analysis, it is useful to bear in mind that most feminist scholars adopt a constructive perspective, according to which 'how things naturally are is instead an expression of a historically specific way of structuring some set of social interactions'.[7] This emphasis on the constructive potential of social relationships for citizens' agency and their subjectivity is particularly interesting when we explore the status of EU citizenship which is clearly a constructed, rather than organic, source of subjectivity.

Feminist theory is relevant to the analysis of EU citizenship both methodologically because of its constructive starting point and substantively because of its critique of assimilation. Most ideologies that emphasise the pre-political aspects of identity base equality on citizens' 'presumed commonality and sameness'.[8] What is too often neglected in the nationalist or communitarian accounts of citizenship is the understanding that these identities can also be transformed by 'the exercise of rights themselves and the practice of political agency'.[9] Moreover, the critics have noted that the 'equality of a shared identity', from which political solidarity emerges, is 'at least in part self-determined and chosen'[10] and that the 'communities of choice' can lead to the 'reconstitution' of subjects.[11] These arguments about the constructed nature of political identity are relevant for EU citizenship because it cannot rely on a sense of belonging based on the shared 'culture' or 'origin'. However, it is not enough to simply refer to the possibility of the 'choosing of a political identity',[12] but we must also explore the conditions under which this choice becomes possible in the case of EU citizens, that is, their agency and subjectivity as EU citizens. The emergence of transnational political identity can thus be understood as one particular mode or expression of EU citizens' subjectivity as EU citizens.

Feminist theory has sometimes criticised the vision of the citizen as the bearer of rights on the basis that it reinforces the liberal principles of individual freedom and formal equality.[13] However, a response to this criticism is that citizenship

[7] Naomi Scheman, 'Individualism and the Objects of Psychology' in Sandra Harding and Merrill B Hintikka (eds), *Discovering Reality: Feminist Perspectives on Epistemology, Metaphysics, Methodology, and Philosophy of Science* (D Reidel Publishing Company, 1983) 231.

[8] Seyla Benhabib, *The Rights of Others—Aliens, Residents, and Citizens* (Cambridge University Press, 2004) 62.

[9] Ibid 168.

[10] Adrian Oldfield, *Citizenship and Community—Civic Republicanism and the Modern World* (Routledge, 1990) 7.

[11] Friedman (n 6) 157. Friedman also argues that 'resources and skills derived from communities which are not merely found and discovered may equally well contribute to the constitution of identity'. Ibid 153.

[12] Oldfield (n 10) 8.

[13] For instance, May Dietz has noted that '[o]nce in the domain of "equal access talk", we are tied into a whole network of liberal concepts—rights, interests, contracts, individualism, representative government, negative liberty'. Mary Dietz, 'Context Is All: Feminism and Theories of Citizenship' (1987) 116 *Daedalus* 1. However, unlike both the Marxist and maternal feminists, Dietz argues for 'the virtues, relations and practices that are expressly political and, more explicitly, participatory and democratic'. Anne Phillips is another author who links feminism with democracy. In Anne Phillips,

rights also enable people to 'act as agents'.[14] Historically, the relationship between feminism and citizenship has been 'ambivalent'.[15] The concern has been that the idea of citizenship might not adequately accommodate human diversity.[16] This concern for particularity has its roots in the old controversy over whether the claims for women's inclusion in public life should have been based on their equality with men or on their difference to men.[17] In practice, the feminist interest in diversity and difference has meant that feminist theory directs attention to the question of 'otherness'[18] which is often undermined both in the liberal and the communitarian accounts of citizenship. Feminist theory can therefore provide a useful critical tool for understanding the reception of difference even outside the gender-context.

For the first feminist thinkers, the liberation of women was identified as access to civil and political rights on equal terms with men.[19] However, the later feminist critique of political theory has distanced itself from the liberal and contractarian ideas of equality and rationality on the basis that they are 'deeply marred by masculine biases about what it means to be human'.[20] The feminist concern is that the liberal self as 'the equal and abstract bearer of rights' fails to pay adequate attention to the identity of this self 'as a gendered subject'.[21] On this basis, it has been argued that the modern political theory advances an ideal of citizenship which fails to recognise 'most particular aspects of a person'.[22] The analysis of EU citizenship shows that the assimilationist tendencies of a liberal conception of citizenship are not limited to the mere gender context. This means that the way in which feminist scholarship has problematised the requirement of assimilation as part of the

Engendering Democracy (Polity Press, 1991) 159, she notes that '[f]eminism multiplies the places within which democracy appears relevant'.

[14] Ruth Lister, *Citizenship: Feminist Perspective* (Palgrave Macmillan, 1997) 37. Lister underlines that '[c]itizenship as the expression of agency can contribute to the recasting of women as political actors'. Thus, for Lister, '[t]o be a citizen, in the legal and sociological sense, means to enjoy the rights of citizenship necessary for agency and social and political participation'. Ibid 39 and 42.

[15] Birte Siim, *Gender and Citizenship: Politics and Agency in France, Britain and Denmark* (Cambridge University Press, 2000) 1. The feminist critique of citizenship rejects the 'false universalism' of the traditional citizenship theory. For instance, Ruth Lister explains how feminist scholars object to 'the way in which abstraction has served to hide the essentially male characteristics of the individual qua citizen'. Lister (n 14) 68 and 71.

[16] Lister (n 14) 89.

[17] Ibid 93.

[18] For instance, Seyla Benhabib has noted that the need to take the standpoint of the other in moral deliberation has been restricted to the 'generalized other' at the expense of ignoring the 'moral identity of the concrete other'. Seyla Benhabib, 'The Generalized and the Concrete Other: The Kohlberg-Gilligan Controversy and Feminist Theory' in Seyla Benhabib and Drucilla Cornell (eds), *Feminism as Critique: Essays on the Politics of Gender in Late-Capitalist Societies* (Polity Press, 1987) 91–92.

[19] See more about this eg in Iris-Marion Young, 'Impartiality and the Civic Public: Some Implications of Feminist Critiques of Moral and Political Theory' in Benhabib and Cornell (n 18) 58.

[20] Ibid 58.

[21] Dietz (n 13) 10. See also Carole Pateman, *The Disorder of Women: Democracy, Feminism and Political Theory* (Polity Press, 1989) 220–21 and Susan Moller Okin, *Women in Western Political Thought* (Princeton University Press, 1979).

[22] Young (n 19) 74.

constitution of political identity can help us to rethink the boundaries of national and transnational citizenship.

At the heart of the feminist critique lies the concern that the general, human standpoint is assimilated with the masculine viewpoint 'thereby confining the feminine to the structural position of the "other"', meaning that 'the masculine qua human is taken as the "norm", and the feminine qua other is seen as marking the "difference"'.[23] From this common starting point, however, different feminist traditions have made radically different claims about the nature of citizenship, agency, and subjectivity—as well as about the relationship between the three. A central distinction can be made between liberal feminism and the so-called maternalist communitarian approach. The former has focused on criticising the classical notions of citizenship based on women's exclusion and male domination as integral aspects of modern political philosophy.[24] The latter advocates caring and other 'practices of mothering'[25] as central political values.[26] Moreover, different forms of socialist,[27] Marxist,[28] and radical[29] feminism, as well as the postmodern theories[30] that focus on deconstructing essentialist (gender) categories and differences, have also emerged within feminist theory. For the purposes of this chapter, it is important to note that, despite sharing the critical stance towards the unity of the liberal self, the feminist and postmodern philosophies differ radically in their approaches to the constitution of self and subjectivity.[31]

In general, feminist authors, such as Judith Butler, distinguish themselves from the postmodern deconstruction of subjectivity by noting that 'to claim that the

[23] Rosi Braidotti, *Embodiment and Sexual Difference in Contemporary Feminist Theory* (Columbia University Press, 1994) 152.

[24] eg Martha C Nussbaum, *Sex & Social Justice* (Oxford University Press, 1999).

[25] eg Virginia Held, *The Ethics of Care—Personal, Political, and Global* (Oxford University Press, 2006).

[26] See eg Sara Ruddick, 'Maternal Thinking' in Marilyn Pearsall (ed), *Women and Values Readings in Recent Feminist Philosophy* (Wadsworth Publishing Company, 1999) for the argument that 'maternal' is a 'social category' and that it must shape a theory of justice. See also Nel Noddings, 'Ethics from the Standpoint of Women' in Pearsall (n 26) who argues for 'an ethics of care based on women's traditional role as nurturers'. A helpful summary of maternal feminism is included in Jane Mansbridge, 'Feminism and Democratic Community' in Weiss and Friedman (n 4) 350.

[27] The socialist feminist critique of citizenship builds on the idea that 'male dominance is intrinsic rather than accidental to classical capitalism' and that the concept of citizenship has, therefore 'an implicit gender subtext'. See eg Nancy Fraser, 'What's Critical about Critical Theory? The Case of Habermas and Gender' in Benhabib and Cornell (n 18) 45–46.

[28] See eg Zillah R Eisenstein, *The Radical Future of Liberal Feminism* (Northern University Press, 1986). The relationships between feminist theories and Marxism is complex and it remains controversial how far gender can be unified with class and whether the feminist concept of reproduction must also challenge the primacy of production within Marxist theories.

[29] eg Catherine MacKinnon, *Toward a Feminist Theory of the State* (Harvard University Press, 1991).

[30] eg Judith Butler, 'Contingent Foundations: Feminism and the Question of "Postmodernism"' in Judith Butler and Joan W Scott (eds), *Feminists Theorize The Political* (Routledge, 1992).

[31] Jane Flax, *Thinking Fragments: Psychoanalysis, Feminism, and Postmodernism in the Contemporary West* (University of California Press, 1990) 15. Postmodernists reject what they call the 'metaphysics of presence', including the 'philosophies of mind, truth, language, and the Real that underlie and ground any such transcendental or foundational claims'. Instead, postmodernists view self as a 'position in language' (Derrida) or as an 'effect of discourse' (Foucault). Ibid 35 and 231.

subject is constituted is not to claim that it is determined; on the contrary, the constituted character of the subject is the very precondition of its agency'.[32] This shift from 'deconstruction' to 'reconstruction'[33] makes the feminist critique of citizenship particularly relevant for the analysis of EU citizenship. Namely, unlike postmodernism, feminism cannot altogether deconstruct the claim for agency and subjectivity. In contrast, the need to deconstruct the essentialist (gender) categories and difference must be balanced against the danger of making the feminist agency disappear. The feminist critique of citizenship as agency therefore provides an analytic framework within which the current parameters for EU citizens' agency can be critically assessed in the light of their subjectivity.

The ideal of agency lies at the heart of the feminist critique of citizenship. In particular, feminist scholars have expressed the concern that the discussion on citizenship has focused on the 'questions of identity' at the expense of the 'questions of agency and morality'.[34] According to them, it is questionable whether the concept of identity can provide an adequate basis for political action.[35] At the same time, however, it has been noted that human identity cannot be reduced to 'its capacity for agency alone'.[36] For instance, Seyla Benhabib concludes that '[i]dentity does not refer to my potential for choice alone, but to the actuality of my choices'.[37] The inadequacy of the traditional notions of citizenship to accommodate 'vulnerability, ambiguity and dependency'[38] illustrate that the relationship between 'agency' and the 'conditions within which that potential originates' are central themes of the feminist understanding of citizenship.[39] It is therefore important to direct more attention to the feminist claim that our understanding of citizenship must build on a more realistic view of a person whose existence is relational rather than atomistic.

4.2.2 Affirming Intersubjective Relations Between Citizens

The attempt to reconstruct the parameters for relevant political and social agency has led feminist scholars to show particular interest in '*how* social selves are constituted, toward what ends, and with what costs and benefits'.[40] The feminist

[32] Butler (n 30) 12.

[33] Seyla Benhabib and Drucilla Cornell, 'Introduction—Beyond the Politics of Gender' in Benhabib and Cornell (n 18) 1.

[34] Sevenhuijsen (n 3) 25.

[35] Ibid 14.

[36] Seyla Benhabib, *Situating the Self: Gender, Community and Postmodernism in Contemporary Ethics* (Polity Press, 1992) 161.

[37] Ibid 161.

[38] Sevenhuijsen (n 3) 57.

[39] Shelley Budgeon, *Third Wave Feminism and the Politics of Gender in Late Modernity* (Palgrave Macmillan, 2011) 139.

[40] Weiss (n 4) 169.

critique of the self is usually directed against the ideal of '*homo economicus*—the free and rational chooser and actor whose desires are ranked in a coherent order and whose aim is to maximize desire satisfaction'.[41] A similar ideal of 'Economic Man' is familiar to us from EU law. It is problematic how this conception of the self disengages the individual from both 'personal relationships' and from 'social forces' in general.[42] One of the major contributions of the feminist critique of citizenship has therefore been to strengthen the link between social rights and the democratic citizenship.[43] This development is closely connected to the interest in women's agency in the feminist rethinking of citizenship.[44] The notion of agency can arguably provide 'a bridge between the social and the political'.[45] By defining citizens' agency inter-subjectively, the feminist critique of citizenship can help us to rethink the parameters for relevant agency in the case of EU citizens.

The feminist critique of citizenship attempts to challenge the vision of the 'unencumbered Self' that is arguably advocated by liberal political thought.[46] For feminists, the liberal contractual models of human relations are based on 'a certain historically specific conception of "economic man" as representative of humanity'.[47] According to this criticism, the ideals of 'separateness' and 'independence' embedded in the liberal view of the self, have never been true for women to the same extent as for men.[48] The feminist idea of citizenship responds to the idea of independence by arguing that citizens' agency and subjectivity can only be developed in and through social relationships.[49] It is this attempt to reconceptualise the link between '(economic) independence' and 'citizenship' which can help us to reconceptualise the relevant parameters for EU citizens' agency through their subjectivity.[50] Namely, for feminists, the question is not one of 'dependence versus

[41] Diana Tietjens Meyers, 'Introduction' in Diana Tietjens Meyers (ed), *Feminist Rethinking the Self* (Westview Press, 1997) 2.

[42] Ibid.

[43] Siim (n 15) 1.

[44] Ibid 2. The feminist vision of agency has its roots in a 'normative vision that aims at increasing women's political participation and representation in politics'. Ibid.

[45] Ibid 158.

[46] Benhabib and Cornell (n 33) 10. This criticism has its roots in the claim that both the market liberals (eg Hayek and Nozick) and the welfare liberals (eg Rawls and Dworkin) 'proceed from a conception of the self as public persona, as a bearer of individual rights'. Ibid.

[47] Virginia Held, 'Non-Contractual Society: A Feminist View' in Weiss and Friedman (n 4) 209–10. This critique is based on the view that the individualistic notion of the self is connected to the human development in 'a patriarchal culture where childcare in primarily in the hands of women'. See eg Scheman (n 7) 230.

[48] Benhabib and Cornell (n 33) 12.

[49] Ann Ferguson, 'Can I Choose Who I Am? And How Would That Empower Me? Gender, Race, Identities and the Self' in Ann Garry and Marilyn Pearsall (eds), *Women Knowledge, and Reality: Explorations in Feminist Philosophy* (Routledge, 1996) 111.

[50] Martha Ackelsberg, *Resisting Citizenship—Feminist Essays on Politics, Community, and Democracy* (Routledge, 2010) 61. On this basis, it has also been argued that 'engaging in waged' must not be seen as 'a necessary condition for individuals to deserve the social standing and to warrant the rights and dignity associated with citizenship'. Uma Narayan, 'Towards a Feminist Vision of Citizenship: Rethinking the Implications of Dignity, Political Participation, and Nationality' in Mary Lyndon Shanley and Uma Narayan (eds), *Reconstructing Political Theory—Feminist Perspectives* (Polity Press, 1997) 50–51.

independence' because 'virtually no one in this society is totally independent in any meaningful sense'.[51] In contrast, feminists argue that 'societies' consist of 'networks of relationships, characterized by *inter* dependence'.[52]

It has been noted that excluding the relations of dependency from the 'circumstances of justice' will distort our understanding of 'the sort of individual who warranted the dignity of citizenship'.[53] Thus, the feminist theories of citizenship refuse to include individual dignity and worth in the capacity to be 'autonomous' and 'self-governing'.[54] What is problematic from the feminist perspective is 'not dependency, per se, but *unequal* dependence resulting in relationships of domination and subordination'.[55] The feminist vision of social policy is focused on enabling people 'to achieve relationships of meaningful interdependence and mutuality'.[56] Similarly, it needs to be considered whether the stark dichotomy between 'dependence' and 'independence' could be replaced with the ideal of 'interdependence' when we consider justifications for EU citizens' access to equal treatment under EU law. What remains of this section will discuss in more detail how a more realistic view of human interdependence in the case of EU citizens can complete the ideals of individual activity, responsibility, and economic self-sufficiency.

What is central to the feminist approach is the claim that human agency that is relevant to citizenship is constituted in 'social and cultural relations'.[57] This tendency to see relationships as constitutive for citizens' subjectivity and, thus, for their agency, forms the basis of a specific ideal of the 'ethics of care' which inspires many feminist accounts of citizenship. Those feminists who defend 'care' as a practice of moral thinking argue that care involves a 'distinctive moral orientation' towards other persons.[58] All of these accounts of 'caring' underline the importance of the 'ability to adopt the standpoint of others'.[59] This approach was originally rooted in Carol Gilligan's now contested argument that two different modes of moral reasoning are typically reflected in feminine and masculine thought.[60] But the major theorists of care have rejected the simplistic claim that the differences between the feminist 'ethics of care' and the liberal 'ethics of justice' could be derived from 'invariable differences' between the moral thinking of men and

[51] Ackelsberg (n 50) 67.
[52] Ibid.
[53] Narayan (n 50) 52.
[54] Ibid 53.
[55] Ibid 68.
[56] Ibid 69.
[57] Lister (n 14) 38.
[58] Alison Jaggar, 'Caring as a Feminist Practice of Moral Reason' in Virginia Held (ed), *Justice and Care—Essential Readings in Feminist Ethics* (Westview Press, 1995) 180.
[59] Lister (n 14) 103.
[60] Carol Gilligan, *In a Different Voice—Psychological Theory of Women's Development* (Harvard University Press, 1982) 179. Carol Gilligan criticised Lawrence Kohlberg's theory of moral development by distinguishing between the ethical orientation of justice and rights and the ethical orientation of care. She argued further that women's moral development would in general come closer to a 'vision of moral maturity that views the self as a being immersed in a network of relationships with others'. For further analysis and critique of Gilligan's argument, see eg Benhabib (n 36) 149.

women.[61] In contrast, the idea of care has been generalised and contextualised politically. For instance, Joan Tronto has suggested that caring as a political perspective can provide a new insight into the principles of justice because it requires us to start from the 'standpoint of the one needing care and attention'.[62]

Thus, the relationship between justice and care ethics is more complex than some of the early care theorists were willing to acknowledge.[63] The values of impartiality and neutrality may often need to overcome the particularity of any specific situation in the application of the principles of justice. What is nonetheless interesting from the perspective of EU citizenship is the way in which the care-thinking underlines the reality of human life as fundamentally interdependent. To adopt a particular standpoint is both the most 'distinctive' and the most 'controversial' feature of care ethics.[64] It has been noted that, although some theorists envision how care-thinking could expand our 'moral imagination' and could thus apply to 'large-scale social or global issues', that would be in conflict with the importance of the 'characteristically interactive and personal relation' which is characteristic of care-thinking.[65] However, Tronto, for instance, has replied to this criticism that adopting the practice of care as one of the 'qualities necessary for democratic citizens to live together well in pluralistic society' would change not just the 'conception of self' but also 'relations with others'.[66] On this basis, she claims that '[r]ather than assuming the fiction that all citizens are equal, a care perspective would have us recognize the achievement of equality as a political goal'.[67]

The arguments for adopting the standpoint of the other have their roots in a relational view of the self. It is characteristic of care ethics that the 'interests of the self' are regarded as inherently connected to the interests of others.[68] Social relations are seen as part of what constitutes identity, and autonomy is defined as the

[61] Jaggar (n 58) 182. One approach is to view them as 'different aspects of moral reasoning'. Another approach suggests that they 'originate from the experience of public and private life respectively' (Ibid 185).

[62] Joan Tronto, *Moral Boundaries—A Political Argument for an Ethic of Care* (Routledge, 1993) 19.

[63] It has been underlined that '[m]ost proponents of the ethics of care now dispute the possibility of any easy synthesis of care with justice' (Jaggar (n 58) 187). Virginia Held is one of those feminist thinkers who argue that the ethics of care is a 'distinct moral theory' and not 'a concern that can be added on to or included within other more established approaches' (Held (n 25) 3). But even she acknowledges that care may not in itself contain 'adequate theoretical resources for dealing with issues of justice'. However, according to Held, the idea of care can nonetheless be seen as 'the wider and deeper ethics within which justice should be sought'. Held (n 25) 17.

[64] Jaggar (n 58) 180.

[65] Ibid 197. It has also been noted that care ethics may struggle with distinguishing between 'felt or expressed needs' and 'genuine needs' (Ibid 189). Moreover, care ethics often fails to establish 'how to identify' morally relevant care (Ibid 192). Despite this criticism, Virginia Held, for instance, has envisioned 'how caring relations extend—to the social ties that bind groups together, to the bonds on which political and social institutions can be built, and even to the global concerns that citizens of the world can share'. Held (n 25) 31. Her argument is two-fold. Firstly, she notes that '[c]aring relations form the small societies of family and friendship on which larger societies depend'. Secondly, she suggests that '[c]aring relations of a weaker but still evident kind between more distant persons allow them to trust one another enough to live in peace and respect each other's rights'. Ibid 43.

[66] Tronto (n 62) 161–62.

[67] Ibid 164.

[68] Jaggar (n 58) 188.

capacity 'to reshape and cultivate new relations'.[69] At the same time, it has been noted that the political idea of care cannot be equated with 'benevolence' because it describes 'a social relation' rather than 'an individual disposition'.[70] In practice, the way in which agency is constituted under the ethics of care is connected with a specific view of moral subjectivity which leads to a 'relational image of human nature' which can be contrasted with the 'individualized subject of liberal political philosophy'.[71] Thus, the ethics of care views persons as 'interdependent'.[72] This means that persons are 'at least partly constituted by their social ties'.[73] From this starting point, it can be argued that the current parameters for EU citizens' agency are distorted '[i]n equating dependence with weakness and incapacity for citizenship'.[74] This defect becomes apparent if we consider the way in which the needy and economically dependent EU citizens are currently excluded from being recognised as relevant agents in the EU.

In sum, the way in which feminist theory highlights the connection between the social and political dimensions of citizenship through the relational notion of agency provides a basis for a critique of individual activity and economic self-sufficiency as the main parameters for EU citizens' agency. It has been seen in this section that the feminist idea of 'citizenship as agency' is connected to the argument that citizens' agency can only be developed in and through social relationships. However, for many feminists, the importance of social relationships for citizens' agency is rooted in the view that the constitution of subjectivity in relation to the 'Other' at the early levels of human development informs the later stages of cultural, political, and legal identity-building. This chapter will therefore move on to examine EU citizenship in the light of the psycho-dynamic theories of subject-formation that often underlie the feminist idea of 'citizenship as agency'.

Developmental psychology has provided an important analytical tool for feminist political theory and philosophy in its attempt to view human nature as a 'product of social relations in interaction with biology'.[75] Some feminist theorists still claim that the constitution of gender in modern societies is split between 'unencumbered' male selves and 'situated' female selves. However, it is widely acknowledged that the relationship between the biological and the cultural attributes of gender is more complex than this. It has been noted that '[t]he simple identification of the subject with its social roles reinstates the very logic of identity that feminists have sought to critique in their examinations of the psychosexual

[69] Held (n 25) 14.

[70] Ibid 42.

[71] Sevenhuijsen (n 3) 34.

[72] Held (n 25) 46.

[73] Ibid 46. For instance, Virginia Held captures this vision of relationality in the following statement: 'We can decide to treat such persons as individuals, to be the bearers of individual rights, for the sake of constructing just political and legal and other institutions. But we should not forget the reality and the morality this view obscures. Persons are relational and interdependent. Ibid 72.

[74] Lister (n 14) 109.

[75] Jane Flax, 'Political Philosophy and the Patriarchal Unconscious: A Psychoanalytic Perspective on Epistemology and Metaphysics' in Harding and Hintikka (n 7)249.

constitution of the gender.'[76] Thus, questioning the unity of the subject is one of the central themes in the work of feminist theorists. On a more constructive note, the feminist theory has challenged the logic of binary oppositions between the self and the Other by using the psycho-dynamic theories of subjectivity as analytical tools.[77]

Understanding the psycho-dynamic foundations of the feminist rethinking of citizenship is important for two reasons. Firstly, shifting the focus to the connection between citizens' agency and their subjectivity demonstrates that the feminist critique of citizenship has relevance outside the gender context. Secondly, and more importantly, this analysis illustrates how several political theorists take the leap from the psychological to the political by arguing that the constitution of human subjectivity in and through intimate social relations at the early level of human development has implications for how social relations in general inform and shape political identity-building. Their concern is that, as the (m)other has been 'internalised' by the child in early infancy and, in so far as patriarchy requires the rejection of the m/Other,[78] the relationship to the 'Other' becomes repressed 'as complete as possible so that this internal object can be kept separate from the conscious self'.[79] From this follows the claim that later attempts of political, legal, and cultural identity-building are often affected by the unconscious responses to the early interaction between the 'self' and the 'Other'.

4.3 SUBJECTIVITY AS A PROCESS: A PSYCHO-DYNAMIC APPROACH TO EU CITIZENSHIP

Psycho-dynamic theories of subject-formation are interested in the period of psychological development during which children become aware of themselves as social persons who are distinct from all others.[80] The central question in these theories is what constitutes the sense of a separate self/subject. The classic psycho-dynamic theories of subjectivity have two main branches. The object-relation theories see the 'relational life of the infant' prior to any 'psychic development', whereas

[76] Benhabib and Cornell (n 33) 13. Benhabib and Cornell also note that women have been more 'situated' than men in terms of social roles and expectations '[p]recisely because to be a biological female has always been interpreted in gendered terms as dictating a certain psychosexual and cultural identity'. Ibid 12.

[77] It is worth noting that feminist scholarship originally disregarded psychoanalysis. Until the early 1970s, most feminist scholars were more likely to be influenced by the so-called 'ego psychology' which views the ego as the 'centre of the self' and underlines the positive adaptation between 'inner psychic organization' and 'outer social organization' than by the psychoanalytic theories of the self. See further eg Hazel Rowley and Elizabeth Grosz, 'Psychoanalysis and Feminism' in Gunew (n 1) 181. However, Juliet Mitchell's book *Psychoanalysis and Feminism* (1974) changed this by suggesting that 'psychoanalysis is not a recommendation for a patriarchal society, but an analysis of one'. Juliet Mitchell, *Psychoanalysis and Feminism: Freud, Reich, Laing and Women* (Allen Lane, 1974) xv.

[78] Flax (n 75) 246.

[79] Ibid 246–47.

[80] Scheman (n 7) 236.

the Lacanian and post-Lacanian structural theorists emphasise the unconscious as a 'source of discontinuous and chaotic drives or significations'.[81] The object-relations theorists have taken root in Anglo-American feminism, whereas the Lacanian tradition has been more prominent in continental Europe, especially amongst French feminists. These two approaches to human development can be seen as opposites when it comes to the role of relatedness/inter-subjective relationships in constructing human subjectivity and identity. However, as analytical tools, both of them provide a valuable insight into the importance of the 'Other' for human subjectivity and for the development of the 'Self'.

Unlike developmental psychologists, political theorists do not need to choose between these two approaches to subject-formation. Instead, these two accounts of subjectivity together can help us to better understand the constitution of transnational subjectivity as a complex cognitive process both *between* subjects and *within* the subject.[82] Many political theorists now suggest that the development of political and legal subjectivity is linked to how human subjectivity is constituted psychologically.[83] At the heart of this critique lies the claim that '[k]nowing other people in relationships' has a crucial role in the production of human subjectivity and that more attention should be paid to the 'epistemic significance of early experiences with other people'.[84] This section will accordingly address the question of what it means for EU citizenship if the relationship to the 'Other' at the early level of human development is reflected in the later attempts of cultural, social, political, and legal identity-building. This analysis goes beyond the individual psychological need to examine (1) what theoretical principles of subjectivity can be drawn out of developmental psychology and (2) how these principles can be extrapolated to the theory of transnational subjectivity and identity-building.

The psycho-dynamic accounts of subjectivity will direct our attention to the complexity of human subjectivity. Firstly, it will be seen in Section 4.3.1 how the object-relations theory provides a basis for the concept of a 'relational subject', which suggests that the relationship to the 'Other' plays a positive role in constituting the subject's sense of self. The analytic category of a 'relational subject' allows us to view the relations to the 'Other' as a positive source of transnational subjectivity. Secondly, Section 4.3.2 will explain how the structural psychoanalytic accounts of human subjectivity assign a more negative role to the 'Other' in constituting human subjectivity. These theories focus on the unconscious split between

[81] See further eg Judith Butler, 'Gender, Trouble, Feminist Theory, and Psychoanalytic Discourse' in Nicholson (n 5) 328.

[82] These two psycho-dynamic accounts of subjectivity are discussed in this book because they inform the work of those political theorists who argue for more relational accounts of political subjectivity. It is important to note that they do not give a full or an up-to-date picture of debates on human subjectivity in developmental psychology.

[83] See eg Leonie Huddy, David O Sears and Jack S Levy, 'Introduction: Theoretical Foundations of Political Psychology' in Leonie Huddy, David O Sears and Jack S Levy (eds), *The Oxford Handbook of Political Psychology* (Oxford University Press, 2013).

[84] Lorraine Code, 'Taking Subjectivity into Account' in Ann Garry and Marilyn Pearsall (eds), *Women, Knowledge, and Reality: Explorations in Feminist Philosophy* (Routledge, 1996) 287.

the subject and the Other as a precondition for a sense of subjectivity. However, it will also be seen how the feminist rethinking of structural psychoanalytic theories through the idea of a 'subject-in-process'[85] reconciles the intrapersonal complexity of subject-formation with the importance of intersubjective relations for the constitution of subjectivity. The analytic category of a 'subject-in-process' requires that our account of transnational subjectivity also recognises the complex and partly unconscious dimensions of subjectivity. Lastly, Section 4.3.3 will consider these theoretical considerations about EU citizens' subjectivity from a more critical (feminist) perspective which underlines the role of social power relations in shaping the conditions for meaningful political and social agency.

4.3.1 Self as a 'Relational Subject'

The analytic category of a 'relational subject' has its origins in the object-relations theory of human subjectivity. Object-relations theorists underline the 'central importance of sustained, intimate relations with other persons or the repression of such relations in the constitution, structure, and ongoing experiences of a self'.[86] These theories account for the origin of a self 'in and out of relations with others' and they view human beings as 'object seeking' by nature.[87] One of the best-known advocates of the object-relations theory has been Donald Winnicott whose work deals with the earliest stages of infancy, which are not subjected to repression because they relate to the pre-Oedipal stages of psychological development and the construction of the self.[88] Winnicott proceeds in his analysis from the assumption that the infant and the giver of parental care together form a 'unit'.[89] This starting point allows him to envisage how the infant ego gradually becomes free from the parental 'ego-support', so that the infant achieves 'mental detachment' as a 'separate personal self'.[90] According to Winnicott, the development of the ego can thus be described by means of 'the theory of the infant's journey from absolute dependence, through relative dependence, to independence'.[91]

[85] Julia Kristeva, *Desire in Language—A Semiotic Approach to Literature and Art* (Blackwell, 1980) 135.

[86] Flax (n 75) 229–30.

[87] Flax (n 31) 111. It is important to bear in mind that an 'object' in development psychology is a concept for experiences which refer to someone or something outside the self that has significance for the self. See eg Josephine Klein, *Our Need for Others and its Roots in Infancy* (Tavistock Publications, 1987) 152. From this follows the argument that human beings 'seek objects for the intrinsic satisfaction of such relating, not merely to reduce drive tension'. On this basis, the object relations theorists argue that '"instinctual" impulses cannot be distinguished or treated apart from their relational aspects'. Flax (n 31) 111.

[88] Donald Winnicott, *The Maturational Process and the Facilitating Environment—Studies in the Theory of Emotional Development* (The Hogarth Press, 1965) 38.

[89] Ibid 39. At the heart of Winnicott's theory lies the claim that the 'infant ego' becomes 'powerful and stable' by virtue of the 'parental ego' which implements it during this period. Ibid 41.

[90] Ibid 41.

[91] Ibid 42.

The central question for the object-relations theorists is how the infant develops his/her 'perception of objects as external to the self'.[92] For Winnicott, this development is closely related to the transition of the infant from being merged with the giver of parental care to the state of relating to her/him as 'separate and "not-me"'.[93] In other words, it is essential for Winnicott's argument that the constitution of human subjectivity consists of the development towards 'the subject's perception of the object as an external phenomenon, not as a projective entity'.[94] On this basis, he concludes that '[i]ndependence is never absolute' and that '[t]he healthy individual does not become isolated, but becomes related to the environment in such a way that the individual and the environment can be said to be interdependent'.[95] This capacity to relate to the 'Other' provides a key to the constitution of transnational political and legal subjectivity as will be discussed below in this section.

Similarly, for instance, Margaret Mahler has argued that the 'psychological birth of the individual' can be examined as a 'separation-individuation process' which focuses on the development of a 'sense of separateness from, and relation to, a world of reality'.[96] Like Winnicott, Mahler suggests that the 'structural differentiation' which leads to the 'functioning ego' takes its place within the 'matrix of physiological and sociobiological dependency' on the giver of parental care.[97] Interestingly, she underlines that '[l]ike any intrapsychic process, this one reverberates throughout the life cycle. It is never finished; it remains always active; new phases of the life cycle see new derivatives of the earliest processes still at work.'[98] This emphasis on the way in which the self's early relationships with objects shape its later developments explains why these theories are relevant for a more general analysis of the conditions of political and legal agency and subjectivity.

What is common to all of these accounts is to claim that the capacity to establish 'genuinely reciprocal relationships' with others at the later stages of human development has its roots in the gradual separation-individuation process in

[92] Ibid 44.

[93] Ibid 45. Winnicott argues that it is only through the phase of 'structured integration' that the infant becomes able to 'experience anxiety associated with disintegration'. Ibid 44. This means that the capacity for genuine object relationships, ie for relationships in which the subject is capable of distinguishing between the self and the Other, develops when 'the infant changes from a relationship to a subjectively conceived object to a relationship to an object objectively perceived'. Ibid 45. This emphasis on object relations leads Winnicott to argue that successful parental care will 'build up in the infant a continuity of being which is the basis of ego-strength'. Ibid 52. Winnicott also notes that 'ego-functioning needs to be taken as a concept that is inseparable from that of the existence of the infant as a person' and that 'the ego offers itself for study long before the word self has relevance'. Ibid 59–60.

[94] Donald Winnicott, *Playing and Reality* (Routledge, 1971) 120.

[95] Ibid 84.

[96] Margaret Mahler, *The Psychological Birth of the Human Infant—Symbiosis and Individuation* (Hutchinson of London, 1975) 3. By the term 'separation', Mahler refers to 'the child's emergence from a symbiotic fusion with the mother'. By the term 'individuation', she means 'those achievements marking the child's assumption of his own individual characteristics'. Ibid 4.

[97] Ibid 45.

[98] Ibid 3.

early childhood.[99] Moreover, it is important to note that this common starting point leads most object-relations theorists to argue that '[m]aturity is not equated with independence though it includes a certain capacity for independence.'[100] For instance, Harry Guntrip has framed this principle as follows:

> Mature dependence is characterized by full differentiation of ego and object (emergence from primary identification) and therewith a capacity for valuing the object for its own sake and for giving as well as receiving; a condition which should be described not as independence but as mature dependence.[101]

In other words, the account of human subjectivity under the object-relations theory connects the mature subjectivity with the ability to be relational and to recognise the value of interdependence for the coming into existence of the subject.

The idea of psychological maturity as interdependence is particularly clear in WRD Fairbairn's account of ego-development through the following three stages: (1) 'infantile dependence'; (2) a 'transitional stage'; and (3) 'mature dependence'.[102] It has been noted that Fairbairn's theory of psycho-dynamic development presents normal development 'as that of growing out of the starting-point of infantile dependence on the mother to a capacity for the mature dependence of "equals" in an adult relationship'.[103] It seems important to consider whether and, if yes how, this argument of 'mature dependence' can inform the theories of subjectivity outside developmental psychology. By analogy, it can be suggested that defining the political subjectivity through the lens of 'mature dependence' presumes the analytic category of a 'relational subject', which describes the subject that has reached maturity through recognising the necessity of interdependence in the constitution of its subjectivity and the sense of self.

As seen above, for object-relations theorists, the acknowledgement of external reality and the discovery of the Other through 'separation' and 'individuation' are not seen as primarily painful or a product of frustration.[104] On this basis, it has been suggested that the object-relations psychology is able to explain 'the different fundamental ways in which human beings relate themselves to one another, both

[99] Flax (n 75) 252.

[100] Harry Guntrip, *Personality Structure and Human Interactions—The Developing Synthesis of Psychodynamic Theory* (The Hogarth Press, 1961) 293.

[101] Ibid 291.

[102] WRD Fairbairn, *Psychoanalytic Studies of the Personality* (Routledge, 1952) 162–63. Fairbairn argues that '[a]ny theory of ego-development that is to be satisfactory must be conceived in terms of relationships with objects, and in particular relationships with objects which have been internalized during early life under the pressure of deprivation and frustration'. However, it has been noted that, under Fairbairn's account, 'what are primarily repressed are neither intolerably guilty impulses nor intolerably unpleasant memories, but intolerably bad internalized object'. See eg Guntrip (n 100) 323.

[103] Guntrip (n 100) 321.

[104] Flax (n 31) 114–15. Unlike in the case of the 'orthodox' Freudian psychoanalysis, the main focus is on the mother-child relationship rather than on the father-child relationship. The object relation theories do not make a rigid distinction between primary and secondary processes and this arguably allows them to view reason as an 'innate potential capacity' rather than a 'faculty painfully acquired through the internalization of the authority of the father'. Flax (n 75) 249.

as disturbed and as mature persons'.[105] Recognising the positive value of interdependence for constructing transnational political subjectivity implies that the establishment of *ex ante* belonging is not the only available justification for a more relational conception of equality in EU law. Instead, an alternative justification is to focus on how more just and equal social relationships between EU citizens can increase the sense of 'mature interdependence' between EU citizens, which enables the full subjectivity of EU citizens as EU citizens.

The analytic category of a 'relational self' underlines that 'subjects come to understand themselves to an important degree through their relationships with others'.[106] The relevance of this argument for the EU principle of equality is captured in the statement that our '"sameness-and-difference" depends upon the relations in which we stand'.[107] Understanding the self 'as situated in a network of complex and ever-changing relationships' will arguably lead to a 'richer account of moral agents and agency'.[108] It has been argued on this basis that 'the descriptive question of identity (whether our labels correspond with reality) is less important than the relational question (how law and life generate and transform relations)'.[109] Similarly, a relational account of equal treatment between EU citizens can find its normative justification from the claim that just and equal relationships between EU citizens enable EU citizens to become 'mature' subjects of EU law. Firstly, this would mean that the focus of discrimination analysis must be shifted towards enhancing the equality of relationships between EU citizens. Secondly, it would allow us to replace the argument of more comparability between EU citizens with that of stronger relationships between them.

4.3.2 Self as a 'Subject-in-Process'

Approaching EU citizens as 'relational subjects' could justify a more positive approach to equal treatment between EU citizens, providing that focus of discrimination analysis moves from the negative relationship of dependence towards the positive relationships of interdependence. However, the story of 'primary relatedness' is more complex than the above insight into the object-relations theory might imply—and our attempt to reconstruct EU citizenship as a source of transnational subjectivity must also take that complexity into account.

The view of human beings as fundamentally rational and conscious is questioned by the structural psychoanalytic theory which stresses the role of the unconscious in constructing subjectivity.[110] The central finding of the psychoanalytic

[105] Guntrip (n 100) 357.
[106] Sevenhuijsen (n 3) 61.
[107] Victoria Nourse, 'Law's Constitution: A Relational Critique' (2002) 17 *Wisconsin Women's Law Journal* 23. 27.
[108] Ibid.
[109] Ibid 28.
[110] The so-called humanist accounts of subjectivity build upon the idea of human beings as 'fundamentally equal, rational, conscious beings, whose autonomy incorporates the potential to make

theory is the idea of 'differences within each subject'.[111] What is important for EU citizenship is the way in which these theories direct us to consider the constitution of subjectivity as a process. Understanding EU citizenship as a source of transnational political and legal subjectivity can benefit from the analytic category of a 'subject-in-process',[112] which is rooted in structural psychoanalysis, because complexity and fragmentation are axiomatic for transnational subjectivity which cannot argue for a unified/categorical subject. Moreover, recognising the intrapersonal complexity of human subjectivity helps us to understand better why just and equal relationships between EU citizens matter for constructing subjectivity in the transnational context. Namely, in so far as that the development of subjectivity through the identification with the Other is partly repressed, the unconscious levels of subjectivity can only be accessed indirectly, that is, when they are reflected in the self's relations to a more concrete 'Other'.

The psychoanalytic theory builds on Freud's iconic and controversial ideas of the Oedipus complex and the castration complex which he saw as being at the core of human identity.[113] However, despite Freud's emphasis on human development as a biological process, post-Freudian psychoanalysts tend to view the ability of 'significance attaching' as a social rather than a biological construction.[114] One example of this more structural approach is Jacques Lacan's work which has placed the psychoanalysis within the framework of linguistics. For Lacan, both the unconscious and sexuality are 'products of the subject's constitution in language' through what he calls the 'imaginary' and 'symbolic' orders, rather than 'natural or biological essences'.[115] Lacan's work is relevant for the analysis of EU citizenship in so far as it has provided the basis for Julia Kristeva's argument of the 'subject-in-process' which is used to explain the multiple and fragmented nature of transnational subjectivity below in this section.

For Lacan, the symbolic order, which constitutes social law and language, is the domain in which the child can reach the ability to 'signify' and can, thus, refer

informed, free choices', whereas the subject within anti-humanism is always 'secondary for any social explanation'. See eg Rothfield (n 1) 123–25. It has also been noted that the notion of 'subject' is sometimes used in psychoanalytic theory to simply 'avoid running into the very concepts of selfhood, personhood, and individuality'. Rowley and Grosz (n 77) 183.

111 Braidotti (n 23) 166.

112 Kristeva (n 85) 135.

113 For a summary of Freud's arguments, see eg Rowley and Grosz (n 77) 178. For Freud, the super ego is formed when the Oedipus complex is resolved and its task is to ensure that the values it represents are internalised, ie that they will regulate the subject from within. Its repressive force reflects the struggle against the temptation of the Oedipus complex. Freud argues that the Oedipus complex is stronger in men than women and it is also resolved more definitely in their case when they identify with the father's law.

114 See eg Diana Tietjen Meyers, *Self, Society, and Personal Choice* (Columbia University Press, 1989) 136. However, it has also been suggested that Freud did not use the terms 'masculine' and 'feminine' as 'anatomical terms', but conceived of them in terms of the following three oppositions: 'active and passive', 'subject and object', and 'phallic and castrated'. Rowley and Grosz (n 77) 178. Rowley and Grosz note that 'Masculine and feminine are thus not tied to the child's biological sex, but to the ways in which the child is able to resolve, and identify with, the social expectations surrounding the meaning of its sex'. Rowley and Grosz (n 77) 179.

115 Rowley and Grosz (n 77) 183.

to itself as an 'I'.[116] The child becomes a subject through a specific social intervention when it simultaneously becomes a 'social and speaking subject' and a 'being separated from others'.[117] After the emergence of the subject through the ability to signify, '"other scene" of thought and desire' is limited to the operation of the unconscious.[118] The subject therefore becomes 'split' between its unconscious 'identification with the image of another as the model for itself' and its conscious 'ability to signify' within the symbolic order of law, language, and social exchange.[119] The 'split' of subjectivity arguably leads to repression within which consciousness cannot explain the 'whole of subjectivity'.[120]

The separation between the child and the (m)other is experienced by the child both as a loss of the sense of wholeness, as well as the gaining of an identity.[121] In other words, the constitution of subjectivity leaves the subjects as 'the victims of the desire for the other—which is also a part of ourselves—that can never be satisfied'.[122] Lacan himself argues that 'the first object of desire is to be recognized by the other'.[123] The unconscious can, therefore, be conceptualised as a repressed 'discourse of the other'.[124] What is interesting for the analysis of EU citizenship is the way in which Lacan's theory models the self through its unconscious identifications with others/the 'Other'.[125] The subject is marked by its desire for the Other, but this desire is to a large extent repressed and unconscious. It is important to consider what this complexity in the subject's identification with the 'Other'

116 Ibid 185.

117 Lacan argues that the 'function of symbolic identification' requires the recognition of the 'Name of the Father' or 'paternal function' which concentrates in itself both the 'Imaginary' and 'Real' relations and which is, therefore, always 'more or less inadequate' to the 'Symbolic' relation which constitutes it. Jacques Lacan, *The Language of the Self—The Function of Language in Psychoanalysis* (The John Hopkins University Press, 1968) 41. This inadequacy of the 'Symbolic' relation, ie language or social law, to constitute the 'Imaginary' relation between the subject and the 'Other' indicates that the subject can emerge only when it is first disassociated from its primary identification with the '(m)other'. See further in Rowley-Grosz (n 77) 186.

118 Rowley and Grosz (n 77) 186.

119 Ibid 185–86. For Lacan, the distinction between the 'Imaginary' and 'Symbolic' orders has its roots in the so-called 'mirror stage' of child development. It has been noted that, for Lacan, the mirror stage is the 'root of all later identifications' as 'the ego depends upon this primary identification'. See more about this in the Introduction in Lacan (n 117) xiii.

120 Rowley and Grosz (n 77) 186. The term 'repression' refers to the process which 'removes unconscious memories and wishes from access to consciousness; at the same time, it permanently preserves unconscious contents'. Ibid 187.

121 Drucilla Cornell and Adam Thurschwell, 'Feminism, Negativity, Intersubjectivity' in Benhabib and Cornell (n 18) 146. Cornell and Thurschwell have summarised the consequences of this process by noting that: 'The pain of this loss results in a primary repression that on one hand buries the memory of the relationship to the archaic mother in the unconscious, and on the other hand catapults the infant into the symbolic realm of meaningful discourse, in order to fulfil its desire to restablish a relationship with an Other. But once projected into language this desire can never be satisfied in the unmediated form of the primary identification with the mother, and so for speaking subjects our discourse is always marked by a lack.' Ibid.

122 Ibid 146.

123 Lacan (n 117) 31.

124 Ibid 27.

125 Elizabeth Grosz, 'Contemporary Theories of Power and Subjectivity' in Gunew (n 1) 76.

means for EU citizens' subjectivity as EU citizens if, as will be argued in the next section, the relationships between EU citizens can be seen as an archetype of the relationships between the self and the 'Other'.

Lacan's approach challenges the presumption of an autonomous subject. Instead, the subject is seen as fundamentally socio-linguistically constituted. Although the Lacanian subject is always 'based on identifications with others', it arguably remains a 'paranoid and alienated construct' because the subject is always split between the conscious 'stability and unity' of the self in relation to the Other and the unconscious fear of the 'power of the other in defining the self'.[126] Moreover, the critics have argued that Lacan's 'narcissistic premise' under which the 'Other' is only seen as a model for the self is mistaken because it claims that the process of signifying has no connection to the 'relations with actual "others"' but only with the 'child's image of the other as self'.[127] This criticism explains why it is necessary to move beyond Lacan's analysis in order to grasp the critical potential of a 'split subject' for the analysis of EU citizenship without altogether denying the possibility of 'reciprocal social relations'[128] in constructing EU citizenship as a source of subjectivity, as has been discussed in Section 4.2.2.

Lacan's re-reading of Freud has played a central role in the French feminist tradition. His theory has become popular amongst feminist scholars because the interpretation of sexual identity through structural linguistics is not 'biologically reductionist'.[129] Authors such as Julia Kristeva, Luce Irigaray, and Hélène Cixous have referred to Lacan in their analysis of subjectivity. Julia Kristeva's reinterpretation of Lacan is particularly interesting for the analysis of EU citizenship because it combines the argument of a 'split subject' with a more diverse picture of the self's relations to the Other. Like Lacan, Kristeva suggests that the symbolic and social orders are 'maintained by virtue of a sacrifice' because the emergence of the subject through the signifying process happens 'at the cost of repressing instinctual drive and continuous relation to the mother'.[130] On this basis, Kristeva, too, argues that the becoming of the subject requires 'a stance involving otherness, distance, even limitation'.[131] However, for Kristeva, the (speaking) subject is constituted not just by the 'Symbolic' order but also by what she calls the 'Semiotic' processes.[132]

[126] Ibid 74.

[127] Flax (n 31) 92.

[128] Ibid 106.

[129] For this observation, see eg Lois McNay, *Gender and Agency Reconfiguring the Subject in Feminist and Social Theory* (Polity Press, 2000) 6.

[130] Kristeva (n 85) 136 and 138.

[131] Ibid ix.

[132] Kristeva's analysis builds upon the attempt 'to describe the signifying phenomenon' by means of what she calls 'semanalysis'. The goal of 'semiology' is to scrutinise 'the most deeply buried logic of those unities and ultimate relations that weave an identity for subject, or sign, or sentence'. From this follows her focus on the 'underlying speaking subject'. Kristeva (n 85) vii–viii and x. It has been noted that the object of the analysis is not language in itself but the 'discourse of a split subject'. See Introduction in Kristeva (n 85) 6. By 'semiotic', Kristeva refers to 'a distinctiveness admitting of an uncertain and indeterminate articulation because it does not yet refer (for young children) or no longer refers (in psychotic discourse) to a signified object for a thetic consciousness'. Ibid 133. By 'symbolic', she refers to the 'attribute of meaning, sign, and the signified object for consciousness'. Ibid 134.

She envisages the 'semiotic body' which '[b]efore recognizing itself as identical in a mirror and, consequently, as signifying, … is dependent vis-à-vis mother'.[133] Envisaging the 'dialectical opposition' between the semiotic processes and the symbolic order allows Kristeva to assign a more positive role to the self's relation to the 'Other' in constituting subjectivity than what is possible under Lacan's account.[134]

Thus, Kristeva's theory of subjectivity does not collapse into 'narcissism' in the same way as Lacan's theory seems to do. The idea of the 'semiotic heterogenity' makes it possible to include the reality of the intra-personal complexity of human subjectivity in the account of subjectivity without rejecting the constructive potential of inter-subjective relationships in constituting subjectivity. This is important for the analysis of EU citizenship as a source of transnational political and legal subjectivity because it indicates that recognising the reality of 'split subjectivity' does not automatically undermine the possibility of 'reciprocal social relations' between the subject and the Other. Moreover, the assumption of heterogeneity leads Kristeva to conclude: 'If it is true that there would unavoidably be a speaking subject since the signifying set exists, it is nonetheless evident that this subject, in order to tally with its heterogeneity, must be, let say, a questionable *subject-in-process*.'[135] This argument of the 'subject-in-process' provides an interesting vantage point for the analysis of transnational subjectivity.

The theory of a signifying subject as presented in Kristeva's work associates the signifying phenomenon with 'the *crisis* or the *unsettling process* of meaning and subject' rather than with the 'coherence or identity of either *one* or a *multiplicity* of structures'.[136] These references to multiplicity and fragmentation are particularly relevant in the transnational context in which sense of subjectivity and identity-building would need to accommodate several different levels or layers, including regional, national, and transnational sources of political and legal subjectivity. Kristeva emphasises that 'what is censured at the level of semantic complexity re-emerges in the form of a becoming'.[137] Similarly, it needs to be considered how the unconscious and repressed sides of the subject's relationships to the 'Other' re-emerge when subjectivity is constituted at the transnational level, ie when EU citizens become subjects on the basis of EU citizenship. Above all, the interesting question to the study of EU citizenship is whether recognising 'difference' as

[133] Ibid 136. These processes are significant because they will 'prepare the future speaker for entrance into meaning and signification (the symbolic)'. Kristeva argues on this basis that the 'semiotic heterogeneity' is 'inseparable' from 'the symbolic function of significance' and that language as social practice always presupposes both of these two dispositions. Ibid 134. See further Julia Kristeva, 'The System and the Speaking Subject' in T Moi (ed), *The Kristeva Reader* (Basil Blackwell, 1986).

[134] See Introduction in Kristeva (n 85) 19.

[135] Ibid 135. Kristeva suggests that the speaking subject 'maintains himself or herself as such to the extent that he/she allows for the presence of two brinks'. By this, she means that one both 'recognizes oneself as subject of (others') discourse, hence tributary of a universal Law' and finds 'oneself different, irreducible, for one is borne by a simply singular speech, not merging with others'. Ibid x.

[136] Ibid 125.

[137] Ibid 127.

something internal to each subject could change the perception of otherness when the Other takes the form of non-belonging and dependent EU citizens.

At the same time, it is important not to lose touch with the political dimension of this analysis which is expressed in the claim that, although the unconscious identification with the other plays an important role in subject-formation, the subject's conscious identity is shaped and transformed through its capability of agency. Thus, the argument of EU citizens as 'subjects-in-process' must not be understood as inward-looking or apolitical. On the contrary, the analysis of transnational subjectivity must consider the intra-psychic and partly unconscious identification with the Other within each subject against the fact that subjects become agents inter-subjectively, that is, in and through their social relations with others. For instance, Kristeva's work has inspired comments that 'any politics will fail unless it takes the pre-symbolic realm into account'.[138] Kristeva herself has framed this thought by stating that 'the economic-political differences refer not only to visions of society but, more precisely and in the last resort for me as a psychoanalyst, to very different conceptions of the *human person* or *subject*'.[139] Moreover, she claims that it is important to 'envisage the differing conceptions of the human person and of subjectivity that are asserted and contested in this European space'.[140]

In the light of these comments, it is important to consider in more detail how the analytic category of a 'subject-in-process' can provide us with a tool for including the unconscious and repressed relationship to the 'Other' in our account of EU citizens' subjectivity and agency. Firstly, seeing subjectivity as a process shifts the focus of analysis to the 'concrete' conditions which 'structure' subjectivity.[141] Secondly, the argument that subjectivity has 'levels' implies that these different levels or 'self-aspects' may also be in conflict.[142] This account of subjectivity as a process that functions at multiple different levels implies that what political and legal subjectivity mean in a national context may need to be reconsidered to enable the development of transnational subjectivity. It has been suggested that subjectivity can be seen as a 'multiple and discontinuous process of becoming'[143] that can best be understood in a 'nonhierarchical way'.[144] This argument for a 'non-hierarchical' subjectivity can also support the claim that 'singling out'[145] just one aspect of self-identity, whether national or supranational, is not helpful in the light of the

[138] Rowley and Grosz (n 77) 194.

[139] Julia Kristeva, *Crisis of the European Subject* (Other Press, 2000) 115.

[140] Ibid.

[141] Braidotti (n 23) 98.

[142] Ferguson (n 49) 117.

[143] Braidotti (n 23) 110. From this starting point, identity can be defined as 'a play of multiple, fractured aspects of the self; it is relational, in that it requires a bond to the "other"; it is retrospective, in that it is fixed through memories and recollections, in a genealogical process' and, at the same time, as something that is 'made of successive identifications, that is to say unconscious internalized images that escape rational control'. Ibid 166.

[144] Ibid 146.

[145] Ferguson (n 49) 122.

inter- and intra-personal complexity of human subjectivity. From this starting point, viewing EU citizens as 'subjects-in-process' allows a more complex and multi-layered conception of what subjectivity means in the case of EU citizens.

4.3.3 Why Political Subjects Need Agency

The analysis of subjectivity in Sections 4.3.1 and 4.3.2 has contributed a theoretical perspective which is generally not there when EU citizens' subjectivity and agency are discussed in academic literature. By outlining some basic convergences between the psycho-dynamic theories of subjectivity and the constitution of political and legal subjectivity, this analysis extrapolated two analytic categories of subject-formation which are helpful in explaining the conditions for transnational political and legal subjectivity. The object-relations theory stresses the importance of inter-personal social relationships for constituting a 'relational subject', while the structural psychoanalytic theory introduces a cognitively complex and more fragmented conception of a 'subject-in-process'. What is central to both of these accounts is that the identification with the Other explains human subjectivity in important ways. This section will discuss how recognising the relational dynamics of subject-formation can also provide a new approach to EU citizens' agency.

The brief insight into developmental psychology emphasised the following two premises: (1) '[s]ubjects come to understand themselves to an important degree through their relationships with others'; and (2) 'the fragmented and multiple subject has more possibilities of experiencing the other within the self'.[146] In the light of this analysis, EU citizens' sense of subjectivity as EU citizens can be seen as a two-fold process which must recognise *both* the constructive potential of inter-personal relationships between those who share the status of EU citizenship *and* the intra-personal complexity within the subject who needs to mediate between the local, national, and transnational attributes of subjectivity. It follows from this complexity that 'difference' is internalised within each subject—as opposed to only being external to the subject.

The validity of this analysis to EU citizenship depends on whether the psycho-dynamic theories of subjectivity, which are primarily focused on intimate relations and the individual psychological need, can have wider relevance for political and legal identity and subjectivity. There are two levels to look at when this question is addressed. Firstly, the need for a conceptually coherent account of subjectivity can justify the argument that the different forms of subjectivity are composed of similar elements. Secondly, however, there are political theorists who take the leap from the psychological to the political and the legal, not just at the level of conceptual coherence, but also by arguing for a more substantive connection between

[146] Sevenhuijsen (n 3) 60–61. On this basis, it has been suggested that an alternative account of the self must recognise 'the multiple, sometimes fractious sources of social identity', as well as 'the complexity of the intrapsychic world of unconscious fantasies, fears, and desires'. Meyers (n 41) 2.

different modes of subjectivity. This chapter has followed in their footsteps to explore how these ideas of subjectivity can be applied to EU citizenship. However, what has been said about the psycho-dynamic constitution of subjects through unconscious identification with the Other must not be understood as an argument for apolitical inward-lookingness in rethinking the role of EU citizenship in European integration. On the contrary, these observations concerning subject-formation can lay the foundations for a more substantive theory of agency in the case of EU citizens.

The reason for discussing EU citizens' subjectivity has been to rethink their agency.[147] This analytic approach is based on the fact that agents are also subjects and, thus, their ability to act meaningfully in part depends on their subjectivity.[148] This means that understanding the conditions for transnational subject-formation is an important step for rethinking the parameters for EU citizens' agency. It is therefore essential to consider how the two-fold framework of EU citizens as both 'relational subjects' and 'subjects-in-process' can bridge the gap from inward-looking psychological theories to more outward-looking accounts of meaningful political and legal agency. Subjectivity emerges from a complex set of different 'social, economic, cultural or biographical' factors.[149] The 'fundamental epistemological insight' of psychoanalysis in this context is to show how 'pre-rational matter' shapes our thinking processes.[150] Taking this perspective seriously means that the 'desire' for the Other is assigned a central role in subject-formation.[151] However, the crucial question is whether the 'subjective desire' can intersect with the 'willed social transformation'.[152] In other words, what are the political and legal implications of the epistemological insight that follows from shifting the analytical focus to 'subjectivity'?

It is clear that the concept of subjectivity that 'bears a privileged bond to unconscious processes' cannot be assimilated with political identity as 'a conscious and wilful position'.[153] At the same time, however, it can be argued that 'both levels are the site of political agency' and that they are 'different but interrelated moments of in the process of defining a subject position'.[154] Recognising this connection between the complexity of human subjectivity, on the one hand, and political identity and agency, on the other, supports the view that the 'politics of subjectivity' must amount to the rejection of 'assimilation'.[155] Moreover,

[147] See Chapter 3, Section 3.5.3, p 128.

[148] See eg John Macmurray, *The Self as Agent* (Faber and Faber, 1957) 100–02 and *Persons in Relation* (Faber and Faber, 1961) 160.

[149] Patrizia Violi, 'Gender, Subjectivity and Language' in Gisela Bock and Susan James (eds), *Beyond Equality and Difference Citizenship, Feminist Politics and Female Subjectivity* (Routledge, 1992) 167.

[150] Rosi Braidotti, 'On the Female Feminist Subject, or: From "She-Self" to "She-Other"' in Bock and James (n 149) 183.

[151] Ibid.

[152] Ibid 188.

[153] Braidotti (n 23) 166.

[154] Ibid 196.

[155] Ibid 160.

the idea of 'self-difference' as part of the subject also supports the argument that the construction of subjectivity at multiple levels (eg both national and transnational) becomes easier if the subject recognises the 'Other' as something not entirely external to its own subjectivity. It follows from this that understanding EU citizens' subjectivity as a process can challenge the assimilating tendencies of the discrimination analysis when the parameters for EU citizens' agency are defined.

But the complexity of transnational subject-formation can only be understood in connection with the relational and social nature of subjectivity. Feminist theory, in particular, claims that the assumption of the man as 'a solitary creature by nature' in modern political philosophy follows from the denial of the 'primary relatedness' between the infant and the caretaker, as well as from the 'consequences of this denial for conceptions of human nature'.[156] Moreover, it has been argued that philosophy in general and political and legal philosophy in particular are not 'immune' to these consequences and the 'influence of the unconscious'.[157] The importance of recognising the role of the unconscious in understanding subjectivity and, thus, agency, is captured in Jane Flax's statement that 'childhood experience is repressed on a social and individual level' and that '[o]nly thus it is possible to deny the most fundamental proof of necessity of human bonding and its effects, which extend far beyond mere utility, and reverberate throughout adult life'.[158] It arguably follows from this that 'true reciprocity' is not possible 'if the "other" must be dominated and/or repressed rather than incorporated into the self while simultaneously acknowledging the difference'.[159]

However, it has been suggested that the central question to understanding political subjectivity is not so much about how to strike the balance between 'equality' and 'difference' but about how to fight the 'relation of domination' that emerges from these differences.[160] Any attempt to construct EU citizenship as a source of subjectivity therefore leads us back to the questions of emancipation and justice, as discussed at the end of Chapter three. This is also clear in Jane Flax's argument that:

> Discourse about justice cannot do without concepts of subjectivity. The necessity for and problems about justice arise in part out of the complexity of human subjectivity and our relations with others.[161]

But the critics have noted that understanding subject formation 'negatively' through lack and desire in structural psycho-analytic theory leads to 'a partial account of agency' and fails to provide 'a broad enough understanding of subjectification'.[162] As stated above, an important element of this critique is that

[156] Flax (n 75) 261.
[157] Ibid 255.
[158] Ibid 268.
[159] Ibid 269.
[160] See eg Jane Flax, 'Beyond Equality: Gender, Justice and Difference' in Bock and James (n 149) 193–94.
[161] Ibid 203.
[162] McNay (n 129) 2–3.

'difference' must be understood 'in more sociological terms, as the differentiated power relations constitutive of the social realm'.[163]

For instance, Lois McNay argues that the Lacanian accounts of subjectivity are not able to adequately explain the subject's various relations to the other and its ability to cope with difference.[164] In particular, she argues that they ignore 'the capabilities of individuals to respond to difference in a less defensive and even, at times, a more creative fashion'.[165] In McNay's view, it is also problematic that the unconscious is often seen as 'a source of some, as yet, unexpressed identity'.[166] As an example of this tendency, she mentions Julia Kristeva's work, which arguably lacks 'any mediatory notion of political agency' and thus fails to explain how the idea of Semiotic 'may have an emancipatory impact on social practices'.[167] Kristeva's work is valuable for the analysis of EU citizens' subjectivity for the reasons discussed at the end of Section 4.3.2. Namely, her re-reading of Lacan demonstrates that recognising the internal complexity of the subject does not automatically need to mean that the subject is unable to meaningfully relate to the Other. However, the above criticism is justified in so far as it emphasises the need for a more developed notion of political agency in this context.

From a feminist perspective, it is clearly problematic if identity is defined by virtue of 'a process of exclusion of the other or denial of difference'.[168] But it has also been noted that the solution to this 'dilemma of difference'[169] is not to invoke a 'domesticated view of otherness or difference'.[170] Instead, it has been suggested that recognising the 'active role' of the subject in shaping a 'coherent identity' can lead to a more substantive theory of agency.[171] On this basis, it has also been suggested that 'the way in which subjectivity may be transformed' is limited by the fact that 'a coherent sense of self is a necessary dimension of subject formation'.[172] However, the 'transformation' of social relations could emerge from agency understood as 'the ability to act in an unexpected fashion or to institute new and unanticipated modes of behaviour'.[173] Along similar lines, but from a different theoretical perspective, Lea Ypi has presented an argument of cosmopolitan 'avant-garde political agents', as seen in Section 3.4.3.[174]

163 Ibid 14.
164 Ibid 3.
165 Ibid.
166 Ibid 137–38.
167 Ibid 140.
168 Ibid 77–78.
169 Martha Minow, *Making All the Difference—Inclusion, Exclusion, and American Law* (Cornell University Press, 1990).
170 McNay (n 129) 102.
171 Ibid 73.
172 Ibid 74.
173 Ibid 22.
174 Lea Ypi, *Global Justice and Avant-Garde Political Agency* (Oxford University Press, 2012), as discussed in Chapter three, Section 3.4.3.

Lois Mc Nay argues for a conception of feminist agency which is based on the capacity to 'manage actively … the relations of power'.[175] It is central to her understanding of agency that it recognises 'reflexivity' which emerges from 'a self-conscious relation with the other'.[176] At the same time, however, she acknowledges that understanding the 'psychic dimension' of subjectivity 'adds depth to an account of agency and guards against voluntarism by showing how action may be subverted or intensified by unconscious motivations'.[177] Similarly, the important question for this book is how to mediate between the psycho-dynamic understanding of subjectivity and the socially-aware account of agency if we recognise the inherent connection between the two. In particular, it can be asked whether EU citizenship as a legal and political status could play any role in mediating between transnational subjectivity and agency. This enquiry is based on the view that citizenship can become a 'transitional practice' between the 'subjective' experience and need, on the one hand, and 'public' and 'intersubjective' action, on the other.[178]

The mediating role assigned to EU citizenship as a source of transnational subjectivity would mean that the 'self' is no longer 'driven by necessity but as part of a community'.[179] At the same time, the feminist understanding of citizenship as agency indicates that a more substantive theory of agency is needed to let the achieved knowledge of transnational subject-formation actually shape or transform the political and social interaction between EU citizens.However, it has been seen in this section that this theory of agency would need to take into account that 'difference' is internalised within each subject—as opposed to only being external to the subject. EU citizens' agency and their subjectivity are in this sense inherently connected. The next section will conclude the analysis of subjectivity by considering its ethical implications for EU citizenship in the light of phenomenological philosophy.

4.4 SUBJECTIVITY AND THE SECOND-PERSON PERSPECTIVE: A PHENOMENOLOGICAL APPROACH TO EU CITIZENSHIP

This section develops a more philosophical argument about just and equal relationships between EU citizens as the basis for their subjectivity. It will be seen that EU citizens becoming subjects of EU law also depends on their treatment as

175 McNay (n 129) 16.

176 Ibid 5.

177 Ibid 117. McNay acknowledges that some authors have aimed at 'reversing the causal privilege that the psychic is accorded in respect of the social' in the psychoanalytic accounts. However, in her view, a more developed concept of agency would require a clearer move 'beyond the essentially negative account of subject formation in Lacan and Foucault'. For her, this should include 'looking beyond the interface between psyche and social to consider the political as an effect of the shifting power relations between groups of social actors and between institutional and non-institutional structures'. Ibid 130–32.

178 Flax (n 160) 206.

179 Ibid 207.

persons, which can only happen in relation to the 'Other'. First, some basic ideas of phenomenological philosophy are used to show how a 'second-person perspective' as a condition for the full personhood and subjectivity can only emerge in relation to the 'Other' (or stranger or 'Thou') for whom the subject accepts responsibility (Section 4.4.1). It will then be explained how a 'second-person perspective' as a condition for full personhood and subjectivity can provide an independent source of responsibility between EU citizens and how constructing EU citizenship as a source of subjectivity can therefore create new 'meaningful relationships' for the purposes of non-discrimination and equal treatment between EU citizens (Section 4.4.2).

4.4.1 Subjectivity Through the 'Second-Person Perspective'

At its simplest, the sense of subjectivity can refer to the self 'as reflexively understood by the person'. However, it has been noted that becoming a person 'is not just to be a reflexive actor, but to have a concept of a person (as applied both to the self and others)'.[180] For philosophical and political personalists, a genuine understanding of the person and the recognition of her as a personal subject are therefore closely intertwined. The idea of the uniqueness of the person in relation to the material world leads to the argument that the person is 'someone' rather than 'something'.[181] Besides the difference between persons and non-persons, personalists distinguish between the two ways in which one can relate to the reality: the 'I-Thou' relationships are open to the Other, whereas the 'I-It' relationships lead to the objectivisation of the Other.[182] Thus, although personalism defends an understanding of personhood as a unique and inviolable status, it is not so much a theory of the person, but a theory of how persons interact, communicate, and relate to one another. As a political theory, personalism is strongly relational. The central paradigm is that persons never exist in isolation.[183] Relationships form the essence of personhood and the ethical claim for responsibility follows from this, as will be seen in this section.

The inherent connection between 'personhood' and 'relationships' is beautifully articulated in Emmanuel Levinas' phenomenological account of our original experience of the other person. This analysis is relevant for EU citizenship because

[180] See eg Anthony Giddens, *Modernity and Self-Identity: Self and Society in the Late Modern Age* (Polity Press, 1991) 53. Cf Foucault's argument of the 'techniques of the self' as procedures that 'determine', 'maintain', and 'transform' individual identity. Michel Foucault, 'Technologies of the Self' in Paul Rainbow (ed), *Ethics: Subjectivity and Truth (Essential Works of Michel Foucault, 1954-1984)* (Penguin, 2000).

[181] Robert Spaemann, *Persons—The Difference between 'Someone' and 'Something'* (Oxford University Press, 2006).

[182] Martin Buber, *I and Thou* (1923, translated into English in 1937). Buber also argues that the fundamental difference between these two relationships draws from a man's attitude towards the reality, even if the sphere in which the relationship arises may also affect the form it takes.

[183] See eg Jacques Maritain, *The Person and the Common Good* (Geoffrey Bles, 1948).

the argument about the 'second-person perspective' can provide a philosophical basis for the idea of 'subjectivity through relationships', as discussed in this chapter. According to Levinas, our 'metaphysical desire' is always directed towards 'the absolutely other'.[184] From this starting point, he envisions how the choice for communication allows us to welcome the stranger and to 'receive from the Other beyond the capacity of the I, which means exactly: to have the idea of infinity'.[185] Moreover, Levinas also suggests that 'I' has access to the Other 'not through a comparison of myself with the other' but 'from the society I maintain with him'.[186] This move from comparison to communion is particularly interesting for the analysis of transnational subjectivity.

The possibility of communication and discourse implies that the self can have 'an existence that is more than his interior existence'.[187] This metaphysical starting point leads Levinas to suggest that the subject's 'interiority' is something which is 'at the same time closed and open'. The subject's capability of being is partly defined by the Other who is always 'exterior' to the subject.[188] By making this connection between the interior and exterior constitution of subjectivity, Levinas is able to claim that only 'in approaching the Other I attend to myself'.[189] Moreover, he argues that the 'urgency of response' to the Other induces responsibility and 'as responsible I am brought to my final reality'.[190] On this basis, Levinas concludes that '[t]o be in oneself is to express oneself, that is, already to serve the Other'.[191] What is equally important, however, is that the Other does not 'negate' the subject in 'calling it to responsibility', but, on the contrary, the subject is 'found and justified' in that call to responsibility for the Other.[192]

The analysis of EU citizenship as a source of subjectivity can benefit from considering how Levinas' ideas of subjectivity and infinity are produced 'in sociality'.[193] The central idea in Levinas' account of subjectivity is that meeting

[184] Emmanuel Levinas, *Totality and Infinity: An Essay on Exteriority* (Duquesne University Press, 1969) 33.

[185] Ibid 51. Levinas' vision is that the Other does 'reveal himself in his face'. For Levinas, '[t]he face to face' represents 'an ultimate situation' which 'involves a calling into question of oneself, a critical attitude which is itself produced in face of the other and under his authority'. Ibid 75 and 81.

[186] Ibid 121. For Levinas, 'pluralism' refers to 'an attitude of an I with regard to the Other' which 'implies a radical alterity of the other, whom I do not simply conceive by relation to myself, but confront out of my egoism'. Levinas develops this thought further by noting that '[t]he alterity of the Other is in him and is not relative to me; it reveals itself'. Ibid.

[187] Ibid 182.

[188] Ibid 147 and 149. It also means that '[t]he I is not a being that always remains the same, but it is the being whose existing consists in identifying itself, in recovering its identity throughout all that happens to it.' Ibid 36.

[189] Ibid 178.

[190] Ibid.

[191] Ibid 183.

[192] Ibid 194 and 197. Levinas suggests that '[t]he other precisely reveals himself in his alterity not in a shock negating the I, but as the primordial phenomenon of gentleness'. This means that the very 'dwelling which makes the separation of the human being possible' will already 'imply a first revelation of the Other'. Ibid 150–51.

[193] Ibid.

the Other in his/her 'alterity' constitutes the self. What he calls the 'resistance' of the Other is, therefore, given 'a positive structure: ethical'.[194] Namely, the relation with the Other in the form of discourse will assign the self to responsibility.[195] Subjectivity can then be understood as 'the coming to pass of responsibility itself' when 'the "I" is singled out by the other'.[196] This same intuitive idea is articulated more clearly in John Macmurray's argument that, in order to grasp the essence of subjectivity and, thus, agency, it is important to bear in mind that 'the Self exists only in dynamic relation with the Other', ie 'the Self is constituted by its relation to the Other'.[197]

When we consider how the relationship to the 'Other' shapes EU citizens' subjectivity as EU citizens, it is good to bear in mind that Macmurray's relational account of subjectivity emphasises that while '[e]ach realizes himself in and through the other', 'the other remains really other'.[198] What is important is that 'they are then related *as equals*' but 'equality is intentional: it is an aspect of the mutuality of the relation'.[199] The argument of just and equal relations as a source of subjectivity has therefore nothing to do with 'assimilation'. On the contrary, it simply indicates that persons 'know themselves to be persons among persons' by using the 'second personal pronoun'.[200] For instance, Annette Baier has captured this constitutive connection between the self and the 'Other' in her statement that '[p]ersons essentially are second persons who grow up with other persons'.[201] On this basis, she suggests that 'we are second persons before we are first or third persons'.[202] Similarly, recognising and deepening the connection between the

[194] Ibid.

[195] Ibid 213.

[196] Thomas D Williams and Jan Olof Bengtsson, 'Personalism' in Edward N Zalta (ed), *The Stanford Encyclopedia of Philosophy (Summer 2013 Edition)* http://plato.stanford.edu/archives/sum2013/entires/personalism/

[197] Macmurray (n 148) 17. MacMurray distinguishes between 'personal' and 'impersonal' relations and 'direct' and 'indirect' relations. Ibid 30. He argues that only 'direct relations' may be 'personal'. Ibid 43. For Macmurray, a community is 'a unity of persons as persons' and it 'cannot be defined in functional terms'. Ibid 157. This leads Macmurray to argue that 'the unity of a community of persons, each in personal relationship with all the others' can only be represented symbolically through 'the idea of a personal Other who stands in the same mutual relation to every member of the community'. Macmurray notes that '[i]n its full development, the idea of a universal personal Other is the idea of God'. Ibid 164. However, Macmurray also considers the implications of his argument for 'indirect' relations in the field of politics. He writes: 'Where relations are indirect it can only be potential; and this means that if we did come into direct relation with another person the relation would be positively motivated'. Ibid 189. This is where 'law' steps in. Namely, Macmurray notes that 'where our practical relations are indirect, … the justice of our actions depends upon a system of law'. Ibid 196. On this basis, he underlines that '[t]he primary presupposition of law is then the will of justice in society'. Ibid 202.

[198] Ibid 158.

[199] Ibid. Macmurray concludes on this basis that '[t]he unity of the personal is, then, to be sought in the community' and that 'since persons are agents, this community is not merely matter of fact, but also matter of intention'. Ibid 27. This emphasis on 'intention' leads Macmurray to suggest that 'the conception we have of our relations to one another determines the relations themselves'. Ibid 148.

[200] Annette Baier, *Postures of the Mind—Essays on Mind and Morals* (Methuen, 1985) 89.

[201] Ibid 84. According to Baier, 'a person, perhaps, is best seen as one who was long enough dependent upon other persons to acquire the essential arts of personhood'. Ibid.

[202] Ibid 90.

first-person and the second-person perspectives can be regarded as crucial for the emergence of EU citizens' subjectivity as EU citizens.

However, it has been noted that the debate about 'personhood' is inadequate for addressing the specific concerns related to citizenship.[203] The (political) agency of citizens cannot be reduced to the mere claim of personhood if we do not want to collapse into cosmopolitanism. But, in so far as it is the presence of subjectivity that makes (political) agency in its full potential possible, it is nevertheless important to understand what the conditions of subjectivity are in the case of EU citizens, ie under what conditions the 'Self' which can be an agent exists. This section has argued that ignoring the 'second-person perspective' leaves EU citizens deprived as persons and, thus, prevents EU citizenship from developing into a source of subjectivity. Namely, treating someone as a person is a precondition for their full subjectivity and, thus, for their agency. At the same time, however, this analysis leads to a more positive conclusion: If the genuine second-person perspective is possible, as has been discussed in this section, and if it follows from the way in which the subject emerges from its relationships to the Other through accepting responsibility for the Other, a new source of 'meaningful relationships' for the purposes of equal treatment will arise from recognising EU citizens as full subjects of EU law and European integration.

4.4.2 A Meaningful Relationship to the Other

The subject as a person can only come into existence in and through its relations to the 'Other'. In particular, the previous section showed that those relationships within which subjectivity finds its existence require a 'second-person perspective'. This section will discuss in more detail how this connection between subjectivity and the 'second-person perspective' can inform our understanding of what constitutes a 'meaningful relationship' for the purposes of non-discrimination and equal treatment between EU citizens. Here the key argument is that the emergence of EU citizens' subjectivity through a second-person perspective can transform 'meaningful relationships' because it creates a new sense of responsibility, that is, a new ethical obligation in relation to the 'Other' who is still a stranger. In relying on their fundamental right to equal treatment and non-discrimination irrespective of nationality, economically inactive and needy EU citizens embody the role of the 'Other' when they claim access to social equality in the Member State other than their state of origin.

There seems to be little doubt about the fact that EU citizens are often perceived through 'otherness'. The first three chapters of this book have drawn our attention to the fact that the implicit comparability between EU citizens has significantly been qualified at the level of reasonableness analysis and integration requirements

[203] John Shotter, 'Psychology and Citizenship: Identity and Belonging' in Bryan S Turner (ed), *Citizenship and Social Theory* (SAGE Publications, 1993) 116.

as part of the discrimination analysis. Moreover, it has been seen in this book that embracing the idea of more explicit comparability between EU citizens is not an adequate solution to the EU equality problem because it would emphasise the value of similarity at the expense of diversity in EU equality law. But it must also be considered whether the general premise that social relationships are important for the constitution of political subjectivity can justify the argument that *special legal relationships* between EU citizens will advance their subjectivity as EU citizens. That is, can legal relations between EU citizens count as those social relations in which their subjectivity as EU citizens is constituted? This question is important because the positive answer to it would also mean that these relationships count as new meaningful relationships for the purposes of non-discrimination and equal treatment in EU law.

It has been noted that 'subjects are formed through exclusionary operations'.[204] Underlying this claim is a social constructivist viewpoint that our relations 'are open to revision through the modification of powerful social institutions such as law'.[205] The law can accordingly be seen as an 'important discursive apparatus' which may have 'enabling and/or constraining effects on human agency'.[206] Law can give birth to relations that did not exist before and these relations may be discriminatory.[207] It therefore seems convincing that legal relations between EU citizens provide one category of those social relations in and through which EU citizens' subjectivity as EU citizens is constituted. Namely, the relationships which matter most for EU citizens' subjectivity as EU citizens are those social relationships that are formed in relation to other holders of the status of EU citizenship. Although the analysis of subjectivity in this chapter cannot give a direct answer to the question of how the principle of equality should be defined between EU citizens when it comes to their access to social benefits in the host Member Sate, it can provide a justification for recognising equality as a 'normative ideal of human relationships' in a transnational context and, thus, introduce one solution to the EU 'Equality Problem', as discussed in this book.

It must therefore be asked whether EU citizenship aims at creating a sense of transnational legal and political subjectivity beyond the existing patterns of cultural, ethnic and democratic belonging within the Member States. If we answer this question positively, new meaningful relationships between EU citizens for the purposes of non-discrimination and equal treatment emerge from the fact that subjectivity is constituted in relation to the 'Other' and from accepting a new ethical responsibility for the 'Other'. This argument for more just and equal relationships between EU citizens as a source of their subjectivity as EU citizens is important because it does not collapse into vague cosmopolitanism. The

[204] Butler (n 30) 14.

[205] Nicola Lacey, *Unspeakable Subjects: Feminist Essays in Legal and Social Theory* (Hart Publishing, 1998) 3.

[206] Sevenhuijsen (n 3) 31.

[207] See eg Nourse (n 107) 30. By discrimination, Nourse refers to 'discrimination of relation, a rule that re-enacts a relation of inferiority and invisibility'. Ibid 39.

normativity of just and equal relationships under this account is derived from EU citizens becoming subjects of European integration, rather than from their mere humanity—although, as mentioned above, this sense of subjectivity is only possible if EU citizens are first treated as persons. It follows from this that the relationship between 'us' and the 'Other' defines the project of European integration in a positive way because that relationship makes it possible for EU citizens to become full subjects of European integration—as opposed to being its mere objects.

4.5 TRANSNATIONAL SUBJECTIVITY AS A DYADIC PROCESS OF BECOMING BETWEEN THE SELF AND THE OTHER

It has been argued that a person experiences herself as a subject from the inside and that self-determination in relation to the 'I' of the acting subject can be viewed as the 'efficient cause' of responsibility for action.[208] However, things appear more complicated if the focus of analysis is shifted to the question of what 'signifies interiority to self', that is, what makes a person experience herself as a subject from the inside. This question can be narrowed down as follows: What makes an EU citizen experience him- or herself as a transnational political and legal subject from the inside? In this chapter, this question has been examined in the light of the psycho-dynamic and phenomenological accounts of subjectivity. It is now time to pull these theoretical considerations together and outline what it means to view EU citizenship as a source of transnational subjectivity. How this question about the conditions for EU citizens' subjectivity is answered is important because it also defines whether EU citizenship can provide a new source of meaningful relationships for the purposes of non-discrimination and equal treatment in the absence of *ex ante* belonging and, thus, introduce a new justification for a more relational account of equality within the EU.

The theoretical analysis of subjectivity highlighted the following three conditions of subjectivity: (1) its dependence on social relationships/interactions; (2) its emergence as a process at several different levels; and (3) its complexity, ie 'the self is always an other'. Accordingly, EU citizens can be considered *both* as 'relational subjects' whose sense of subjectivity as EU citizens is constituted in and through their social relations with other EU citizens *and* as 'subjects-in-process' whose relations to the 'Other' are affected by complex unconscious processes. Bringing these two dimensions of subjectivity together indicates that any successful attempt to construct EU citizenship as a source of subjectivity, either politically or legally, would need advance just and equal legal relationships between EU citizens both (1) as a means of creating and protecting the space in which the inter-relational construction of subjectivity becomes, even in theory, possible and (2) as a means of creating and protecting the space in which the unconscious relation to the

[208] eg John Macmurray has argued that '[t]he Self must be conceived not theoretically as subject, but practically, as agent'. Macmurray (n 148) 38.

'Other' can be reshaped indirectly in so far as the 'Other' now takes the form of the economically inactive and needy EU citizens who do not yet belong to the society of the host Member State.

Thus, understanding transnational subjectivity as a process that is defined by the self's identification with the 'Other', both inter-personally and intra-personally, supports the argument that constructing EU citizenship as a source of subjectivity depends on more just and equal relationships between EU citizens.[209] Moreover, accepting a second-person perspective as part of subject-formation engages the Self in a constitutive relationship with the Other, which may become a source of ethical responsibility for the Other and, thus, of new meaningful relationships for the purposes of non-discrimination and equal treatment. At the same time, however, conceptualising EU citizens' relationships as relationships between the self and the Other also means that the potential of EU citizenship to become a source of subjectivity in its own right requires that the 'Other' is internalised more consciously and that the unconscious fear of the Other is no longer projected on another EU citizen. It follows from this that (re)constructing EU citizenship as a source of subjectivity can be defined as a dyadic process of becoming between those who hold the status of EU citizenship. Affirming EU citizens as subjects of EU law and European integration involves recognising their capability of self-determination and, thus, their capability for responsible actions—however, not responsible for the exercise of individual (economic) responsibility, as discussed in Chapter three, but for the becoming of transnational subjects, as outlined in this chapter.

This chapter has suggested that EU citizens become subjects of EU law and European integration in relation to other EU citizens (horizontally) and not just in relation to the Member States or the Union (vertically). It follows from this conclusion that the 'equality of relationships' between EU citizens forms a necessary, even if not sufficient, condition for EU citizens' status as subjects of EU law and European integration. Moreover, as will be discussed in the next chapter, these relationships between EU citizens need to be constructed by EU law because they do not emerge organically on the basis of ethnic, cultural or democratic belonging. Under this account EU citizens' fundamental right to non-discrimination and

[209] The psychoanalytic insight into social theory can arguably grasp 'a broader concept of relevant figures of Otherness'. Lacey (n 205) 134. Lacey suggests that '[w]hat is central is that the logical relation of identity to otherness has to be denied, but constantly threatens to surface again'. On this basis, she argues that there is 'a very close connection between the project of psychoanalytic interpretation and that of reflection upon the institutional structure of social orders'. Ibid 134–35. Lacey explains this by noting that: 'In the quest for identity, the Other thus becomes an object of hatred and fear; but this hatred of the Other is in fact a displaced hatred of the self'. Ibid 135. However, some have noted that '[b]y claiming that some identifications are more primary than others', the psychoanalytic theories may also fail to recognise discriminating practices which are embedded in 'that particular narrative of identity formation'. Butler (n 81). For instance, Judith Butler suggests that the method of existential critique can, therefore, provide analytical tools for understanding subjectivity through 'the metaphysical order of becoming' instead of the 'metaphysical order of being'. Judith Butler, 'Variations on Sex and Gender: Beauvoir, Witting, and Foucault' in Benhabib and Cornell (n 18) 141.

equal treatment gains a positive role as a means of enabling those relationships in and through which EU citizens' subjectivity as EU citizens is constituted. What is significant in this account of EU citizens' subjectivity is that it provides one normatively and theoretically coherent solution to the EU equality problem, that is, to the question of whether the principle of just and equal relations between citizens as the fundamental premise of political and social justice can be justified transnationally.

4.6 CONCLUSION

This chapter used the feminist critique of citizenship to support the claim that the idea of subjectivity is central for a more balanced view of agency in the case of EU citizens. It then moved on to explore how the conditions of subjectivity are defined in those psycho-dynamic theories of subject-formation which underlie the feminist arguments of citizens' agency and their subjectivity. On the basis of this analysis, the chapter suggested that the two historical psychoanalytic traditions, the object-relations theory and the structural psycho-analytic model, can provide useful analytical tools for understanding EU citizens as subjects of EU law and European integration. The findings of this analysis were conceptualised by suggesting that EU citizens can be understood both (1) as 'relational subjects' whose sense of subjectivity depends on inter-subjective relations with other EU citizens and (2) as 'subjects-in-process' whose sense of subjectivity is marked by the unconscious and fragmented intra-personal relationship to the 'Other'. A more balanced account of agency in the case of EU citizens can therefore emerge from recognising that difference is internal to each subject, and that the self who can become an agent emerges in and through social relations.

This chapter then suggested that EU citizens can become full and equal subjects of European integration in and through relationships in which they accept responsibility for the 'Other', ie for the stranger who does not yet belong. This argument was based on the phenomenological view that the Self's relationship to the 'Other' can simultaneously become both a source of subjectivity and a source of new ethical responsibility for the Other. What is central to this argument is that the relations between EU citizens can be seen as an archetype of the dyadic and constitutive relationships between the Self and the Other. A more relational interpretation of the EU principle of equality can therefore be justified by referring to how just and equal relationships between EU citizens are essential for constituting their subjectivity as EU citizens. And, if the equality of relationships matters for EU citizens' full subjectivity as EU citizens, that implies that those relationships must also be constructed by law because they will not emerge organically. The final chapter of this book will discuss in more detail what theoretical and practical implications this premise of EU citizens as subjects of European integration will have for EU law and integration theory.

5

EU Citizens as Equal Subjects of European Integration: Practice and Theory

5.1 INTRODUCTION

THIS CHAPTER DISCUSSES what practical and theoretical implications EU citizens' subjectivity would have for EU law, including EU citizens' fundamental right to non-discrimination and equal treatment. It will first briefly explain how a constitutional constructivist perspective on EU citizenship provides a methodological framework within which the idea of 'subjectivity through relationships' can be introduced into EU law (Section 5.2). It will then move on to examine the 'equality of relationships' paradigm both in practice, that is, at the level of discrimination analysis, and in theory, that is, at the level of integration theory. It will be seen how the structural and the substantive equality problem can be addressed by introducing just and equal relationships between EU citizens as the essence of EU citizens' general right to equal treatment (Section 5.3). The chapter will then conclude with a more theoretical argument about how 'interdependence' as the key hermeneutic principle of European political and legal integration would support the idea of EU citizens as full and equal subjects of European integration (Section 5.4).

5.2 A CONSTITUTIONAL CONSTRUCTIVE PERSPECTIVE ON EU CITIZENSHIP

Some argue that the EU's constitutional development should focus on reshaping relations amongst the states, and not on empowering individuals vis-à-vis the states.[1] This means that the 'individual's existence' is understood as secondary to the 'union of peoples' and the underlying rationale of individual rights is seen as purely 'institutional'.[2] This book has adopted an opposite view of transnational constitutionalisation by claiming that what is genuinely novel in EU citizenship is its promise to fulfil the Court's early reference to private individuals as full and

[1] Gianluigi Palombella, 'Whose Europe? After the Constitution: A Goal-Based Citizenship' (2005) *International Journal of Constitutional Law* 357, 374.
[2] Ibid 358–59.

equal subjects of political and legal integration.[3] However, as will be discussed in this section, realising this promise without falling into the trap of 'transnational individualism'[4] requires a constructive approach to EU law as the analytical framework within which the idea of EU citizens' subjectivity can be implemented.

As a methodological approach, social constructivism does not present any substantive demands for EU law or European integration.[5] But, in order to fulfil its promise to proceed from 'critique' to 'construct', any constructive theory must develop new 'conceptual tools' to demonstrate that the existing rules and principles are not the 'only possibilities' but that they can be replaced with alternative norms and ideals.[6] Similarly, the critique of EU citizenship in this book has looked for new conceptual tools which can help us critique the EU equality problem as outlined in Part I, as well as to construct a solution to it in Part II. When the idea of theory 'as critique and normative intervention'[7] enters into the field of EU constitutional law, it makes sense to speak of *constitutional constructivism* as a specific mode of scholarship on EU law. This analysis is based on the assumption that the European Union has been a constructive project from the outset. That is, the constitutionalisation of EU law is understood as a process that is also focused on instituting the 'conceivability' of the social practice it sets up.[8]

A constructive approach to European integration means that the 'European identities' and not just 'institutions and policies' become the target of theoretical analysis.[9] Social constructivism as a theory of European integration focuses on

[3] See eg 26/62 *NV Algemene Transport- en Expeditie Onderneming van Gend & Loos v Netherlands Inland Revenue Administration* [1963] ECR 3.

[4] Alexander Somek, *Individualism: An Essay on the Authority of the European Union* (Oxford University Press, 2008) 240.

[5] Thomas Risse, 'Social Constructivism and European Integration' in Antje Wiener and Thomas Dietz (eds), *European Integration Theory*, 2nd edn (Oxford University Press, 2009) 144.

[6] Elizabeth Grosz, 'Contemporary Theories of Power and Subjectivity' in Senja Gunew (ed), *Feminist Knowledge: Critique and Construct* (Routledge, 1990) 59–60. It has been noted that, as part of this endeavour, theory must develop a capacity to recognise both the 'underlying' and 'more apparent' forms of commitments that are embedded in the prevailing norms and ideals. Ibid. A more 'critical' or 'problematising' theoretical approach to European integration does not just differ from the traditional forms of integration theory (such as neo-functionalism or different governmental theories) on the basis of its methods, but the idea of why European integration needs to be theorised is also different. See more about this eg in Thomas Dietz and Antje Wiener, 'Introducing the Mosaic of Integration Theory' in Wiener and Dietz (n 5)3 and 10.

[7] Dietz and Wiener (n 6) 18.

[8] Palombella (n 1) 362.

[9] Dietz and Wiener (n 6) 11. It is possible to distinguish between the 'structural-institutionalist' and the 'normative' social constructivist approaches. The former has its focus on institutional developments in a particular social context, while the latter underlines the ways in which European constitutionalisation is 'shaped by law'. Ulrike Liebert, 'Reconciling Market with Social Europe? The EU under the Lisbon Treaty' in Dagmar Schiek, Ulrike Liebert and Hildegard Schneider (eds), *European Economic and Social Constitutionalism after the Treaty of Lisbon* (Cambridge University Press, 2011) 73. However, what is common to both of these approaches is that the focus of analysis is on how structure and agency interact. Jeffrey T Checkel, 'Social Construction and European Integration' in Thomas Christiansen, Knud Erik Jørgensen and Antje Wiener (eds), *The Social Construction of Europe* (SAGE Publications, 2001) 62.

the question of how social actors constitute social reality.[10] Instead of identifying reality with what is thought to be 'objectively knowable', social constructivism suggests that our attributions of reality can be conferred 'by virtue of some relevant social fact'.[11] Firstly, social constructivists claim that social reality is constructed and reproduced by human agents through social practices.[12] Secondly, they claim that the existence of human agents is not independent of 'social environment and its collectively shared systems of meaning'.[13] Thirdly, the emphasis on the 'mutual *constitutiveness*' between social structures and agents forms a central premise in research informed by social constructivism.[14] For these theorists, the central question is therefore 'how things are related to us'.[15] On this basis, 'human beings and their interactions' are seen as central to understanding reality.[16] It follows from this starting point that the question of European identity appears as one of those areas to which social constructivism can particularly contribute.[17]

This book applies the constitutional constructivist approach to one specific norm and practice of EU law, namely that of EU citizenship. The psycho-dynamic and phenomenological analysis of subjectivity through the self's identification with the Other in Chapter four introduced a set of theoretical principles which form the basis for strengthening EU citizens' legal and political subjectivity as EU citizens. However, it has been noted that any attempt to deconstruct and reconstruct 'essential identities' needs to grasp the 'variety of social relations' which are relevant for applying the principle of equality.[18] It has also been noted that 'a process whereby the identity of European citizens is negotiated in emotional reflex with a concrete other, is not easily explained in formal legal categories'.[19] Moreover, reshaping essentialist identity categories must arguably locate the self 'in concrete social relations, not only in fictive or purely textual conventions'.[20] What these statements have in common is the attempt to challenge the 'categories of the person' which define narrowly 'what would constitute equality'.[21] Similarly,

[10] See eg Dagmar Schiek, 'Re-Embedding Economic and Social Constitutionalism: Normative Perspectives for the EU' in Schiek, Liebert and Schneider (n 9) 22.

[11] Sally Haslanger, 'Objective Reality, Male Reality, and Social Construction' in Ann Garry and Marilyn Pearsall (eds), *Women, Knowledge, and Reality: Explorations in Feminist Philosophy* (Routledge, 1996) 101.

[12] Risse (n 5) 145.

[13] Ibid.

[14] Ibid.

[15] Haslanger (n 11) 101.

[16] Schiek (n 10) 22.

[17] Risse (n 5) 144.

[18] Chantal Mouffe, 'Feminism, Citzenship and Radical Democratic Politics', in Judith Butler and Joan W. Scott (eds), *Feminists Theorize the Political* (Routledge, 1992) 371–72.

[19] Michelle Everson, 'A Very Cosmopolitan Citizenship: But Who Pays the Price?' in Michael Dougan, Niamh Nic Shuibhne and Eleanora Spaventa (eds), *Empowerment and Disempowerment of the European Citizen* (Hart Publishing, 2012) 636.

[20] Jane Flax, *Thinking Fragments: Psychoanalysis, Feminism, and Postmodernism in the Contemporary West* (University of California Press, 1990) 232.

[21] Drucilla Cornell, 'Gender, Sex, and Equivalent Rights' in Judith Butler and Joan W Scott (eds), *Feminists Theorize the Political* (Routledge, 1992) 293.

it is necessary to consider what role EU equality law can play in shaping those relations in and through which EU citizens' subjectivity as EU citizens is constituted.

For instance, Nicola Lacey has suggested that we must pay more attention to how law promises 'identity for those who are both eligible for and willing to accept membership of its community'.[22] From this starting point, she claims that the 'challenge of reconstructing a notion of legal subjectivity or subjecthood' is closely connected to 'the possibility of extending law's communities—in terms of both of access to powerful interpretative communities and of examining substantive questions about the meaning of membership of law's community as subject'.[23] A similar argument has been presented in the context of European and international law by those who underline the need to consider 'why and for whom do such legal systems exist'.[24] On this basis, it has been suggested that more attention needs to be paid to how the 'paradigm subject of law' is defined.[25] The need to rethink the legal subject is particularly strong in the field of anti-discrimination law, where the traditional rights discourse tends to emphasise the 'sameness' between people.[26] It has been noted that a 'reconstruction of equality' needs to address those 'limitations' which follow from the accepted standard of comparability.[27] This concern is also captured in the statement that '[b]etter theories of justice will require different accounts of what subjectivity might be'.[28]

The analysis of subjectivity can arguably contribute to a better understanding of its political and legal 'consequences'.[29] It has been seen in the previous chapter that constructing political subjectivity is a process which is shaped by those social and legal relationships in which citizens interact with one another. However, it still needs to be asked what kind of relationships law ought to create and why. In particular, what kind of relations EU law ought to create between EU citizens and why? In this book, this question has been addressed in the light of EU citizens' subjectivity. This means that new relationships, which would perhaps not exist otherwise, can become relevant as part of the discrimination analysis because they would strengthen EU citizens' subjectivity by enabling the genuine 'second-person perspective' in relation to the 'Other'. This approach is based on the constructive view that EU citizens' agency, and their subjectivity as part of it, are developed in relation to the external world.

[22] Nicola Lacey, *Unspeakable Subjects: Feminist Essays in Legal and Social Theory* (Hart Publishing, 1998) 125.

[23] Ibid.

[24] Christopher Harding, 'Legal Subjectivity as a Fundamental Value: the Emergence of Non-State Actors in Europe' in Kim Economides, Lammy Betten, John Bridge, Andrew Tettenborn and Vivien Shrubsall (eds), *Fundamental Values* (Hart Publishing, 2000) 115.

[25] Lacey (n 22) 14.

[26] Martha Minow, *Making All the Difference—Inclusion, Exclusion, and American Law* (Cornell University Press, 1990) 146 and Lacey (n 22) 28.

[27] See eg Lacey (n 22) 30. See also Minow (n 26) 174 and 213. Minow argues that what she calls the 'social-relations approach' enables 'critiques of the ways issues about difference have been framed'.

[28] Jane Flax, *Disputed Subjects: Essays on Pyschoanalysis, Politics and Philosophy* (Routledge, 1993) 111.

[29] Ibid 109.

Instead of adopting the view of the 'third-person, external observer standpoint', a constructivist perspective both allows and requires us to approach political subjectivity as 'the situation between the first and the second-persons'.[30] From this starting point, it seems logical to argue that the relationships which matter most for EU citizens' subjectivity as EU citizens are those (specific) social and legal relationships that are formed in relation to other holders of the status of EU citizenship. This is not to say that horizontal relations between EU citizens would form the only relevant category of inter-relations for the project of European integration. Other types of relations, such as intergovernmental relations, are also important for achieving the objectives of European integration as outlined in the EU Treaties. However, horizontal relations between EU citizens are unique constitutive relations because they enable EU citizens to become full and equal subjects of EU law and European integration. Moreover, if just and equal relationships between EU citizens are crucial for their subjectivity as EU citizens, as has been shown in this book, EU law has a central role in constructing these relationships in the absence of cultural or ethnic belonging or a full democratic pedigree at the EU level.

Thus, EU citizens becoming more noticeable subjects of EU law depends on the quality of relationships between EU citizens. These findings about how central just and equal relationships between EU citizens are for constituting EU citizens' subjectivity as EU citizens can be conceptualised as the 'equality of relationships' paradigm. This paradigm holds that the relationships in which EU citizens can become full and equal subjects of EU law and European integration must in part be constructed by EU law because they will not emerge otherwise. It has been seen in this section that a constitutional constructive perspective on EU citizenship can help us to incorporate the 'equality of relationships' paradigm into EU law as a means of giving more substance to EU citizens' subjectivity. The practical and theoretical implications of this suggestion will be explored further in the next sections of this chapter.

5.3 EU CITIZENS' SUBJECTIVITY AS A MATTER OF LAW

The constructive perspective on EU citizenship directs our attention to the way in which law in general and the discrimination analysis in particular create and shape those relationships in which EU citizens can become full and equal subjects of EU law. This section will discuss how the 'equality of relationships' paradigm as a means of giving more substance to EU citizens' subjectivity as EU citizens can provide a way forward with the EU equality problem as outlined in this book. The EU equality problem emerges from the fact that EU citizens' general right to equal treatment under Article 18 TFEU lacks independence both at the level of

[30] John Shotter, 'Psychology and Citizenship: Identity and Belonging' in Bryan S Turner (ed), *Citizenship and Social Theory* (SAGE Publications, 1993) 119 and 121.

its *de facto* scope and at the level of limitations which have been accepted on that right.[31] This problem can be re-framed by returning to the original research question of whether EU citizenship has the potential to transform those relationships within which the principles of distributive justice gain relevance in EU law. In this section, it will first be seen how the relational understanding of equality can provide a more independent objective for EU law. It will then be considered how a new, more inter-relational, test for legitimate differential treatment between EU citizens emerges from this understanding of the EU principle of equality.

5.3.1 A More Independent Equality Objective for EU Law

The claim for more comparability between EU citizens does not provide an adequate solution to the EU equality problem if the value of diversity is taken seriously in EU law.[32] In considering the practical consequences of the 'equality of relationships' paradigm for EU law, it is therefore important to distinguish between 'relative' and 'relational' accounts of equality. Relative justifications for equal treatment are based on the idea that the people are identified as equals on the basis of a certain 'standard of comparison'.[33] Understanding equality as a relational idea is to value equal relationships more intrinsically, in which case access to equal treatment is no longer about identifying comparability on the basis of citizenship status, but about the realisation of just and equal relationships between citizens. The argument about more just and equal (legal) relationships between EU citizens as a source of their subjectivity as EU citizens comes closer to this latter view of equality. Shifting the focus of EU equality law from comparability between EU citizens to just and equal relationships between them could therefore help us to overcome the structural equality problem as discussed in Chapter two.

The notion of a structural equality problem refers to the fact that EU citizens' fundamental right to non-discrimination and equal treatment under Article 18 TFEU has *de facto* no independent scope of application. The important question for overcoming the structural equality problem is whether the EU constitutional order can provide a normative justification for a more independent equality objective. The idea of EU citizenship as a source of subjectivity would allow us to answer this question positively. Namely, recognising EU citizens as full subjects

[31] The analysis of the EU 'equality problem' in chapter 2 referred to (1) the lack of (de facto) independent scope of EU citizens' general right to equal treatment under Article 18 of the Consolidated Version of the Treaty on the Functioning of the European Union (TFEU) [2012] OJ C326/47, which may cause circularity because the reliance on the right to equal treatment can lead to termination of lawful residence which, at the same time, is a necessary precondition for the enjoyment of the right to equal treatment (the structural equality problem) and (2) to the lack of independent, non-economic, criteria for legitimate differential treatment between EU citizens because the 'real link' test is merged with the 'unreasonable burden' test in the case law (the substantive equality problem).

[32] See more about this in Section 3.5, p 122.

[33] Christine M Koggel, *Perspectives on Equality: Constructing a Relational Theory* (Rowman & Littlefield Publishers Ltd, 1998) 2.

of European integration would indicate that their very subjectivity constitutes integration. And, if becoming EU citizens as full and equal subjects of European integration depends on the (e)quality of their relationships with other EU citizens, as has been argued in Chapter four, the equality of those relationships can be seen as an independent objective of European integration on the basis that it provides a precondition for their full subjectivity under EU law. It follows from this that the 'equality of relationships' paradigm can provide one solution to the structural EU equality problem by justifying a more independent equality objective in the case of economically inactive and dependent EU citizens, even when they lack a sufficient degree of *ex ante* belonging under the 'unreasonable burden' test.

5.3.2 A New Test for Legitimate Differential Treatment Between EU Citizens

The 'equality of relationships' paradigm opens the door for a more independent equality objective in EU law and, thus, sheds new light on the EU equality problem. However, implementing this paradigm in EU law would also require changes in the interpretation of EU citizens' general right to equal treatment. What remains of this section will discuss in more detail what these changes are and how the legal analysis of Article 18 TFEU is affected. In practice, the 'equality of relationships' paradigm shifts the focus of discrimination analysis from individual activity and responsibility to the quality of relationships between EU citizens. And the quality of these relationships is affected when the limits of legitimate differential treatment between EU citizens are defined. It is therefore important to consider in more detail how the argument of EU citizens as full and equal subjects of EU law can shape the substantive criteria under which legitimate differential treatment between EU citizens is defined.

The accepted justifications for legitimate differential treatment are currently based on the activity-based ideal of equality which reduces EU citizens' agency to individual responsibility to prove economic or social integration. The 'equality of relationships' paradigm requires that the criteria for legitimate differential treatment become interpersonal. Adopting a more 'interpersonal test'[34] for legitimate differential treatment would mean that the way in which 'needy' migrant EU citizens are treated in the host Member State is not examined merely in terms of the vertical relationship of belonging between an individual and the state. Instead, more weight must be given to the impact which this treatment may have on the equality of horizontal relationships between EU citizens.

It has been noted in academic commentary that the case law on social rights has already redefined the '*vertical* relationship' between the individuals and the Member States but the same process of reconstruction has not yet happened

[34] The 'interpersonal test' can have a dual justificatory role both as a source of individual responsibility for 'action that affect other members' and as a test for 'whether all people are treated as members of a community'. See Koggel (n 33) 120.

'at the *horizontal* level, ie between states or between European citizens in terms of European solidarity spaces'.[35] However, there is an increasing need to go beyond the ideas of 'vertical integration' as a means of identity-building to explore 'a more horizontal and dynamic theory of political recognition'.[36] According to this view, being a European citizen is not about 'feeling European' but about 'having a bond of mutual recognition with nationals of other Member States'.[37] A similar idea of more just and equal relationships between EU citizens has gained more normative weight from the analysis of EU citizenship as a source of transnational subjectivity in this book. This means that the 'equality of relationships' paradigm can also provide a means of tackling the substantive equality problem as discussed in Chapter two.

In practice, the 'equality of relationships' paradigm challenges the current symbiosis between the 'real link' test and the 'unreasonable burden' test by shifting the focus of discrimination analysis from the vertical belonging between a Union citizen and the Member State to the question of how equal treatment, or the lack of it, affects the (e)quality of relationships between EU citizens. Formal criteria, such as the length of residence, or economic criteria, such as prior economic activity, may still gain relevance in this assessment. But the 'interpersonal test' which emerges from the 'equality of relationships' paradigm differs from the current 'real link' test under which the primary relationship of integration appears between the host Member State and the Union citizen. Moreover, the 'interpersonal' test views the establishment of a 'real link' not just as an expression of individual activity but also as a shared commitment with the nationals of the host Member State to pursue one's life project under the same rights and duties as the nationals of the host Member State. The normative difference between economically active and inactive EU citizens would therefore become less significant if it is accepted that EU citizens also constitute integration as the subjects of EU law and European integration and not just on the basis of their economic and social activity.

The 'equality of relationships' paradigm will not solve the problems related to the *ad hoc* character of discrimination analysis in general. But it can justify a more extensive use of non-economic criteria in this analysis. The Court's reference to 'other social and economic factors' in *Commission v Austria* and *Prinz and Seeberger* can be seen as a sign of increasing willingness to explore this field.[38] But the 'equality of relationships' paradigm underlines that these 'other social and economic factors' are valid considerations and must be given more weight in the

[35] Wolfram Lamping, 'Mission Impossible? Limits and Perils of Institutionalizing Post-National Social Policy' in Yuri Borgmann-Prebil and Malcolm Ross (eds), *Promoting Solidarity in the European Union* (Oxford University Press, 2010) 70.

[36] Paul Magnette, 'How Can One Be European? Reflections on the Pillars of European Civic Identity' (2007) 13 *European Law Journal* 664, 665–68.

[37] Ibid 668.

[38] Case C-75/11 *European Commission v Republic of Austria*, 4 October 2012, paras 62–63 and Cases C-532/11 and C-585/11 *Laurence Prinz v Region Hannover and Philipp Seeberger v Studentenwerk Heidelberg*, 18 July 2013, paras 36–38.

discrimination analysis because they shape those social/horizontal relationships in which EU citizens' subjectivity is constituted as EU citizens and not just because they prove *ex ante* integration or activity. However, the aim is not to secure the equality of outcomes between EU citizens in every possible respect. Rather, what is seen as decisive is the promotion of the equality of those relationships which can strengthen and advance EU citizens' status as subjects of European integration. Under the 'interpersonal test', more attention would therefore be paid to how the refusal to grant equal treatment, may create an obstacle to the Union citizen's ability to integrate into the society of the host Member State and to relate to the nationals of that state on an equal basis. This would mean that EU citizens are granted a more status-based right to equal treatment under which justifications for legitimate differential treatment must be interpreted narrowly.

Assessing justificatory criteria for legitimate differential treatment becomes more positive, for it will take into account how equal access to the benefit in question would advance the applicant's equal relationships with the nationals of the host Member State, including his/her potential for future integration into the society of the host Member State. Social integration is seen as a dynamic process and the right to equal treatment is not just a reward for individual activity, but also a shared goal which may have positive effects on the future integration of the individual in question. In other words, the 'interpersonal' test would also recognise the *ex post* integrative dimension of equal treatment. The current interpretation of Article 18 TFEU implies that *those who belong deserve to be treated equally*, whereas viewing EU citizens as full and equal subjects of EU law would suggest that *those who are treated equally (will) belong*. The discrimination analysis under the 'equality of relationships' paradigm focuses on the potential of equal treatment to create integration rather than on the evidence of assumed non-integration, such as economic dependence, vulnerability and the lack of long-term resident status of those 'needy' EU citizens who, nonetheless, would benefit from equal treatment as a means of strengthening their sense of subjectivity as EU citizens through further integration into the host Member State.

The EU equality problem as discussed in this book concerned the scope of EU citizenship as an equal status of all Member State nationals in relation to the 'inner limits' of Article 18 TFEU. However, adopting the 'equality of relationships' paradigm as an interpretative key to EU citizens' right to equal treatment, might also have implications on the 'outer limits' of Article 18 TFEU.[39] The fact that the focus here is on the 'equality of relationships' as a source of transnational subjectivity, and not on equality *per se*, means that those relationships which contain no cross-border element might in theory still be excluded from the scope of Article 18 TFEU. This could occur on the basis that they are not as likely to

[39] See more about the 'outer' and 'inner' limits of Article 18 TFEU in Anne Pieter Van de Mei, 'The Outer Limits of The Prohibition of Discrimination on the Grounds of Nationality: A Look Through The Lens of Union Citizenship' (2011) 18 *Maastricht Journal of European and Comparative Law* 62.

advance EU citizens' sense of subjectivity as EU citizens as those relationships which emerge after the Union citizen has already exercised his/her right to free movement and residence as an EU citizen. In the long run, however, the emphasis on just and equal relationships between EU citizens would make it more difficult to justify why 'purely internal situations' are irrelevant for the project of European integration in so far as they include relations between EU citizens which might also increase their sense of subjectivity as subjects of European integration. However, further studies on this question must be left for others to conduct. This book has completed its own task in providing a legally and philosophically coherent normative justification for a more relational account of equality in EU law, which can provide both a solution to the structural and the substantive EU equality problem.

5.4 EU CITIZENS' SUBJECTIVITY AS A MATTER OF INTEGRATION THEORY

A renewed understanding of the EU principle of equality can be based on the claim that just and equal relationships between EU citizens form a precondition for EU citizens becoming full and equal subjects of EU law. However, the EU equality problem is rooted in a deeper uncertainty over what motivates integration in the first place. It is argued that EU citizenship as an equal status must go beyond the establishment of individual rights to examine the relevance of just and equal relationships between EU citizens for the whole project of European integration. This section will accordingly conclude this chapter, and the book, by asking what it would mean for the project of European integration to recognise EU citizens as its subjects.

It has been argued that EU citizenship has already established a substantive right which fundamentally differs from functional rights established by the four fundamental freedoms.[40] To the extent that this is true and the rights of EU citizens are not just instruments for constructing the internal market, what, then, is the justification for requiring their equal treatment as full and equal subjects of European integration? This book responds by saying that deepening the relationships of interdependence between the subjects of European integration as the fundamental value underlying the project of European integration can best explain why the process of integration has taken the direction of constitutionalisation instead of the more traditional forms of intergovernmentalism. Or, at least, that it can be used to give legitimacy to those constitutional developments afterwards even if their origins were more pragmatic in nature. Under this account, European integration is constituted through those relationships in which the deepening interdependence between its subjects is actualised. But why would EU citizens count as those subjects?

[40] See eg Xavier Groussot, 'Principled Citizenship and the Process of European Constitutionalization: From a Pie in the Sky to a Sky with Diamonds' in Ulf Bernitz, Joakin Nergelius and Cecilia Gardner (eds), *General Principles of EC Law in a Process of Development* (Kluwer, 2008).

5.4.1 Meaningful Relationships Between EU Citizens: A Source of New 'Associative Duties'?

The critics of post-national citizenship models argue that duties based on social rights will always require 'strong social and symbolic ties of generalized reciprocity and diffuse solidarity'.[41] However, it is not self-evident that duties which arise out of special relationships must always be reduced to 'duties arising out of discrete interactions'.[42] On the contrary, some argue for a 'non-reductionist' approach under which special responsibilities can be based on 'our relationships to people rather than particular interactions with them'.[43] This approach suggests that to value one's relationships is, in part, to see oneself 'as having such responsibilities'.[44] The central question for this account of 'meaningful relationships' is under what conditions people have reason to value their relations to others in such a way that those relationships become a source of distributive claims. This question can be re-framed by asking whether the process of European integration can provide such reason to value just and equal relationships between EU citizens that those relationships justify access to social equality in the host Member State even in the absence of *ex ante* belonging on the side of the needy and dependent EU citizen.

Many commentators agree that the EU can now be seen an 'emergent polity'.[45] More pessimistic authors nevertheless suggest that '[r]edistribution is not an issue' in the constitutional project beyond national boundaries.[46] For instance, Alexander Somek argues that such 'social facts' which could justify redistributive claims are possible 'only as long as a group experiences certain social practices, such as the practice of politics, as instances of "living together" or as, however conflicted, pursuit of the common good'.[47] But, again, it seems important to consider more carefully whether it is possible that altogether new 'social practices' with the potential to create new shared experiences can also emerge from the project of European integration. The 'politicisation' of the EU has been advocated as one possible solution to this dilemma, as has been discussed in Chapter three. This approach is based on the view that 'the success of any constitutional regime rests on the extent to which it reflects how those governed by it see their political role'.[48]

[41] Thomas Faist, 'Social Citizenship in the European Union: Nested Membership' (2001) 39 *Journal of Common Market Studies* 37, 46.

[42] Samuel Scheffler, *Boundaries and Allegiances: Problems of Justice and Responsibility in Liberal Thought* (Oxford University Press, 2006) 98.

[43] Ibid 100. From Scheffler's point of view, 'only socially salient connections among people' count as relationships in this sense. However, Scheffler outlines that 'two members of a socially recognized group do have a relationship in the relevant sense, even if they have never met'. Ibid 102.

[44] Ibid 103–04. According to Scheffler, the fact that the 'significance of our social relations is not fully under our own control' does not compromise self-determination because the 'relationships that generate responsibilities for an individual are those relationships that the individual has reason to value'. Ibid 100.

[45] See eg Antje Wiener, 'Constitution-Making and Citizenship Practice—Bridging the Democracy Gap in the EU?' (1997) 35 *Journal of Common Market Studies* 595, 596.

[46] Alexander Somek, *The Cosmopolitan Constitution* (Oxford University Press, 2014) 234.

[47] Ibid 237.

[48] Wiener (n 45) 600.

However, it has also been noted that 'constitution-building' cannot be examined as separate from 'how individuals will relate to each other as, possibly, citizens and members of a political community'.[49] This is where the status of EU citizenship as a source of subjectivity could potentially have an important role to play.

This book has suggested that, because equal treatment between EU citizens advances those relationships within which EU citizens can become full subjects of EU law and European integration, there is strong reason to value just and equal relationships between EU citizens, independent of the internal market. Viewing EU citizenship as a source of subjectivity may therefore transform those relationships which are regarded to be meaningful when access to social benefits is defined under EU law. Moreover, meaningful relationships between EU citizens cannot be created without creating new 'associative' duties based on these relationships. Or, as Samuel Scheffler has put it, 'the perception of them as giving rise to such duties is what enables them to make rewarding relationships possible'.[50] In other words, if just and equal relationships between EU citizens *qua* EU citizens are meaningful because they help to construct EU citizenship as a source of transnational political and legal subjectivity, these relationships can also be seen as an independent source of 'associative duties', including distributive claims in EU law. The crucial question is therefore whether EU citizens can be seen as subjects of EU law and European integration, not just in the judicial rhetoric but also in the application of EU equality law.

5.4.2 European Integration: A Dynamic Process of Deepening Interdependence?

The idea of transnational solidarity has often been offered as a moral justification for the existence of the EU beyond the internal market and free movement.[51] For instance, Floris de Witte has suggested that, since the EU cannot at present be regarded as a fully functioning 'transnational political system', the EU's quest for justice must be examined in the light of different expressions of 'transnational solidarity'.[52] The status of EU citizenship has accordingly been described as an 'institutionalization of solidarity'.[53] However, solidarity, whether national or transnational, is based on the existing sense of community or belonging.[54] It has been noted on this basis that this approach is problematic in the context of the

[49] Ibid 601.

[50] Scheffler (n 42) 62.

[51] See eg Yuri Borgmann-Prebil and Malcolm Ross, 'Promoting European Solidarity: Between Rhetoric and Reality' in Borgmann-Prebil and Ross (n 35)20.

[52] See eg Floris de Witte, 'Transnational Solidarity and the Mediation of Conflicts of Justice in Europe' (2012) 18 *European Law Journal* 694, 696.

[53] Malcolm Ross, 'Solidarity—A New Constitutional Paradigm for the EU' in Borgmann-Prebil and Ross (n 35)27.

[54] The principle of solidarity is usually based on 'gradations according to differing degrees of integration in and membership of the (national) redistribution collectivity'. Stefano Giubboni, 'Free Movement of Persons and European Solidarity' (2007) 13 *European Law Journal* 360, 375.

EU because it 'presupposes something which it simultaneously needs to develop: common values and the willingness to share'.[55] It is true that what has been called 'aspirational solidarity' could emerge from carefully considering what rights and obligations are 'implicit' in the 'communal objectives' of the EU.[56] But even this approach to transnational solidarity seems to place more weighton 'aspirational' belonging than on the constructive potential of EU citizenship to redefine on what basis EU citizens are sufficiently related to one another to be treated equally under European Union law.

Unlike the idea of transnational solidarity, the argument of EU citizenship as a source of subjectivity necessarily transforms what constitutes a 'meaningful relationship' for the purposes of non-discrimination and equal treatment within the EU. However, the legitimacy of this vision depends on the hermeneutics of integration, ie on the values and principles of interpretation which underlie the project of European integration as a whole. It must therefore be considered which ideal of integration would support the view of EU citizens' subjectivity as something that constitutes integration in itself. It will be suggested below in this section that this ideal is to conceive European integration as a dynamic process of deepening interdependence between the subjects of integration because it also places a distinct value on creating and enabling such relationships of interdependence (between its subjects) which would not exist otherwise.

For instance, Miguel Poiares Maduro suggests that 'lack of European solidarity is the result of that very lack of internalization of the consequences of interdependence'.[57] However, some respond to him stating that there is no reason to take for granted the claim that 'European integration generates a deep interdependence between national policies'.[58] This criticism is based on the view that placing so much weight on interdependence leads to a functionalist theory of European integration. This section discusses the question of interdependence from a different perspective; namely, the role of interdependence is here understood as a positive normative value, rather than a functionalist necessity. This approach radically differs, for instance, from Alexander Somek's negative understanding of interdependence, according to which:

> The web of mutual interdependence is the extension of our nature into the social sphere. The resulting quasi-natural social bondage can only be overcome by rising above it. Hence, the *emancipation* from commodification and toil is the task of the real polity.[59]

The process of integration can be understood as striving for more just and equal relationships between its subjects as a means of deepening their mutual interdependence—instead of seeing (inter)dependence merely as a vice which needs

[55] Lamping (n 35) 47.

[56] de Witte (n 52) 708.

[57] Miguel Poiares Maduro, 'A New Governance for the European Union and the Euro: Democracy and Justice', RSCAS Policy Papers 2012/11, 5.

[58] eg Alexander Somek, 'What Is Political Union' (2013) German Law Journal 561.

[59] Somek (n 46) 170.

to be overcome by political or legal cooperation. A political and legal system which derives its existence from the deepening relationships of interdependence between its subjects needs to value their relationships non-instrumentally in order not to become self-contradictory. Thus, interpreting the objectives of European integration in the light of the ideal of interdependence indicates that just and equal relationships between the subjects of integration become involuntary, ie not chosen, for the integration project and theory. This is a claim for a political, rather than cosmopolitan, conception of justice[60] in the sense that conditioning the project of European integration on just and equal relations of interdependence between the subjects of integration creates an obligation to live in a just society with other subjects of integration who commit themselves to the values and objectives of European integration—and not with just anyone. However, the 'articulation of the problem as one of relationships and associations' must still address the question of 'why people might want to transfer even some of their loyalty to abstract and so far incoherent and incomplete institutions such as the EU and its constitution'.[61]

How far the dynamic process of deepening interdependence can extend therefore remains undefined in this book. But to define European integration in terms of interdependence implies that just and equal relationships between the subjects of integration (whether individuals or States) have a distinct value for the project of integration. Moreover, European integration then appears as a dynamic process which does not just value the existing relationships of interdependence between its subjects, but which also searches for opportunities to create new 'meaningful relationships' of interdependence. Thus, explaining European integration in terms of interdependence places intrinsic value both on deepening the existing relationships between the subjects of integration and on creating new relationships which would not otherwise exist between them. One condition for genuine relationships of interdependence is the self-governance of those who are involved in those relationships. This would mean that recognising EU citizens as subjects of European integration would also make such 'meaningful relationships' of interdependence possible which would not exist otherwise because their materialisation and existence depend on the subjectivity of those EU citizens who are involved in these relationships.

The previous paragraph explains how the argument of EU citizens' subjectivity is in line with defining European integration in terms of 'constitutive interdependence'. This scenario may seem disconcerting to some because it indicates that we recognise the process of integration as something *that actively creates its own subjects*. This dimension of political and legal integration can be described as transcendental, meaning that it is difficult to plan or predict the outcomes of European

[60] See more about the difference between these two forms of justice in Thomas Nagel, 'The Problem of Global Justice' (2005) 33 *Philosophy & Public Affairs* 113, 121 and 132.

[61] Jo Shaw, 'The Interpretation of European Union Citizenship' (1998) 61 *Modern Law Review* 293, 306.

integration in advance in so far as they turn out to be more than the mere sum of its parts. Viewing the constitutionalisation of EU law as a dynamic process of deepening interdependence between its subjects is in accordance with the argument that integration is incremental. Mutual interdependence was first recognised just between the Member States and only in the context of economic policy, above all, free and undistorted competition. The so-called 'constitutional moments'[62] of EU law, including the emergence of the doctrines of direct effect and supremacy, the creation of Union citizenship, and the inclusion of the EU Charter of Fundamental Rights in primary law, have provided significant signposts on this journey. The next step could have been the Union's long-debated accession to the European Convention on Human Rights. What the effects of this step on EU citizenship would be remains to be seen. However, all of these developments can be interpreted as steps towards (and not away from) giving more substance to the idea of EU citizens as full and equal subjects of European integration.

5.5 CONCLUSION

This chapter applied the argument of 'subjectivity through relationships' into EU law and the integration theory. It first considered how EU law can construct those social relationships within which the emergence of EU citizens' subjectivity as EU citizens is enabled and maintained. This analysis is built on a constitutional constructive perspective on EU citizenship, which gives rise to the 'equality of relationships' paradigm. The chapter then discussed how the 'equality of relationships' paradigm can justify a more independent equality objective in relation to Article 18 TFEU, as a solution to the structural equality problem, and how it can give birth to a new, more interpersonal, test for legitimate differential treatment between EU citizens, as a solution to the substantive equality problem. This analysis was completed by considering which hermeneutic principle of integration would justify the argument of EU citizens as full and equal subjects of European integration.

This final part of the chapter defined European integration as a process of dynamic recognition of mutual interdependence between its subjects, including not just the Member States but also the nationals of the Member States as EU citizens. The justification for EU citizens' subjectivity was based on the argument that those social and legal relations in which EU citizens' sense of subjectivity as EU citizens is constituted create an entirely new category of meaningful relations of interdependence within the project of European integration. Thus, as there is a whole array of relationships of interdependence which become possible when the Union gives birth to its own subjects (= EU citizens), it seems logical that this is what happens in due course. On this basis, the chapter concluded that EU citizenship as a source of subjectivity can transform what constitutes a 'meaningful relationship' for the purposes of non-discrimination and equal treatment within the EU.

[62] eg Síonaidh Douglas-Scott, *Constitutional Law of the European Union* (Longman, 2002) 522.

Conclusions

THE CRUCIAL QUESTION for rethinking EU citizenship as an equal status is whether EU citizens are fully recognised as subjects of European integration. If the answer is 'yes', the essence of EU citizens' right to equal treatment must be seen as inherently relational and just and equal relationships between EU citizens become a decisive criterion for interpreting the EU principle of equality. What is novel and intriguing in the status of EU citizenship is that it promises to put more flesh on the bones of the Court's early promise to recognise private individuals as subjects of political and legal integration. The positive outcome of this analysis is that a more relational conception of equality can be established within the existing constitutional framework of EU law if the idea of private individuals as subjects of European integration is given more substance in the application of EU law. The more negative side of this analysis is that constructing EU citizenship as a source of transnational political and legal subjectivity depends essentially on more just and equal relationships between EU citizens but cannot be reduced to them alone. Namely, transnational subject-formation appears as a complex process which also depends on the reception of difference through the subject's unconscious and conscious identification with the Other.

EU citizenship is more normative than its national counterparts because it emerges from the objectives of the founding Treaties and its aim is to secure the realisation of the values and aims of European integration. The EU's fundamental purpose is sometimes defined as to create a 'level-playing field', that is, to create rules that are applicable cross-border. It is nonetheless important to ask why this is so. This book argued that the *Telos* of integration is to transform our understanding of what constitutes a 'meaningful relationship' between its subjects for the purposes of non-discrimination and equal treatment. The ideal of EU citizens as full and equal subjects of European integration as discussed in this book therefore offers a positive approach to the ontology of relationships: For a project involving political and legal integration in the triangular relationships between states, individuals, and transnational institutions, interdependence is no longer an unfortunate imperative or vice which must be overcome, but a virtue which should be fostered. The non-economic objective of European integration can thus be seen as opposite to what has been called 'transnational individualism', which claims that 'once we move beyond the purview of family life and friendship, we live in mutual isolation from one another'.[1]

[1] Alexander Somek, *Individualism: An Essay on the Authority of the European Union* (Oxford University Press, 2008) 240.

Recognising the inherent connection between EU citizens' agency and their subjectivity introduces a compelling normative justification for advancing more just and equal relationships between EU citizens. The language of individual rights has failed to provide enough substance for the status of EU citizenship as a 'fundamental' or 'equal' status. It has also been noted that it would be 'unrealistic (at least at present) to offer an overarching, substantive, redistributionist theory of justice for the EU'.[2] However, this book adopted the view that there must be a meaningful connection between 'equality' and 'citizenship'. It follows from this that the analysis of EU citizenship cannot avoid the difficult question of whether distributive social justice, understood as a quest for just and equal relations between citizens, can be justified transnationally in the absence of a full democratic pedigree at the EU level. The question, 'Should the EU pursue a quest for justice?' cannot be examined separately from the question of what justice means for the EU. The relevance of 'justice as fairness' amongst those who are united by 'common sympathies', as Rawls framed it, must not be rejected, but the project of European integration is fundamentally a project which emerges from the need to redefine what political and social justice means in a world in which no one can claim to be fully self-sufficient.

This question concerning transnational justice gives birth to the EU equality problem as discussed in this book. Namely, the EU principle of equality suffers from structural and substantive indeterminacy in so far as it needs to define the connection between equal treatment and EU citizenship. EU citizenship, as the 'fundamental status' of all Member State nationals, is still deeply rooted in the narrow individualistic view of agency. The philosophical foundations of the EU principle of equality must therefore be critically evaluated and replaced with a more relational account of equality. However, the difficult question is whether meaningful relationships between EU citizens can emerge transnationally. On a more positive note, the lack of relationality as the core of the EU equality problem can be faced by (re)constructing EU citizenship as a source of subjectivity. Analysis of the conditions of subjectivity shows that EU citizens' full subjectivity as EU citizens can only emerge within just and equal relationships between EU citizens. Hence, where national citizenship can primarily be seen as an instrument for political legitimacy in a representative democracy, EU citizenship can be seen as an instrument for creating new subjects of European integration. In this book, the analysis of EU citizenship involved the following four different levels.

Firstly, the book used the case law of the CJEU to show that the status of EU citizenship has not reached its full potential as a 'fundamental status'. Although the Court now frequently bases its decisions on the status of EU citizenship, the parameters for EU citizens' agency and, thus, the enjoyment of their fundamental

[2] Síonaidh Douglas Scott, 'The Problem of Justice in the European Union—Values, Pluralism, and Critical Legal Justice' in Julie Dickson and Pavlos Eleftheriadis (eds), *Philosophical Foundations of European Union Law* (Oxford University Press, 2012) 432.

right to equality and non-discrimination are still conditioned on the individual responsibility to prove value through economic and social activity. The book argued that, in order to actualise the potential of EU citizenship as an equal status, it is important to have a closer look at the concepts of social equality and distributive justice that underlie the EU principle of equality (Chapters one to two).

Secondly, an insight into philosophical egalitarianism laid the ground for a theoretical critique of the EU principle of equality as it emerges from the case law. The EU principle of equality suffers from a 'deontological bias' in so far as it conditions EU citizens' access to social equality on the individual responsibility to prove economic or social integration. The EU principle of equality is therefore vulnerable to a similar criticism as that which has been directed against the so-called responsibility-sensitive theories of egalitarian justice on the basis that they fail to adequately consider social equality as a 'normative ideal of human relationships'. Placing more weight on the idea of just and equal relationships between EU citizens could provide an alternative account of equality for the EU, but the difficult question is how a relational account of justice could be justified in a transnational context (Chapter three).

Thirdly, the book moved from the deconstruct to the reconstruct by exploring how the ideal of more just and equal relationships between citizens can be justified in the absence of a full democratic pedigree at the level of the EU. One such approach is to construct EU citizenship as a source of subjectivity. This approach to EU citizenship is built on the feminist argument that citizens' political and legal agency cannot be separated from their sense of subjectivity. Exploring this connection between citizens' agency and their subjectivity in developmental psychology and phenomenological philosophy paved the way for the argument that the normative significance of just and equal relationships between EU citizens can be derived from the claim that their sense of subjectivity as EU citizens is constituted in and through their relationships with other EU citizens (Chapter four).

Finally, the book applied the theoretical argument of 'subjectivity through relationships' into EU law and the integration theory. This was done, first, by considering how transnational law in general and EU citizens' fundamental right to non-discrimination and equal treatment in particular can be used to construct those social relationships within which the emergence of EU citizens' subjectivity as EU citizens is enabled and maintained and, then, by suggesting that the hermeneutic principle of interdependence can support the argument of EU citizens as full and equal subjects of European integration (Chapter five).

This study of EU citizenship was based on the fact that EU equality law suffers from normative indeterminacy. The emergence of EU citizenship has moved the EU principle of equality from the realm of 'nationality discrimination' to that of 'equal citizenship'. However, the question of what 'equal citizenship' means in a transnational context has remained unclear and under-theorised. EU citizenship needs more 'philosophy' because both the history and the tradition of the EU legal system are still thin compared to national or international law. The inadequacy of legal positivism is multiplied in the realm of transnational law where the existing democratic structure does not provide validity and recognition (Hart) for the law and its application. What remains is, at its worst, a technocratic system of rules and regulations that consume private individuals and their human potential for a neo-liberal and potentially discriminating economic agenda or, even more appallingly, a technocratic system which exists for the sake of its own existence, rather than for the sake of justice or any other human value, including economic growth. For pessimists, EU law seems to approach a travesty of justice in instrumentalising private individuals and their fundamental rights in the name of European economic integration.

The *status quo* has been challenged by suggesting that the status of EU citizenship should be interpreted 'in such a way that both the "rich" and the "poor" can enjoy the rights that come with it'.[3] This book explored whether the philosophical foundations of the EU principle of equality can be transformed within the existing constitutional system of the EU in such a way that 'needy' EU citizens could gain agency and enjoy the status of EU citizenship. This analysis went beyond the claim that Articles 18 and 21 TFEU should be read as fundamental rights or that the status of EU citizenship can be seen as a proxy for more explicit comparability between EU citizens to examine where the normativity of these claims comes from in the case of economically inactive and dependent Union citizens. This study did not promote unconditional access to social benefits, but introduced a new conceptual framework for transnational subjectivity within which just and equal legal relationships must be given more weight in discrimination analysis. Even if the political will is to protect the national welfare sovereignty, it is no longer sustainable to mask what implications these choices have on EU citizens' agency and subjectivity as EU citizens. By contrast, it is necessary to discuss more openly what ideological and philosophical presumptions are embedded in the interpretation of the EU principle of equality. In particular, it is important to bear in mind that the question of EU citizenship as an equal status is a question about transnational justice and not just about individual rights.

The key to understanding EU citizenship as an equal status is when differential treatment between EU citizens is legitimate and when it is not. The book engaged in this task from two perspectives. Firstly, the limits on EU citizens' right to non-discrimination and equal treatment were critically assessed as parameters for their agency as EU citizens. Secondly, the book contributed to the ongoing debate on transnational justice by demonstrating how a normative justification for a more relational conception of equality emerges from recognising the connection between EU citizens' agency and their subjectivity. Namely, just and equal legal relationships between EU citizens create the social space in which EU citizenship can be constructed as a source of political and legal subjectivity. This kind of subjectivity is not what is meant by 'political subjectivity' in the context

[3] See eg Anne Pieter Van der Mei, *Free Movement of Persons within the European Community—Cross-Border Access to Public Benefits* (Hart Publishing, 2003) 220.

of a democratic nation state. However, the ideal of transnational subjectivity as advanced in this book is able to justify the political value of just and equal relationships between EU citizens even in the absence of a full democratic pedigree at the EU level. Moreover, this attempt to engage with the substantive democratic values in a transnational context can and, hopefully, will strengthen the transnational democratic institutions and structures in the long run.

This is clearly a bottom-up approach which requires both time and faith in the possibility of such cognitive changes in regard to how a 'polity' can emerge transnationally. However, it seems clear that any top-down ideal of transnational politics is deemed to fail as long as it finds no echo from EU citizens' sense of subjectivity as EU citizens. It is also clear that this is not a one-way process in which the existing concepts of democracy and citizenship would suffice to determine what can be regarded as legitimate in the context of EU law. The process of integration itself shapes our view of when and how differential treatment can be justified within the EU. An important meta-question is therefore how we can observe and evaluate those changes in our standards of normative critique that follow from the process of integration. Along these lines, the argument that EU citizenship can gain more substance as a fundamental status if advancing more just and equal relationships between EU citizens can be normatively justified as a source of their subjectivity aims to articulate how just and equal relationships between citizens can be introduced to 'a polity without democracy', as the EU has been described.

Any serious attempt to advance a more relational account of egalitarian social justice transnationally must also consider what consequences these developments would have for the existing national welfare systems. The concern for the 'race to the bottom'[4] assumes that needy and dependent EU citizens are more mobile than those who are able to contribute financially to the economic system of the host Member State.[5] The fear of increasing movement may encourage the Member States to stagnate the level of welfare protection and would, thus, 'hamper a "race to the top"'.[6] For instance, Gareth Davies draws the following scenario for the future:

> There will be ever more persons present on the soil who are not fully integrated into the welfare system, and so who follow relatively precarious lives by comparison with the long-term resident or worker. Yet the alternative to inequality is closure and Europe's love affair with equality since the war has been made possible by its protection from outside. It has been said that 'the poor will always be with us'. For a long time it seemed that it did not have to be so—they were safely outside our borders. Now, as borders come down to

[4] See eg Catherine Barnard, 'Social Dumping and Race to the Bottom: Some Lessons for the EU from Delaware?' (2000) *European Law Review* 57.

[5] For a critique of this assumption, see eg Van der Mei (n 3) 206–07.

[6] Ibid 208.

> the east, but also, with increasing immigration, more generally, we can be sure that they once again are, at least until wealth has spread throughout the world.[7]

If these fears are correct and, in the light of the fact that it would be against both the Union's *Telos* and its competences to harmonise benefit levels in the different Member States, it seems correct to argue that a more just EU can only follow from rethinking what role the vulnerable groups, such as economically inactive and dependent EU citizens, play in the overall project of European integration. Recognising the case of the 'needy' EU citizens as a valuable touchstone of how the European Union lives up to the ideal of interdependence between its subjects, and not their closure of the project on European integration, may ultimately provide the only protection for the welfare systems of all Member States and, above all, of those Member States who value the 'race to the top' in particular.

The painful news is that there is no easy or costless way to protect the social welfare systems against the challenge imposed on them by the EU principles of equality and free movement. Instead, the available choices seem to vary between social dumping or the blunt harmonisation of national benefit levels. However, in this book, it has been shown that there is also a third way which is both more difficult and more faithful to the core values of European integration: the case of the 'needy' Union citizens allows us to test and develop the ideal of interdependence that arguably underlies the project of European integration. This means that the EU's quest for justice can gain more substance if we first acknowledge the central role of just and equal relationships between EU citizens for the project of European integration as a whole. It is only the commitment to mutual interdependence and vulnerability between the subjects of integration that can both explain what being just means in the transnational context (enabling just and equal relationships between the subjects of integration to deepen their mutual interdependence) and why it should be pursued (it is a necessary precondition for creating EU citizens as new subjects of integration).

In this book, the constitution of transnational political and legal subjectivity was viewed as a complex psychological and social process which depends on just and equal relationships between EU citizens but which can never be reduced to the mere conscious elements of *cognitio*.[8] Conceptualising the relationships between EU citizens as relationships between the Self and the Other will ultimately direct us to contemplate the transcendental element embedded in the ideal of European integration. The necessary cognitive and social reforms for (re)constructing EU citizenship as a source of subjectivity may require a Revelation, which still

[7] Gareth Davies, 'Comment: The High Water Point of Free Movement of Persons: Ending Benefit Tourism and Rescuing Welfare' (2004) 26 *Journal of Social Welfare and Family Law* 211, 221.

[8] Analysis of the cognitive dimension of (supranational) subjectivity in chapter 4 draws a picture of EU citizenship as a more intentional commitment than the cultural or ethnic emotions of Weiler's 'Eros' but also as a more complex process than the rational reasons for his 'Civilization'. JHH Weiler, 'To be a European Citizen—Eros and Civilization' (1997) 4 *Journal of European Public Policy* 495, 509–11.

eludes the political decision-makers of the Union, as well as us who vote for them. Joseph Weiler has critically observed that many attempts to legitimate the EU are 'politically messianic' in the sense that the justification for the EU is based on the 'ideal pursued'. For him, the danger is that 'the end always trumps the means'.[9] But, perhaps, the legitimacy of the European Union must always partly lie beyond the perception: the project of European integration in its finality is about the promise of something which is yet to be seen and which promises to bring together those who seem otherwise so different by affirming their mutual interdependence. The right question is therefore not whether we can already 'see face to face', but whether integration brings to us 'faith, hope or charity'.[10] For Europe, replying to this question might always include a leap of faith.

[9] JHH Weiler, 'In the Face of Crisis: Input Legitimacy, Output Legitimacy and the Political Messianism of European Integration' (2012) 34 *European Integration* 825.

[10] 1 Cor 13:12–13.

Bibliography

Ackelsberg M, *Resisting Citizenship—Feminist Essays on Politics, Community, and Democracy* (Routledge, 2010).

Alexy R, *A Theory of Constitutional Rights* (Oxford University Press, 2002).

Anderson B, *Imagined Communities Reflections on the Origin and Spread of Nationalism* (Verso, 1983).

Anderson E, 'What Is the Point of Equality' (1999) 109 *Ethic* s 287.

——, *The Imperative of Integration* (Princeton University Press, 2010).

——, 'The Fundamental Disagreement between Luck Egalitarians and Relational Egalitarians' (2010) 40 *Canadian Journal of Philosophy* 1.

Arcarazo D, 'Civic Citizenship Reintroduced? The Long-Term Residence Directive as a Post-National Form of Membership' (2015) 21 *European Law Journal* 200.

Archer M, *Being Human: The Problem of Agency* (Cambridge University Press, 2000).

Armstrong C, *Rethinking Equality: The Challenge of Equal Citizenship* (Manchester University Press, 2006).

Arnardóttir OM, *Equality and Non-Discrimination under the European Convention on Human Rights* (Kluwer, 2003).

Arneson R, 'Equality and Equal Opportunity for Welfare' (1989) 56 *Philosophical Studies* 77.

——, 'Equality of Opportunity for Welfare Defended and Recanted' (1999) 7 *The Journal of Political Philosophy* 488.

——, 'Luck Egalitarianism and Prioritanism' (2000) *Ethics* 110.

——, 'Luck Egalitarianims—A Primer' in Knight C and Stemplowska Z (eds), *Responsibility and Distributive Justice* (Oxford University Press, 2011).

Asscher-Vonk IP, 'Towards One Concept of Objective Justification?' in Loenen T and Rodrigues P (eds), *Non-Discrimination Law: Comparative Perspectives* (Kluwer, 1999).

Azoulai L, 'Transfiguring European Citizenship: From Member State Territory to Union Territory' in 'The (Mis)Construction of the European Individual Two Essays on Union Citizenship Law', EUI Working Papers LAW 2014/14.

Baier A, *Postures of the Mind—Essays on Mind and Morals* (Methuen, 1985).

Bamforth N, 'Setting the Limits of Anti-Discrimination Law: Some Legal and Social Concepts' in Dine J and Watt B (eds), *Discrimination Law: Concepts, Limitations and Justifications* (Longman, 1996).

Barnard C, 'P V. S: Kite Flying or A New Constitutional Approach?' in Dashwood A and O'Leary S (eds), *The Principle of Equal Treatment in EC Law* (Sweet & Maxwell, 1997).

——, 'The Principle of Equality in the Community Context: *P*, *Grant*, *Kalanke*, and *Marschall*: Four Uneasy Bedfellows?' (1998) 57 *Cambridge Law Journal* 352.

——, 'Social Dumping and Race to the Bottom: Some Lessons for the EU from Delaware?' (2000) *European Law Review* 57.

——, 'EU Citizenship and the Principle of Solidarity' in Dougan M and Spaventa E (eds), *Social Welfare and EU Law* (Hart Publishing, 2005).

——, 'Social Policy Revisited in the Light of the Constitutional Debate' in Barnard C (ed), *The Fundamental of EU Law Revisited: Assessing the Impact of the Constitutional Debate* (Oxford University Press, 2007).

Barrett G, 'Re-Examining the Concept and Principle of Equality in EC Law' (2003) 22 *Yearbook of European Law* 117.
——, 'The Concept of Equality in European Community Law' in Costello C and Barry E (eds), *Diversity In Equality: The New Equality Directives* (Irish Centre for European Law, 2003).
Bell M, *Anti-Discrimination Law and the European Union* (Oxford University Press, 2002).
——, 'Civic Citizenship and Migrant Integration' (2007) 13 *European Public Law* 311.
Bellamy R, 'Evaluating Union Citizenship: Belonging, Rights and Participation within the EU' (2008) 12 *Citizenship Studies* 597.
Bengtsson J, *The Worldview of Personalism: Origins and Early Development* (Oxford University Press, 2006).
Benhabib S, 'The Generalized and the Concrete Other: The Kohlberg-Gilligan Controversy and Feminist Theory' in Benhabib S and Cornell D (eds), *Feminism as Critique: Essays on the Politics of Gender in Late-Capitalist Societies* (Polity Press, 1987).
——, *Situating the Self: Gender, Community and Postmodernism in Contemporary Ethics* (Polity Press, 1992).
——, *The Rights of Others—Aliens, Residents, and Citizens* (Cambridge University Press, 2004).
Benhabib S and Cornell D, 'Introduction—Beyond the Politics of Gender' in Benhabib S and Cornell D (eds), *Feminism as Critique: Essays on the Politics of Gender in Late-Capitalist Societies* (Polity Press, 1987).
Bernard N, 'What are the Purposes of EC Discrimination Law?' in Dine J and Watt B (eds), *Discrimination Law: Concepts, Limitations and Justifications* (Longman, 1996).
Besson S and Utzinger A, 'Introduction: Future Challenges of European Citizenship—Facing a Wide-Open Pandora's Box' (2007) 13 *European Law Journal* 573.
Betten L, 'New Equality Provisions in European Law: Some Thoughts on the Fundamental Value of Equality as a Legal Principle' in Economides K, Betten L, Bridge J, Tettenborn A, and Shrubsall V (eds), *Fundamental Values* (Hart Publishing, 2000).
von Bogdandy A, Kottmann M, Antpöhler C, Dickschen J, Hentrei S, and Smrkolj M, 'Reverse *Solange*—Protecting the Essence of Fundamental Rights Against EU Member States' (2012) 49 *Common Market Law Review* 489
Borgmann-Prebil Y, 'The Rule of Reason in European Citizenship' (2008) 14 *European Law Journal* 328.
—— and Ross M, 'Promoting European Solidarity: Between Rhetoric and Reality' in Borgmann-Prebil Y and Ross M (eds), *Promoting Solidarity in the European Union* (Oxford University Press, 2010).
Braidotti R, 'On the Female Feminist Subject, or: From "She-Self" to "She-Other"' in Bock G and James S (eds), *Beyond Equality and Difference Citizenship, Feminist Politics and Female Subjectivity* (Routledge, 1992).
—— *Embodiment and Sexual Difference in Contemporary Feminist Theory* (Columbia University Press, 1994).
Broekman J, 'Justice as Equilibrium' (1986) 5 *Law and Philosophy* 369.
Buber M, *I and Thou* (1923, translated into English in 1937 (Charles Scribner's Sons)).
Budgeon S, *Third Wave Feminism and the Politics of Gender in Late Modernity* (Palgrave Macmillan, 2011).
de Búrca G, 'The Language of Rights and European Integration' in Shaw J and More G (eds), *New Legal Dynamics of European Union* (Clarendon Press, 1995).

——, 'The Role of Equality in European Community' in Dashwood A and O'Leary S (eds), *The Principle of Equal Treatment in EC Law* (Sweet & Maxwell, 1997).
Butler J, 'Variations on Sex and Gender: Beauvoir, Witting, and Foucault' in Benhabib S and Cornell D (eds), *Feminism as Critique: Essays on the Politics of Gender in Late-Capitalist Societies* (Polity Press, 1987).
——, 'Gender, Trouble, Feminist Theory, and Psychoanalytic Discourse' in Nicholson L (ed), *Feminism/Postmodernism* (Routledge, 1989).
——, 'Contingent Foundations: Feminism and the Question of "Postmodernism"' in Butler J and Scott J (eds), *Feminists Theorize the Political* (Routledge, 1992).
Çali B, 'Balancing Human Rights? Methodological Problems with Weights, Scales and Proportions' (2007) 29 *Human Rights Quarterly* 251.
Checkel J, 'Social Construction and European Integration' in Christiansen T, Jørgensen K, and Wiener A (eds), *The Social Construction of Europe* (SAGE Publications, 2001).
Chemirensky E, 'In Defense of Equality: A Reply to Professor Westen' (1983) 81 *Michigan Law Review* 575.
Christensen A and Malmstedt M, 'Lex Loci Laboris versus Lex Loci Domicilii—an Inquiry into the Normative Foundations of European Social Security Law' (2000) 2 *European Journal of Social Security* 69.
Christiano T, *The Constitution of Equality: Democratic Authority and its Limits* (Oxford University Press, 2007).
——, 'A Foundation for Egalitarianism' in Holtug N and Lippert-Rasmussen K (eds), *Egalitarianism: New Essays on the Nature and Value of Equality* (Clarendon Press, 2007).
Closa C, 'Citizenship of the Union and Nationality of the Member States' (1995) 32 *Common Market Law Review* 487.
——, 'Supranational Citizenship and Democracy: Normative and Empirical Dimensions' in La Torre M (ed), *European Citizenship: An Institutional Challenge* (Kluwer, 1998).
Code L, 'Taking Subjectivity into Account' in Garry A and Pearsall M (eds), *Women, Knowledge, and Reality: Explorations in Feminist Philosophy* (Routledge, 1996).
Cohen GA, 'On the Currency of Egalitarian Justice' (1989) 99 *Ethics* 906.
——, 'Where the Action Is: On the Site of Distributive Justice' (1997) 26 *Philosophy & Public Affairs* 3.
Cornell D, 'Gender, Sex, and Equivalent Rights' in Butler J and Scott J (eds), *Feminists Theorize the Political* (Routledge, 1992).
—— and Thurschwell A, 'Feminism, Negativity, Intersubjectivity' in Benhabib S and Cornell D (eds), *Feminism as Critique: Essays on the Politics of Gender in Late-Capitalist Societies* (Polity Press, 1987).
Cousins M, 'Citizenship, Residence and Social Security' (2007) 32 *European Law Review* 386.
Coutts S, 'Union Citizenship as Probationary Citizenship: *Onuekwere*' (2015) 52 *Common Market Law Review* 531.
Dahl R, *On Political Equality* (Yale University Press, 2006).
Damjanovic D and De Witte B, 'Welfare Integration through EU Law: The Overall Picture in the Light of the Lisbon Treaty' in Neergaard U, Nielsen R, and Roseberry L (eds), *Integrating Welfare Functions into EU Law From Rome to Lisbon* (DJØF Publishing, 2009).
Davies G, *Nationality Discrimination in the European Internal Market* (Kluwer, 2002).
——, 'Comment: The High Water Point of Free Movement of Persons: Ending Benefit Tourism and Rescuing Welfare' (2004) 26 *Journal of Social Welfare and Family Law* 211.

——, 'Any Place I Hang My Hat? Or: Residence is the New Nationality' 2005 11 *European Law Journal* 43.
——, 'The Process and Side-Effects of Harmonisation of European Welfare States' Jean Monnet Working Paper No 02/2006 http://jeanmonnetprogram.org/paper/the-process-and-side-effects-of-harmonisation-of-european-welfare-states/.
——, 'The Price of Letting Courts Value Solidarity' in Borgmann-Prebil Y and Ross M (eds), *Promoting Solidarity in the European Union* (Oxford University Press, 2010).
——, 'Discrimination and Beyond in European Economic and Social Law' (2011) 18 *Maastricht Journal of European and Comparative Law* 7.
Davis R, 'Citizenship of the Union ... Rights For All?' (2002) 27 *European Law Review* 121.
Dawson M and De Witte F, 'Self-Determination in the Constitutional Future of the EU' (2015) 21 *European Law Journal* 371.
Delanty G, 'Models of Citizenship: Defining European Identity and Citizenship' (1997) 1 *Citizenship Studies* 285.
Dietz M, 'Context Is All: Feminism and Theories of Citizenship' (1987) 116 *Daedalus* 1.
Dietz T and Wiener A, 'Introducing the Mosaic of Integration Theory' in Wiener A and Dietz T (eds), *European Integration Theory*, 2nd edn (Oxford University Press, 2009).
Dougan M, 'The Constitutional Dimension to the Case Law on Union Citizenship' (2006) 31 *European Law Review* 613.
——, 'Expanding the Frontiers of European Union Citizenship by Dismantling the Territorial Boundaries of the National Welfare States?' in Barnard C and Odudu O (eds), *The Outer Limits of European Union Law* (Hart Publishing, 2009).
——, 'The Spatial Restructuring of National Welfare States within the European Union: The Contribution of Union Citizenship and the Relevance of the Treaty of Lisbon' in Neergaard U, Nielsen R, and Roseberry L (eds), *Integrating Welfare Functions into EU Law From Rome to Lisbon* (DJØF Publishing, 2009).
Douglas-Scott S, *Constitutional Law of the European Union* (Longman, 2002).
——, 'The Problem of Justice in the European Union—Values, Pluralism, and Critical Legal Justice' in Dickson J and Eleftheriadis P (eds), *Philosophical Foundations of European Union Law* (Oxford University Press, 2012).
Dworkin R, *Taking Rights Seriously* (Duckworth, 1977).
——, *Sovereign Virtue: The Theory and Practice of Equality* (Harvard University Press, 2000).
Editorial Comments, 'Two-Speed European Citizenship? Can the Lisbon Treaty Help Close the Gap?' (2008) 45 *Common Market Law Review* 1.
——, 'The Scope of Application of the General Principles of Union Law: An Ever Expanding Union?' (2010) 47 *Common Market Law Review* 1589.
van Eijken H, *EU Citizenship & the Constitutionalisation of the European Union* (European Law Publishing, 2015).
Eisenstein Z, *The Radical Future of Liberal Feminism* (Northern University Press, 1986).
Eleftheriadis P, 'Aspects of European Constitutionalism' (1996) 21 *European Law Review* 32.
Ellis E, 'Social Advantages: A New Lease of Life?' (2003) 40 *Common Market Law Review* 639.
——, *EU Anti-Discrimination Law* (Oxford University Press, 2005).
Elsmore M and Starup P, 'Union Citizenship—Background, Jurisprudence, and Perspective: The Past, Present, and Future of Law and Policy' (2007) 26 *Yearbook of European Law* 57.
Emiliou N, *The Principle of Proportionality in European Law: A Comparative Study* (Kluwer Law, 1996).

Epiney A, 'The Scope of Article 12 EC: Some Remarks on the Influence of European Citizenship' (2007) 13 *European Law Journal* 611.

Evans A, 'Nationality Law and European Integration' (1991) 16 *European Law Review* 190.

——, 'Union Citizenship and the Equality Principle' in Rosas A and Antola E (eds), *A Citizens' Europe: In Search of a New Order* (SAGE Publications, 1995).

——, 'Union Citizenship and the Constitutionalization of Equality in EU Law' in La Torre M (ed), *European Citizenship: An Institutional Challenge* (Kluwer, 1998).

Everson M, 'The Legacy of the Market Citizen' in Shaw J and More G (eds), *New Legal Dynamics of European Union* (Clarendon Press, 1995).

——, 'A Very Cosmopolitan Citizenship: But Who Pays the Price?' in Dougan M, Nic Shuibhne N, and Spaventa E (eds), *Empowerment and Disempowerment of the European Citizen* (Hart Publishing, 2012).

Fairbairn WRD, *Psychoanalytic Studies of the Personality* (Routledge, 1952).

Faist T, 'Social Citizenship in the European Union: Nested Membership' (2001) 39 *Journal of Common Market Studies* 37.

Feinberg J, 'Justice and Personal Desert' in Pojman L and McLeod O (eds), *What Do We Deserve? A Reader on Justice and Desert* (Oxford University Press, 1999).

Ferguson A, 'Can I Choose Who I Am? And How Would that Empower Me? Gender, Race, Identities and the Self' in Garry A and Pearsall A (eds), *Women Knowledge, and Reality: Explorations in Feminist Philosophy* (Routledge, 1996).

Ferrera M, 'European Integration and National Social Citizenship: Changing Boundaries, New Structuring?' (2003) 36 *Comparative Political Studies* 611.

——, 'Towards an "Open" Social Citizenship? The New Boundaries of Welfare in the European Union' in de Búrca G (ed), *EU Law and the Welfare State: In Search of Solidarity* (Oxford University Press, 2005).

Flax J, 'Political Philosophy and the Patriarchal Unconscious: A Psychoanalytic Perspective on Epistemology and Metaphysics' in Harding S and Hintikka M (eds), *Discovering Reality: Feminist Perspectives on Epistemology, Metaphysics, Methodology, and Philosophy of Science* (D Reidel Publishing Company, 1983).

——, *Thinking Fragments: Psychoanalysis, Feminism, and Postmodernism in the Contemporary West* (University of California Press, 1990).

——, 'Beyond Equality: Gender, Justice and Difference' in Bock G and James S (eds), *Beyond Equality and Difference Citizenship, Feminist Politics and Female Subjectivity* (Routledge, 1992).

——, *Disputed Subjects: Essays on Psychoanalysis, Politics and Philosophy* (Routledge, 1993).

Foucault M, 'Technologies of the Self' in Rainbow P (ed), *Ethics: Subjectivity and Truth (Essential Works of Michel Foucault, 1954–1984)* (Penguin, 2000).

Fraser N, 'What's Critical about Critical Theory? The Case of Habermas and Gender' in Benhabib S and Cornell S (eds), *Feminism as Critique: Essays on the Politics of Gender in Late-Capitalist Societies* (Polity Press, 1987).

Fredman S, 'Europe with a Social Face: Equality and Social Rights in the European Union' (2001) 22 *Industrial Law Journal* 1467.

——, *Discrimination Law* (Oxford University Press, 2002).

——, 'Transformation or Dilution: Fundamental Rights in the EU Social Space' (2006) 12 *European Law Journal* 41.

Friedman M, 'Feminism and Modern Friendship: Dislocating the Community' in Sunstein C (ed), *Feminism & Political Theory* (The University Chicago Press, 1982).

Fries S and Shaw J, 'Citizenship of the Union: First Steps in the European Court of Justice' (1998) 4 *European Public Law* 533.
Frost R, *Justification and Critique towards a Critical Theory of Politics* (Polity, 2014).
——, 'Justice, Democracy and the Right to Justification: Reflections on Jürgen Neyer's Normative Theory of the European Union' in Kochenov D, De Búrca G, and Williams A (eds), *Europe's Justice Deficit?* (Hart Publishing, 2015).
Garot M-J, 'A New Basis for European Citizenship: Residence' in Massimo La Torre (ed), *European Citizenship: An Institutional Challenge* (Kluwer, 1998).
Giddens A, *Central Problems in Social Theory: Action, Structure and Contradictions in Social Analysis* (The Macmillan Press Ltd, 1979).
——, *Modernity and Self-Identity: Self and Society in the Late Modern Age* (Polity Press, 1991).
Gilligan C, *In a Different Voice—Psychological Theory of Women's Development* (Harvard University Press, 1982).
Giubboni S, 'Free Movement of Persons and European Solidarity' (2007) 13 *European Law Journal* 360.
——, 'A Certain Degree of Solidarity? Free Movement of Persons and Access to Social Protection in the Case Law of the European Court of Justice' in Borgmann-Prebil Y and Ross M (eds), *Promoting Solidarity in the European Union* (Oxford University Press, 2010).
Goldberg S, 'Discrimination by Comparison' (2010–2011) 120 *The Yale Law Journal* 728.
Golynker O, 'Jobseekers' Rights in the European Union: Challenges of Changing the Paradigm of Social Solidarity' (2005) 30 *European Law Review* 111.
Gordon J, 'Justice or Equality?' (2006) 7 *Zeitschrift für Wirtschafts- und Unternehmensethik (zfwu)* 183.
Greenawalt K, '"Prescriptive Equality": Two Steps Forward' (1997) 110 *Harvard Law Review* 1265.
Grosz E, 'Contemporary Theories of Power and Subjectivity' in Gunew S (ed), *Feminist Knowledge: Critique and Construct* (Routledge, 1990).
Groussot X, 'Principled Citizenship and the Process of European Constitutionalization: From a Pie in the Sky to a Sky with Diamonds' in Bernitz U, Nergelius J, and Gardner C (eds), *General Principles of EC Law in a Process of Development* (Kluwer, 2008).
van Gunsteren H, 'Four Concepts of Citizenship' in Bart van Steenbergen (ed), *The Condition of Citizenship* (SAGE, 1994).
Guntrip H, *Personality Structure and Human Interactions—The Developing Synthesis of Psychodynamic Theory* (The Hogarth Press, 1961).
Habermas J, 'Citizenship and National Identity' in Bart van Steenbergen (ed), *The Condition of Citizenship* (SAGE, 1994).
——, 'The European Nation State. Its Achievements and its Limitations. On the Past and Future of Sovereignty and Citizenship' (1996) 9 *Ratio Juris* 9(2) 125.
Hailbronner K, 'Union Citizenship and Access to Social Benefits' (2005) 42 *Common Market Law Review* 1245, 1266.
Halleskov L, 'The Long-Term Residents Directive: A Fulfilment of the Tampere Objective of Near-Equality' (2005) 7 *European Journal of Migration and Law* 181.
Hanf D, '"Reverse Discrimination" in EU Law: Constitutional Aberration, Constitutional Necessity, or Judicial Choice?' (2011) 18 *Maastricht Journal of European and Comparative Law* 29.

Harding C, 'Legal Subjectivity as a Fundamental Value: the Emergence of Non-State Actors in Europe' in Economides K, Betten L, Bridge J, Tettenborn A, and Shrubsall V (eds), *Fundamental Values* (Hart Publishing, 2000).

Haslanger S, 'Objective Reality, Male Reality, and Social Construction' in Garry A and Pearsall M (eds), *Women, Knowledge, and Reality: Explorations in Feminist Philosophy* (Routledge, 1996).

Hatzopoulos V, 'A (More) Social Europe: A Political Crossroad or a Legal One-Way? Dialogues between Luxembourg and Lisbon' (2005) 42 *Common Market Law Review* 1599.

Held V, 'Non-Contractual Society: A Feminist View' in Weiss P and Friedman M (eds), *Feminism and Community* (Temple University Press, 1995).

——, *The Ethics of Care—Personal, Political, and Global* (Oxford University Press, 2006).

Herdegen M, 'The Relation between the Principles of Equality and Proportionality' (1985) 22 *Common Market Law Review* 683.

Hilson C, 'What's in a Right? The Relationship between Community, Fundamental and Citizenship Rights in EU Law' (2004) 29 *European Law Review* 636.

Hinton T, 'Must Egalitarians Choose Between Fairness and Respect?' (2001) 30 *Philosophy and Public Affairs* 72.

Holmes E, 'Anti_Discrimination Rights Without Equality' (2005) 68 *Modern Law Review* 175.

Holtug N and Lippert-Rasmussen K, 'An Introduction to Contemporary Egalitarianism' in Holtug N and Lippert-Rasmussen K (eds), *Egalitarianism: New Essays on the Nature and Value of Equality* (Clarendon Press, 2007).

Hoogenboom T, 'Free Movement and Integration of Non-EC Nationals and the Logic of the Internal Market' in Schermers HG et al (eds), *Free Movement of Persons in Europe: Legal Problems and Experiences* (Martinus Nijhoff Publishers, 1993).

Huddy L, Sears D, and Levy J, 'Introduction: Theoretical Foundations of Political Psychology' in Huddy L, Sears D, and Levy J (eds), *The Oxford Handbook of Political Psychology* (Oxford University Press, 2013).

Hunter S, 'A Critical Analysis of Approaches to the Concept of Social Identity in Social Policy' (2003) 23 *Critical Social Policy* 322.

Iliopoulou Penot A, 'The Transnational Character of Union Citizenship' in Dougan M, Nic Shuibhne N, and Spaventa E (eds), *Empowerment and Disempowerment of the European Citizen* (Hart Publishing, 2012).

—— and Toner H, 'A New Approach to Discrimination against Free Movers?' (2003) 28 *European Law Review* 389.

Jacobs F, 'Recent Developments in the Principle of Proportionality in European Community Law' in Ellis E (ed), *The Principle of Proportionality in the Laws of Europe* (Hart Publishing, 1999).

——, 'Citizenship of the European Union—A Legal Analysis' (2007) 13 *European Law Journal* 591.

Jacqueson C, 'Union Citizenship and the Court of Justice: Something New under the Sun? Towards Social Citizenship' (2002) 27 *European Law Review* 260.

Jaggar A, 'Caring as a Feminist Practice of Moral Reason' in Held V (ed), *Justice and Care—Essential Readings in Feminist Ethics* (Westview Press, 1995).

Kagan S, 'Equality and Desert' in Pojman L and McLeod O (eds), *What Do We Deserve? A Reader on Justice and Desert* (Oxford University Press, 1999).

Kalypso N, 'The New Constitution as European "Demoi-cracy"?' (2004) 7 *Critical Review of International Social and Political Philosophy* 76.
——, 'European Demoicracy and its Crisis' (2013) 51 *Journal of Common Market Studies* 351.
Karst K, 'Why Equality Matters' (1983) 17 *Georgia Law Review* 245.
Khaitan T, 'An Autonomy-Based Foundation for Legal Protection against Discrimination' (DPhil thesis, University of Oxford, 2010).
Klein J, *Our Need for Others and its Roots in Infancy* (Tavistock Publications, 1987).
Knight C, 'Describing Equality' (2009) 28 *Law and Philosophy* 327.
Kochenov D, '*Ius Tractum* of Many Faces: European Citizenship and the Difficult Relationship between Status and Rights' (2009) 15 *Columbia Journal of European Law* 169.
——, 'Citizenship without Respect: The EU's Troubled Equality Ideal', Jean Monnet Working Paper No 8/10 http://jeanmonnetprogram.org/paper/citizenship-without-respect-the-eus-troubled-equality-ideal/.
——, 'The Right to Have What Rights? EU Citizenship in Need of Clarification' (2013) 19 *European Law Journal* 502.
——, 'The Ought of Justice' in Kochenov D, De Búrca G, and Williams A (eds), *Europe's Justice Deficit?* (Hart Publishing, 2015).
Koggel C, *Perspectives on Equality: Constructing a Relational Theory* (Rowman & Littlefield Publishers Ltd, 1998).
Kon S, 'Aspects of Reverse Discrimination in Community Law' (1981) 6 *European Law Review* 75.
Korsgaard C, *Self-Constitution Agency, Identity, and Integrity* (Oxford University Press, 2009).
Kostakopoulou D, 'Towards a Theory of Constructive Citizenship in Europe' (1996) 4 *The Journal of Political Philosophy* 337.
——, 'Nested "Old" and "New" Citizenship in the European Union: Bringing out the Complexity' (1998–99) 5 *Columbian Journal of European Law* 389.
——, 'European Union Citizenship: Writing the Future' (2007) 13 *European Law Journal* 623.
——, *The Future Governance of Citizenship* (Cambridge University Press, 2008).
——, 'When EU Citizens become Foreigners' (2014) 20 *European Law Journal* 447.
Kristeva J, *Desire in Language—A Semiotic Approach to Literature and Art* (Blackwell, 1980).
——, 'The System and the Speaking Subject' in Moi T (ed), *The Kristeva Reader* (Basil Blackwell, 1986).
——, *Crisis of the European Subject* (Other Press, 2000).
Lacan J, *The Language of the Self—The Function of Language in Psychoanalysis* (The John Hopkins University Press, 1968).
Lacey N, *Unspeakable Subjects: Feminist Essays in Legal and Social Theory* (Hart Publishing, 1998).
Lacroix J, 'Is Transnational Citizenship (Still) Enough?' in Kochenov D, De Búrca G, and Williams A (eds), *Europe's Justice Deficit?* (Hart Publishing, 2015).
Lake C, *Equality and Responsibility* (Oxford University Press, 2001).
Lamping W, 'Mission Impossible? Limits and Perils of Institutionalizing Post-National Social Policy' in Borgmann-Prebil Y and Ross M (eds), *Promoting Solidarity in the European Union* (Oxford University Press, 2010).
La Torre M, 'Citizenship: A European Wager' (1995) 8 *Ratio Juris* 113.

Layton-Henry Z, 'Insiders and Outsiders in the European Union: The Search for a European Identity and Citizenship' in Guild E (ed), *The Legal Framework and Social Consequences of Free Movement of Persons in the European Union* (Kluwer, 1999).
Leader S, 'Proportionality and the Justification of Discrimination' in Dine J and Watt B (eds), *Discrimination Law: Concepts, Limitations and Justifications* (Longman, 1996).
Lenaerts K, 'Union Citizenship and the Principle of Non-Discrimination on Grounds of Nationality' in Fenger N and Hagel-Sørensen K and Vesterdorf B (eds), *Festskrift til Claus Gulmann—Liber amicorum* (Forlaget Thomson, 2006).
Lenaerts K and Heremans H, 'Contours of a European Social Union in the Case-Law of the European Court of Justice' (2006) 2 *European Constitutional Law Review* 101.
Lenaerts K and Gutiérrez-Fons J, 'The Constitutional Allocation of Powers and General Principles of EU Law' (2010) 47 *Common Market Law Review* 1589.
Levinas E, *Totality and Infinity: An Essay on Exteriority* (Duquesne University Press, 1969).
Liebert U, 'Reconciling Market with Social Europe? The EU under the Lisbon Treaty' in Schiek D, Liebert U, and Schneider H (eds), *European Economic and Social Constitutionalism after the Treaty of Lisbon* (Cambridge University Press, 2011).
Lippolis V, 'European Citizenship: What it is and What it Could Be' in La Torre M (ed), *European Citizenship: An Institutional Challenge* (Kluwer, 1998).
Lister R, *Citizenship: Feminist Perspective* (Palgrave Macmillan, 1997).
Loenen T, 'Indirect Discrimination: Oscillating between Containment and Revolution' in Loenen T and Rodrigues P (eds), *Non-Discrimination Law: Comparative Perspectives* (Kluwer, 1999).
MacKinnon C, *Toward a Feminist Theory of the State* (Harvard University Press, 1991).
MacMurray J, *The Self as Agent* (Faber and Faber, 1957).
——, *Persons in Relation* (Faber and Faber, 1961).
Maduro M, *We the Court: The European Court of Justice and the European Economic Constitution A Critical Reading of Article 30 of the EC Treaty* (Hart Publishing, 1998).
——, 'Europe''s Social Self: "The Sickness Unto Death"' in Shaw J (ed), *Social Law and Policy in an Evolving European Union* (Hart Publishing, 2000).
——, 'A New Governance for the European Union and the Euro: Democracy and Justice', RSCAS Policy Papers 2012/11.
Magnette P, 'How Can One Be European? Reflections on the Pillars of European Civic Identity; (2007) 13 *European Law Journal* 664.
Mahler M, *The Psychological Birth of the Human Infant—Symbiosis and Individuation* (Hutchinson of London, 1975).
Majone G, 'Europe's "Democracy Deficit": The Question of Standards' (1998) 4 *European Law Journal* 5.
Malmstedt M, 'From Employee to EU Citizen—A Development from Equal Treatment as a Means to Equal Treatment as a Goal?' in Ann Numhauser-Henning (ed), *Legal Perspectives on Equal Treatment and Non-Discrimination* (Kluwer, 2001).
Mansbridge J, 'Feminism and Democratic Community' in Weiss P and Friedman M (eds), *Feminism and Community* (Temple University Press, 1995).
Marcel G, *Being and Having* (Dacre Press Westminster, 1949).
Maritain J, *The Person and The Common Good* (Geoffrey Bles, 1948).
Mather J, 'The Court of Justice and the Union Citizen' (2005) 11 *European Law Journal* 722.
McColgan A, 'Cracking the Comparator Problem: Discrimination, "Equal" Treatment and the Role of Comparisons' (2006) 6 *European Human Rights Law Review* 650.

McCrudden C, 'Theorising European Equality Law' in Costello C and Barry E (eds), *Equality In Diversity: The New Equality Directives* (Irish Centre for European Law, 2003).
——, 'The New Concept of Equality' Academy of European Law, ERA-Forum, Trier, 2–3 June 2003.
McNay L, *Gender and Agency Reconfiguring the Subject in Feminist and Social Theory* (Polity Press, 2000).
Meyers D, *Self, Society, and Personal Choice* (Columbia University Press, 1989).
——, 'Introduction' in Meyers D (ed), *Feminist Rethinking the Self* (Westview Press, 1997).
Miller D, *Citizenship and National Identity* (Polity Press with Blackwell, 2000).
——, *Principles of Social Justice* (Harvard University Press 2001).
Minow M, *Making All the Difference—Inclusion, Exclusion, and American Law* (Cornell University Press, 1990).
Moller Okin S, *Women in Western Political Thought* (Princeton University Press, 1979).
Morijn J, 'Balancing Fundamental Rights and Common Market Freedoms in Union Law: Schmidberger and Omega in the Light of the European Constitution' (2006) 12 *European Law Journal* 15.
Mouffe C, 'Feminism, Citizenship and Radical Democratic Politics' in Butler J and Scott J (eds), *Feminists Theorize the Political* (Routledge, 1992).
Mounier E, *Personalism* (Routledge & Kegan Paul Ltd, 1950).
Muir E, 'The Transformative Function of EU Equality Law' (2013) 5&6 *European Review of Private Law* 1231.
Muir E and Van der Mei AP, 'Editorial' (2011) 18 *Maastricht Journal of European and Comparative Law* 3.
Nagel T, *Equality and Partiality* (Oxford University Press, 1991).
——, 'The Problem of Global Justice' (2005) 33 *Philosophy & Public Affairs* 113.
Narayan U, 'Towards a Feminist Vision of Citizenship: Rethinking the Implications of Dignity, Political Participation, and Nationality' in Shanley M and Narayan U (eds), *Reconstructing Political Theory—Feminist Perspectives* (Polity Press, 1997).
Nascimbene B, 'Towards a European Law on Citizenship and Nationality?' in Síofra O'Leary and Teija Tiilikainen (eds), *Citizenship and Nationality Status in the New Europe* (Sweet & Maxwell, 1998).
Neuvonen P, 'EU Citizens' Whimsical Status: Persons or Actors on their Way to Full Agency' in Ferreira N and Kostakopoulou D (eds), *The Human Face of the European Union: Are EU Law and Policy Humane Enough?* (Cambridge University Press, forthcoming 2016).
Neyer J, 'Justice, Not Democracy: Legitimacy in the European Union' (2010) 48 *Journal of Common Market Studies* 903.
Nic Shuibhne N, 'Free Movement of Persons and the Wholly Internal Rule: Time to Move On?' (2002) 39 *Common Market Law Review* 731.
——, 'The European Union and Fundamental Rights: Well in Spirit but Considerably Rumpled in Body?' in Beaumont P, Lyons C, and Walker N (eds), *Convergence and Divergence in European Public Law* (Hart Publishing, 2002).
——, 'The Outer Limits of EU Citizenship: Displacing Economic Free Movement Rights?' in Barnard C and Odudu O (eds), *The Outer Limits of European Union Law* (Hart Publishing, 2009).
——, 'The Resilience of EU Market Citizenship' (2010) 47 *Common Market Law Review* 1597.
——, 'Limits Rising, Duties Ascending: The Changing Legal Shape of Union Citizenship' (2015) 52 *Common Market Law Review* 889.

Nourse V, 'Law's Constitution: A Relational Critique' (2002) 17 *Wisconsin Women's Law Journal* 23.
Nussbaum M, *Sex & Social Justice* (Oxford University Press, 1999.)
O'Brien C, 'Real Links, Abstract Rights and False Alarms: The Relationship between the ECJ's "real link" Case Law and National Solidarity' (2008) 33 *European Law Review* 643.
——, 'Social Blind Spots and Monocular Policy Making: The ECJ's Migrant Worker Model' (2009) 46 *Common Market Law Review* 1107.
——, 'I trade, therefore I am: Legal Personhood in the European Union' (2013) 50 *Common Market Law Review* 1643.
O'Cinneide C, 'The Uncertain Foundations of Contemporary Anti-Discrimination Law' (2011) 11 *International Journal of Discrimination and the Law* 7.
O'Keeffe D and Bavasso A, 'Fundamental Rights and the European Citizen' in La Torre M (ed), *European Citizenship: An Institutional Challenge* (Kluwer, 1998).
Ojanen T, *The European Way. The Structure of National Court Obligation under EC Law* (Gummerus, 1998).
Oldfield A, *Citizenship and Community—Civic Republicanism and the Modern World* (Routledge, 1990).
O'Leary S, 'The Relationship between Community Citizenship and the Protection of Fundamental Rights in Community Law' (1995) 32 *Common Market Law Review* 519.
——, *The Evolving Concept of Community Citizenship: From the Free Movement of Persons to Union Citizenship* (Kluwer, 1996).
——, 'Putting Flesh on the Bones of European Union Citizenship' (1999) 21 *European Law Review* 68.
——, 'Solidarity and Citizenship Rights in the Charter of Fundamental Rights of the European Union' in de Búrca G (ed), *EU Law and the Welfare State: In Search of Solidarity* (Oxford University Press, 2005).
——, 'Developing an Ever Closer Union between the Peoples of Europe? A Reappraisal of the Case Law of the Court of Justice on the Free Movement of Persons and EU Citizenship' (2008) 27 *Yearbook of European Law* 167.
——, 'Equal Treatment and EU Citizens: A New Chapter on Cross-Border Educational Mobility and Access to Student Financial Assistance' (2009) 34 *European Law Review* 612.
——, 'The Past, Present and Future of the Purely Internal Rule in EU Law' in Dougan M, Nic Shuibhne N, and Spaventa E (eds), *Empowerment and Disempowerment of the European Citizen* (Hart Publishing, 2012).
Olsaretti S, 'Distributive Justice and Compensatory Desert' in Olsaretti S (ed), *Desert and Justice* (Clarendon Press, 2003).
Palombella G, 'Whose Europe? After the Constitution: A Goal-Based Citizenship' (2005) *International Journal of Constitutional Law* 357.
Pateman C, *The Disorder of Women: Democracy, Feminism and Political Theory* (Polity Press 1989).
Peers S, 'Taking Rights Away? Limitations and Derogations' in Peers S and Wards A (eds), *The European Union Charter of Fundamental Rights* (Hart Publishing, 2004).
Peters C, 'Equality Revisited' (1997) 110 *Harvard Law Review* 1210.
Phillips A, *Engendering Democracy* (Polity Press, 1991)
——, *Which Equalities Matter* (Polity Press, 1999).
Prechal S, 'Equality of Treatment, Non-Discrimination and Social Policy: Achievements in Three Themes' (2004) 41 *Common Market Law Review* 533.

——, 'Competence Creep and General Principles of Law' (2010) 3 *Review of European Administrative Law* 5.
Preuß U, 'Citizenship and Identity: Aspects of a Political Theory of Citizenship' in Bellamy R, Butacchi V, and Castiglione D (eds), *Democracy and Constitutional Culture in the Union of Europe* (Lothian Foundation Press, 1995).
——, 'Problems of a Concept of European Citizenship' (1995) 1 *European Law Journal* 267.
——, 'Two Challenges to European Citizenship' (1996) *Political Studies* XLIV 534.
Rawls J, *A Theory of Justice* (Harvard University Press, 1971).
Raz J, *The Morality of Freedom* (Clarendon Press, 1986).
Reich N, 'Union Citizenship—Metaphor or Source of Rights?' (2001) 7 *European Law Journal* 4.
Ripstein A, *Equality, Responsibility, and the Law* (Cambridge University Press, 1999).
Risse T, 'Social Constructivism and European Integration' in Wiener A and Dietz T (eds), *European Integration Theory*, 2nd edn (Oxford University Press, 2009).
——, 'No Demos? Identities and Public Spheres in the Euro Crisis' (2014) 52 *Journal of Common Market Studies* 1207.
Rivers J, 'Proportionality and Variable Intensity of Review' (2006) 65 *Cambridge Law Journal* 174.
Ross M, 'Solidarity—A New Constitutional Paradigm for the EU' in Borgmann-Prebil Y and Ross M (eds), *Promoting Solidarity in the European Union* (Oxford University Press, 2010).
Rothfield P, 'Feminism, Subjectivity, and Sexual Experience' in Gunew S (ed), *Feminist Knowledge: Critique and Construct* (Routledge, 1990).
Rowley H and Grosz E, 'Psychoanalysis and Feminism' in Gunew S (ed), *Feminist Knowledge: Critique and Construct* (Routledge, 1990).
Rubio Marin R, 'Equal Citizenship and the Difference that Residence Makes' in La Torre M (ed), *European Citizenship: An Institutional Challenge* (Kluwer, 1998).
Sánchez S, 'Fundamental Rights and Citizenship of the Union at a Crossroad: A Promising Alliance or A Dangerous Liaison' (2014) 20 European Law Journal 464.
Sandel M, *Liberalism and the Limits of Justice* (Cambridge University Press, 1982).
Scharpf F, 'Economic Integration, Democracy and the Welfare State' (1997) 4 *Journal of European Public Policy* 18.
——, 'The European Social Model: Coping with the Challenges of Diversity' (2002) 40 *Journal of Common Market Studies* 645.
——, 'After the Crash: A Perspective on Multilevel European Democracy' (2015) 21 *European Law Journal* 384.
Scheffler S, *Boundaries and Allegiances: Problems of Justice and Responsibility in Liberal Thought* (Oxford University Press, 2001).
——, 'Equality as the Virtue of Sovereign: A Reply to Ronald Dworkin' (2003) 3 *Philosophy & Public Affairs* 199.
——, *Equality and Tradition Questions of Value in Moral and Political Theory* (Oxford University Press, 2007).
Scheman N, 'Individualism and the Objects of Psychology' in Harding S and Hintikka M (eds), *Discovering Reality: Feminist Perspectives on Epistemology, Metaphysics, Methodology, and Philosophy of Sience* (D Reidel Publishing Company, 1983).
Schemmel C, 'Distributive and Relational Equality' (2011) 11 *Politics, Philosophy & Economics* 123.

——, 'Why Relational Egalitarians Should Care about Distributions' (2011) 37 *Social Theory and Practice* 365.

Schiek D, 'A New Framework on Equal Treatment of Persons in EC Law? Directives 2000/43/EC, 2000/78/EC and 2002/???/EC Changing Directive 76/207/EEC in context' (2002) 8 *European Law Journal* 290.

——, 'Re-Embedding Economic and Social Constitutionalism: Normative Perspectives for the EU' in Schiek D, Liebert U, and Schneider H (eds), *European Economic and Social Constitutionalism after the Treaty of Lisbon* (Cambridge University Press, 2011).

——, *Economic and Social Integration: The Challenge for EU Constitutional Law* (Edward Elgar Publishing, 2012).

Schwarze J, *European Administrative Law* (Sweet & Maxwell, 1992).

Sen A, *Inequality Reexamined* (Clarendon Press, 1992).

Sevenhuijsen S, *Citizenship and the Ethics of Care* (Routledge, 1998).

Shaw J, 'The Interpretation of European Union Citizenship' (1998) 61 *Modern Law Review* 293.

——, 'Citizenship: Contrasting Dynamics of the Interface of Integration and Constitutionalism' in Craig P and de Búrca G (eds), *The Evolution of EU Law* (Oxford University Press, 2011).

Sher G, *Desert* (Cambridge University Press, 1987).

Shiffrin S, 'Paternalism, Unconscionability Doctrine, and Accommodation' (2000) 29 *Philosophy & Public Affairs* 205.

Shotter J, 'Psychology and Citizenship: Identity and Belonging' in Turner B (ed), *Citizenship and Social Theory* (SAGE Publications, 1993).

Siim B, *Gender and Citizenship: Politics and Agency in France, Britain and Denmark* (Cambridge University Press, 2000).

Simons K, 'Equality as a Comparative Right' (1985) 65 *Boston University Law Review* 387.

Snell J, 'The Notion of Market Access: A Concept or a Slogan?' (2010) 47 *Common Market Law Review* 437.

Snyder F, 'The Unfinished Constitution of the European Union: Principles, Processes and Culture' in JHH Weiler and Marlene Wind (eds), *European Constitutionalism Beyond the State* (Cambridge University Press, 2003).

Somek A, 'A Constitution for Antidiscrimination: Exploring the Vanguard Moment of Community Law' (1999) 5 *European Law Journal* 243.

——, 'Concordantia Catholica: Exploring the Context of European Antidiscrimination Law and Policy' (2005) 14 *Transnational Law & Contemporary Problems* 959.

——, 'Solidarity Decomposed: Being and Time in European Citizenship' (2007) 32 *European Law Review* 787.

——, *Individualism: An Essay on the Authority of the European Union* (Oxford University Press, 2008).

——, *Engineering Equality: An Essay on European Anti-Discrimination Law* (Oxford University Press, 2011).

——, 'What Is Political Union?' (2013) 13 *German Law Journal* 561.

——, 'Europe: Political, Not Cosmopolitan' (2014) 20 *European Law Journal* 142.

——, *The Cosmopolitan Constitution* (Oxford University Press, 2014).

——, 'The Preoccupation with Rights and the Embrace of Inclusion: A Critique' in Kochenov D, De Búrca G, and Williams A (eds), *Europe's Justice Deficit?* (Hart Publishing, 2015).

de Sousa P, 'Quest for the Holy Grail—Is a Unified Approach to the Market Freedoms and European Citizenship Justified?' (2014) 20 *European Law Journal* 499.

Spaemann R, *Persons—The Difference between 'Someone' and 'Something'* (Oxford University Press, 2006).

Spaventa E, 'From Gebhard to Carpenter: Towards a (Non-)Economic European Constitution' (2004) 41 *Common Market Law Review* 743.

Steiner J, 'The Right to Welfare: Equality and Equity under Community Law' (1985) 10 *European Law Review* 21.

Szyszczak E, 'Building a European Constitutional Order: Prospects for a General Non-Discrimination Standard' in Dashwood A and O'Leary S (eds), *The Principle of Equal Treatment in EC Law* (Sweet & Maxwell, 1997).

——, 'The New Paradigm for Social Policy: A Virtuous Circle?' (2001) 38 *Common Market Law Review* 1125.

Taylor C, *Philosophy and the Human Sciences—Philosophical Papers II* (Cambridge University Press, 1985).

——, *Sources of the Self: The Making of the Modern Identity* (Harvard University Press, 1989).

Thym D, 'The Elusive Limits of Solidarity: Residence Rights of and Social Benefits for Economically Inactive Union Citizens' (2015) 52 *Common Market Law Review* 17.

Tomuschat C, 'Comment on Case C-85/96, María Martínez Sala v Freistaat Bayern, Judgment of 12 May 1998, Full Court. [1998] ECR I-2691' (2000) 37 *Common Market Law Review* 449.

Toth AG, 'Human Rights as General Principles of Law, in the Past and in the Future' in Bernitz U and Nergelius J (eds), *General Principles of European Community Law* (Kluwer, 2000).

Tridimas T, 'Proportionality in Community Law: Searching for the Appropriate Standard of Scrutiny' in Ellis E (ed), *The Principle of Proportionality in the Laws of Europe* (Hart Publishing, 1999).

Tronto J, *Moral Boundaries—A Political Argument for an Ethic of Care* (Routledge, 1993).

Tryfonidou A, 'Reverse Discrimination in Purely Internal Situations: An Incongruity in a Citizens' Europe' (2008) 35 *Legal Issues of Economic Integration* 43.

——, *Reverse Discrimination in EC Law* (Kluwer, 2009).

Tsagourias N, 'Introduction—Constitutionalism: A Theoretical Roadmap' in Tsagourias N (ed), *Transnational Constitutionalism: International and European Models* (Cambridge University Press, 2007).

Tuori K, *Critical Legal Positivism* (Ashgate, 2002).

Turner B, 'Outline of a Theory of Citizenship' (1990) 24 *Sociology* 189.

Ulrich H and d'Oliveira J, 'European Citizenship: Its Meaning, its Potential' in Renaud Delhousse (ed), *Europe After Maastricht: An Ever Closer Union?* (Beck Law Books, 1994).

Usher J, *General Principles of EC Law* (Longman, 1998).

Vallentyne P, 'Brute Luck Equality and Desert' in Olsaretti S (ed), *Desert and Justice* (Clarendon Press, 2003).

Van der Mei AP, 'The Elusive and Exclusive Concept of Union Citizenship, A Review Essay' (1998) 5 *Maastricht Journal of European and Comparative Law* 391.

——, *Free Movement of Persons within the European Community—Cross-Border Access to Public Benefits* (Hart Publishing, 2003).

——, 'Union Citizenship and the "De-Nationalisation" of the Territorial, Welfare State' (2005) 7 *European Journal of Migration and Law* 203.

——, 'The Outer Limits of the Prohibition of Discrimination on the Grounds of Nationality: A Look through the Lens of Union Citizenship' (2011) 18 *Maastricht Journal of European and Comparative Law* 62.
Van Parijs P, 'International Distributive Justice' in Goodin R, Pettit P, and Pogge T (eds), *A Companion to Contemporary Political Philosophy* (Blackwell, 2007).
——, 'Should the European Union Become More Democratic?' in Van Parijs P, *Just Democracy: The Rawls—Machiavelli Programme* (ECPR Press, 2011).
Verschueren H, 'Preventing "Benefit Tourism" in the EU: A Narrow or Broad Interpretation of the Possibilities Offered by the ECJ in *Dano*?' (2015) 52 *Common Market Law Review* 363.
Violi P, 'Gender, Subjectivity and Language' in Bock G and James S (eds), *Beyond Equality and Difference Citizenship, Feminist Politics and Female Subjectivity* (Routledge, 1992).
Waldron J, 'The Substance of Equality' (1991) 89 *Michigan Law Review* 1350.
Walker N, 'Denizenship and Deterritorialisation in the European Union' in Lindahl H (ed), *A Right to Inclusion and Exclusion* (Hart Publishing, 2009).
——, 'Justice in and of the European Union' in Kochenov D, De Búrca G, and Williams A (eds), *Europe's Justice Deficit?* (Hart Publishing, 2015).
Walzer M, *Spheres of Justice: A Defense of Pluralism and Equality* (Basic Books, 1983).
Ward I, 'Identity and Difference: The European Union and Postmodernism' in Shaw J and More G (eds), *New Legal Dynamics of European Union* (Clarendon Press, 1995).
Weatherill S, 'After Keck: Some Thoughts on How to Clarify the Clarification' (1996) 33 *Common Market Law Review* 885.
Weiler JHH, 'To be a European Citizen—Eros and Civilization' (1997) 4 *Journal of European Public Policy* 495.
——, *The Constitution of Europe 'Do the New Clothes Have an Emperor?' and Other Essays on European Integration* (Cambridge University Press, 1999).
——, 'In Defence of the Status Quo: Europe's Constitutional Sonderweg' in Weiler JHH and Wind M (eds), *European Constitutionalism Beyond the State* (Cambridge University Press, 2003).
——, 'The Political and Legal Culture of European Integration: An Exploratory Essay' (2011) 9 *International Journal of Constitutional Law* 678.
——, 'In the Face of Crisis: Input Legitimacy, Output Legitimacy and the Political Messianism of European Integration' (2012) 34 *European Integration* 825.
Weiss M, 'Fundamental Social Rights for the European Union' (1997) 18 *Industrial Law Journal* 417.
Weiss P, 'Feminism and Communitarianism' in Weiss P and Friedman M (eds), *Feminism and Community* (Temple University Press, 1995).
Westen P, 'The Empty Idea of Equality' (1982) 95 *Harvard Law Review* 537.
——, 'The Meaning of Equality in Law, Science, Math, and Morals: A Reply' (1983) 81 *Michigan Law Review* 604.
White RCA, 'Free Movement, Equal Treatment, and Citizenship of the Union' (2005) 54 *International and Comparative Law Quarterly* 885.
Wiener A, 'Constitution-Making and Citizenship Practice—Bridging the Democracy Gap in the EU?' (1997) 35 *Journal of Common Market Studies* 595.
Wilkinson M, 'Political Constitutionalism and the European Union' (2013) 76 *Modern Law Review* 191.
——, 'Politicising Europe's Justice Deficit: Some Preliminaries' in Kochenov D, De Búrca G, and Williams A (eds), *Europe's Justice Deficit?* (Hart Publishing, 2015).

Williams A, *EU Human Rights Policies: A Study in Irony* (Oxford University Press, 2004).
——, *The Ethos of Europe: Values, Law and Justice in the EU* (Cambridge University Press, 2010).
——, 'The Problem(s) of Justice in the European Union' in Kochenov D, De Búrca G, and Williams A (eds), *Europe's Justice Deficit?* (Hart Publishing, 2015).
Williams T, *Who Is My Neighbor?* (The Catholic University of America Press, 2005).
Winnicott D, *The Maturational Process and the Facilitating Environment—Studies in the Theory of Emotional Development* (The Hogarth Press, 1965).
——, *Playing and Reality* (Routledge, 1971).
de Witte F, 'The End of EU Citizenship and the Means of Non-Discrimination' (2011) 18 *Maastricht Journal of European and Comparative Law* 86.
—— 'Transnational Solidarity and the Mediation of Conflicts of Justice in Europe' (2012) 18 *European Law Journal* 694.
——, *Justice in the EU: The Emergence of Transnational Solidarity* (Oxford University Press, 2015).
Wolff J, 'Fairness, Respect, and the Egalitarian Ethos' (1998) 27 *Philosophy and Public Affairs* 97.
——, 'The Dilemma of Desert' in Olsaretti S (ed), *Desert and Justice* (Clarendon Press, 2003).
——, 'Fairness, Respect and the Egalitarian *Ethos* Revisited' (2010) 14 *The Journal of Ethics* 335.
Wollenschläger F, 'A New Fundamental Freedom beyond Market Integration: Union Citizenship and its Dynamics for Shifting the Economic Paradigm of European Integration' (2011) 17 *European Law Journal* 1.
Young IM, 'Impartiality and the Civic Public: Some Implications of Feminist Critiques of Moral and Political Theory' in Benhabib S and Cornell D (eds), *Feminism as Critique: Essays on the Politics of Gender in Late-Capitalist Societies* (Polity Press, 1987).
——, 'The Ideal of Community and the Politics of Difference' in Nicholson L (ed), *Feminism/Postmodernism* (Routledge, 1990).
Ypi L, *Global Justice and Avant-Garde Political Agency* (Oxford University Press, 2012).
Yuval-Davis N, *Gender & Nation* (SAGE Publications, 1997).
Ziegler K, 'Strengthening the Rule of Law, but Fragmenting International Law: The *Kadi* Decision of the ECJ from the Perspective of Human Rights' (2009) 9 *Human Rights Law Review* 288.
——, 'International Law and EU Law: Between Asymmetric Constitutionalisation and Fragmentation' in Orakhelashvili A (ed), *Research Handbook on the Theory of International Law* (Edward Elgar Publishing, 2011).

Index

www.ingramcontent.com/pod-product-compliance
Ingram Content Group UK Ltd.
Pitfield, Milton Keynes, MK11 3LW, UK
UKHW020140290926
15471UKWH00003B/619

9 781509 924493